ENVIRONMENTS AND HISTORICAL CHANGE

Environments and Historical Change

The Linacre Lectures 1998

Edited by

PAUL SLACK

Principal of Linacre College
University of Oxford

OXFORD
UNIVERSITY PRESS

OXFORD

UNIVERSITY PRESS

Great Clarendon Street, Oxford OX2 6DP

Oxford University Press is a department of the University of Oxford.
It furthers the University's objective of excellence in research, scholarship,
and education by publishing worldwide in

Oxford New York

Athens Auckland Bangkok Bogotá Buenos Aires Calcutta
Cape Town Chennai Dar es Salaam Delhi Florence Hong Kong Istanbul
Karachi Kuala Lumpur Madrid Melbourne Mexico City Mumbai
Nairobi Paris SãoPaulo Singapore Taipei Tokyo Toronto Warsaw

and associated companies in Berlin Ibadan

Oxford is a registered trade mark of Oxford University Press
in the UK and certain other countries

Published in the United States
by Oxford University Press Inc., New York

British Library Cataloguing in Publication Data

Data available

Library of Congress Cataloging in Publication Data

Data available

ISBN 0-19-823388-4

1 3 5 7 9 10 8 6 4 2

Typeset by Best-set Typesetter Ltd., Hong Kong
Printed in Great Britain
on acid-free paper by
Biddles Ltd., Guildford and King's Lynn

ACKNOWLEDGEMENTS

This eighth series of Linacre Lectures is the second to be sponsored by Riche Monde (Bangkok) Limited. It is a pleasure to record the gratitude of Linacre College to Riche Monde, and especially to the Executive Chairman, Professor Tasman Smith, for making the continuation of the Lectures possible, and for supporting the College in this and other important ways. We were delighted that Professor Smith was able to attend one of the Lectures and contribute to the discussion afterwards. As I hope this volume demonstrates, the series continues to illuminate issues of worldwide interest and concern.

As editor, I must acknowledge a number of other debts. Sir Bryan Cartledge, my predecessor both in this role and as Principal, has been an unfailing source of advice and assistance. Jane Edwards, the College Secretary, has once more been indispensable in coordinating arrangements for the Lectures, and Frances Morphy has prepared the texts for submission to Oxford University Press with her customary expertise. The Lecturers stimulated their audiences and tolerated editorial interference afterwards. It has been a cooperative venture.

P.A.S.
Oxford

CONTENTS

CONTRIBUTORS

M. G. L. Baillie is Professor in the School of Archaeology and Palaeo-ecology, Queen's University, Belfast. He is the author of *A Slice through Time: Dendrochronology and Precision Dating* (1995) and of a number of papers on related themes.

William Beinart is Rhodes Professor of Race Relations, Oxford University. His publications include *Twentieth-Century South Africa* (1994), and *Environment and History: The Taming of Nature in the USA and South Africa* (1995) with Peter Coates.

Andrew S. Goudie is Professor of Geography, Oxford University. His many books on the environment include *Environmental Change* (1977), *The Nature of the Environment* (1984), and *The Human Impact on the Natural Environment* (1993).

Howard Morphy is Senior ARC Research Fellow, Australian National University, and Professor of Social Anthropology, University College London. He is the author of *Ancestral Connections: Art and an Aboriginal System of Knowledge* (1991), editor of *Animals into Art* (1989), and (with Marcus Banks) of *Rethinking Visual Anthropology* (1997).

Charles Phythian-Adams is Professor Emeritus of English Local History, University of Leicester. His books include *Desolation of a City* (1979), *Land of the Cumbrians: A Study in British Provincial Origins 400–1120* (1996) and *Societies, Cultures and Kinship 1580–1850: Cultural Provinces and English Local History* (1993).

Oliver Rackham is a Fellow of Corpus Christi College, Cambridge. He is the author of *Ancient Woodland: Its History, Vegetation and Uses in England* (1980), *The History of the Countryside* (1986), and *Trees and Woodland in the British Landscape* (1996).

Paul Slack, Principal of Linacre College, Oxford, is author of *The Impact of Plague in Tudor and Stuart England* (1985) and editor (with Terence Ranger) of *Epidemics and Ideas* (1992).

Claudio Vita-Finzi is Professor of Geology, University College London. His books include *The Mediterranean Valleys: Geological Changes in Historical Times* (1969), *Recent Earth History* (1973), *Archaeological Sites* (1978), and *Recent Earth Movements* (1986).

E. A. Wrigley is Master of Corpus Christi College, Cambridge. He was formerly Professor of Economic History, University of Cambridge, and is currently President of the British Academy. His publications include *People, Cities and Wealth* (1987), *Continuity, Chance and Change* (1988), and (with R. S. Schofield and others) *English Population History from Family Reconstitution 1580–1832* (1997).

Introduction

Paul Slack

ENVIRONMENTS change. Our current anxieties about environmental deterioration—both local and global—leave us in no doubt about that, even if the causes and likely outcome of such phenomena as global warming are controversial and uncertain. Current concerns also demonstrate that perceptions of the environment—by individuals and social groups—equally alter over time, and are no less complicated in their origins. 'Environmental awareness' is never as objectively 'scientific' as we might like to think, but is shaped by deep-rooted assumptions about actual or ideal relations between man and nature. The essays in this volume, derived from the Linacre Lectures for 1998, are intended to present both kinds of change in their historical contexts. The authors come from a variety of relevant disciplines, from geography and geology as well as history and anthropology, and they were encouraged to look at particular aspects of this large theme from their own specialist standpoints. It was impossible to cover the whole of the subject in only eight lectures, but we hope that the essays which follow illustrate its broad academic interest, its ability to surprise as well as stimulate, and its relevance to present debates and predicaments.

The first three contributions amply demonstrate that past fluctuations in the environment, and especially in climate, have often been both radical and sudden. The Ice Ages are well-known examples of the phenomenon, but Andrew Goudie shows that climatic changes continued to have an extensive impact in the late glacial period and after it. Evidence from what is now the Sahara, for example, suggests greater humidity and hence circumstances favourable for settlement there 6,000 years or so ago. Claudio Vita-Finzi carries the same story forward in time, using the evidence of silting in river valleys as a pointer to climatic deterioration before the 'climatic optimum', which H. H. Lamb detected in medieval Europe (Lamb 1966: 7–8), and to another deterioration after it. Both essays show the importance of fluctuations in rainfall, but they also provide indirect evidence for radical changes in temperature. Goudie suggests that temperature depressions of the order of 5–8°C are not inconceivable in the earliest period, and if later shifts were smaller than that, a change as small as 1°C might well be sufficient to have a measurable impact on patterns of human health and disease, and perhaps cultivation and settlement (Wigley *et al.* 1981: 29, 32).

Several features of these climatic swings remain uncertain. One is their causation, a topic on which the experts are still far from agreeing. While Vita-Finzi emphasizes correlations with sun-spot cycles and changes in solar radiation, Goudie doubts their relevance to changing conditions in the more distant past, in the early Holocene, 8,000 or 9,000 years ago, for example. As he says, palaeoclimatologists are increasingly aware of alternatives, including the radical possibility that the oceanic circulation can 'flip from one state to another, thereby modifying climate on a global basis'. A second set of questions, of particular importance to historians, relates to the impact of these changes on human activity and social development. To put it at its most dramatic, it is tempting to speculate about associations between environmental change and the rise and decline of ancient civilizations. Some of the authors in this volume refer in passing to hypotheses of this kind, but it is not difficult to see the problems involved in trying to substantiate them: not least, the large number of variables which separate supposed cause from presumed effect. In any investigation of links between climate and history, it has been wisely noted, the greater the distance between 'cause' and alleged impact, the 'more interactions intervene to disguise and modify the link.' (Wigley *et al.* 1981: 21).

Before scholars can approach an answer to even the simplest of such questions, however, they require firm evidence of the chronology of past environmental change, firmer evidence than in most cases we currently possess. Andrew Sherratt (1997) has recently emphasized the importance of dating and 'precise punctuation' in analysing the relationship between climatic cycles and the beginning of farming in the Old and New Worlds, the Neolithic revolution or revolutions. He notes the many obstacles to precision, including the subsidiary confusions caused by such scholarly practices as the variant uses of BC and BP (before the present). For later centuries, as Vita-Finzi suggests, essential help comes from dendrochronology, the rapidly advancing study of tree-rings. The present state of knowledge in this important field is summarized in this volume by M. G. L. Baillie. What is immediately remarkable is the general consistency of tree-ring chronologies (not only from European oaks from Ireland to Poland, but from trees in other parts of the northern hemisphere), their near unanimity in identifying short intervals of extremely narrow growth. In the historic period the most important of these environmental traumas appear to have occurred in AD 540 and 1740, and from the mid-1320s to the mid-1340s AD.

Baillie's major and continuing achievement is the construction and measurement of these chronologies (Baillie 1995). In the essay below he goes further and discusses the causation of the abrupt events which they reveal. Previous explanations have tended to focus on the effects of volcanic eruptions. These are known to have affected weather and growth patterns across large areas in the relatively recent past, as in the case of the Tambora eruption in 1815 and those of Vesuvius, Santorini and Fujiyama in 1707 (Baillie 1991; Post 1977: 4–6). However, there is as yet no direct evidence—from the Greenland ice-cores, for example—that volcanic activity immediately preceded some of the most pronounced periods of low growth in the tree-ring record. Baillie therefore turns our attention to the need to take into account other kinds of potential environmental shock, not least impact with cometary dust or debris: a hypothesis which might once have seemed highly speculative, but which recent studies have brought firmly into the realm of the possible (Clube and Napier 1990). Baillie's use of literary evidence from the fourteenth century in support of his case may not entirely persuade medieval historians. Although they are increasingly aware of the possibilities of using myth and legend to throw light on environmental facts (e.g. Horden 1992), they would point out that descriptions of earthly and heavenly perturbations of the kind Baillie cites are not confined to the years or decades which the tree-ring record singles out for attention. Yet even the most sceptical historian can no longer dispute the dendrochronological evidence for abrupt environmental changes across large areas of the globe in the relatively recent past, or doubt the need to investigate the reasons for them.

Their consequences are potentially as interesting and as intricate as their causes. Baillie points to the plagues which immediately followed two of his tree-ring 'events', those of 540 and the mid-1340s. The fact that these were no ordinary epidemics but, respectively, the plague of Justinian and the Black Death, each of them a dramatic beginning to a series of major demographic crises, undoubtedly lends importance to the question of whether the chronological association was more than coincidence. Unfortunately, the links between environmental downturn and these particular demographic disasters are further long chains of supposed causation which it is difficult to unravel. If the demographic disasters were caused by bubonic plague (and even that has been disputed), then there are several areas for investigation, including the movements, whether of humans or of rodents, which may have carried the disease from its long-standing reservoirs in central Asia (McNeill 1977). There seems little doubt that there must have been some major perturbation—environmental, biological, or historical, or some combination of the three—to account for the phenomena. But it is unlikely to have been a simple matter of disease hitting a population weakened by malnutrition brought by bad harvests and hence bad weather. Bad weather and bad harvests certainly occurred in the mid-1340s (Bailey 1998: 247), but they cannot alone account for the Black Death.

Leaving plague on one side, there are other occasions when the links between weather, harvest failure, malnutrition, and mortality are easier to identify: after 1707 and 1815, for example, and, as Baillie points out, after 1740. In 1740–1 adverse environmental conditions damaged humans as well as trees. One further important caveat is necessary here, however. The mortality crises associated with bad weather in 1740–1, though damaging, were not nearly as severe as those of the late medieval 'great famine' in 1315–22 (Post 1985; Jordan 1996). Yet the 'great famine' does not show up in the tree-ring record, while the crises of 1740–1 do. This does more than indicate that historical events cannot be 'read off' from environmental variations in any simple fashion. It also warns us against environmental determinism of any kind. In 1740–1 bad harvests hit a Europe that was able to cope for the most part, through well-established mechanisms of international trade in grain, state-regulated granaries, and relatively sophisticated methods of social welfare. In 1315, by contrast, an environmental downturn of an apparently less severe kind hit an economic system suffering from 'severe structural instability', not least an abundance of smallholders living at the margins of subsistence in many parts of Europe (Bailey 1998: 246). The demographic and social results were, consequently, more severe.

Once again, therefore, we are dealing with a number of variables and hence a multitude of possible outcomes. Historians are beginning to bring new techniques of analysis to bear on these problems, but they need particularly good contemporary records before they can arrive at definite conclusions. One of the few detailed studies in this area, concentrating on Holland between the seventeenth and the nineteenth centuries, found only weak links between climate and economic development (De Vries 1980). Whatever may have been true of other and earlier societies, the rhythms of the 'golden-age' Dutch economy were not determined by the weather. The conclusion is not perhaps surprising, but it is instructive. Economic structures and social organization, strategies of human adaptability and, hence, human culture in the broad sense were at least as important as environmental circumstances in determining the consequences of their interaction.

The point is illustrated across a much wider canvas in E. A. Wrigley's essay on the ways in which human energy needs have been met over time. Wrigley shows how that same solar energy, whose variations in intensity and distribution are discussed in earlier chapters of this book in the context of climate, have been harnessed. In the past there have been important constraints on human access to the energy stored in the environment. One was the 'vicious circle' of the balance between energy consumed in the quest for food and that gained from securing it, especially in situations of poor nutrition like early fourteenth-century Europe. But there have also been opportunities for breaking through such constraints, by harnessing animal, water, or mechanical power, and by utilizing fossil fuels in ever greater quantities. Such devices were vital in preventing an 'ecological crisis' in eighteenth-century Denmark, for example (Kjaergaard, 1994).

More generally, technological and industrial change has undoubtedly allowed output in the right places at the right times to be increased exponentially. Whether that process can continue for much longer, in the absence of new sources of energy, is of course an issue of immediate concern—and another question. Wrigley also touches on historical questions which there is no space to explore in this volume: notably relating to the special circumstances (of both culture and environment) which allowed Britain and Europe to take the lead in energy-capture (cf. Landes 1998; Macfarlane 1997; Wrigley 1988). But in identifying the insatiable search for energy as a main 'determinant of the behaviour and development of most animal species', Wrigley points to a powerful engine of historical change which has moulded the environment at least as much as it has been restrained by it.

The impact of people on the environment is most obvious in the landscape which their activities shape. Forty years ago W. G. Hoskins described 'the making of the English landscape' and showed how it could be read as a historical text (Hoskins 1955; Hoskins and Taylor 1988); and Oliver Rackham's essay in this collection shows the particular interest of boundaries from this point of view. Often the earliest surviving human imprint on countrysides, many of them turn out to be very much older than one might suspect. They may be markers of territory, property, or different agricultural activities. Their shapes may tell us about practical requirements, as in the case of woodland, or about rational colonizing ambitions, as in the straight lines of the Greek and Roman Mediterranean or modern Texas. Once established, however, they 'grow into the landscape', like the reaves on Dartmoor, which are reminders of Bronze Age farming, or the strips of ridge and furrow which Rackham sees as reflecting 'an agricultural and social revolution' in seventh- and eighth-century England.

Natural and man-made boundaries also have cultural meanings and resonances. In the case of England, Charles Phythian-Adams has stressed the importance of watersheds as dividers between 'cultural provinces' (1993). In his essay below he uses three striking new case studies to show the resilience of perceived cultural territories. Places and place-names, and the stories associated with them, whether written or transmitted orally, enabled Cumbrians in the ninth century to re-create mental maps of a lost, heroic, Dark-Age landscape, just as legends of Haveloc, Grim and Hengist preserved perceptions of ethnic differences in twelfth-century Lincolnshire. Folk tales and superstitions as late as the nineteenth century in Somerset and Cornwall served to 'mark out a territory by precisely emphasizing boundaries and edges'. These were methods of appropriating the landscape as effective as separating pasture from arable or woodland from waste, or naming a settlement.

Perceptions of the environment extend far beyond the meanings attached to immediate local settings, of course, and scholars are beginning to reconstruct their histories, with interesting results for both old and new fields of enquiry. The study of agriculture and of alternative routes of agrarian development has benefited from an appreciation of the importance of culture and cultivation in both their senses (Ambrosoli 1997; Thirsk 1997). There have been path-breaking books about imaginative re-creations of scenery, and about attitudes towards animals and plants, and the natural world in general (Schama 1995; Thomas 1983; Goody 1993). There is still work to be done, most notably on cultural perceptions of the environment outside Europe, and within Europe on periods before the sixteenth century; and there is ample material to be quarried, extending from works of fiction and pictorial representations to travel literature and the kinds of legend and annal employed in different ways by Baillie and Phythian-Adams below (cf. Flint and Morphy 2000). It would be interesting to know more about attitudes towards the more threatening aspects of the environment, for example, and how they were related to the chronology of natural catastrophes, storms and fires, floods and earthquakes (cf. Thomas 1971: 3–21; Delumeau 1989; Bennassar 1996).

Thus far the most productive area for investigation has proved to be the impact of European expansion, colonialism, and imperialism both on realities and on attitudes. The process began in famously predatory fashion, with damaging consequences for indigenous environments and peoples, as colonists consciously 'tamed' and 'cultivated' the wild. Yet the process also involved, for the first time, the global exchange of information; and that eventually prompted public appreciation of the differences between environments, of the threats to newly discovered species, and of the dangers of ecological destruction. Richard Grove has persuasively argued that the colonial enterprise promoted conditions conducive to rigorous investigation of ecological processes, and led to pressure for regulation in the interests of conservation (Crosby 1986; Beinart and Coates 1995; Grove 1995, 1997).

William Beinart's essay in this volume takes as its subject a late, almost post-colonial, variation on this theme. The popular appreciation of animals encouraged by British and American films and literature in the 1950s and 1960s embodied a number of not entirely consistent assumptions. There were romantic notions of the exotic and the wild, as well as real concerns about preservation (albeit of animal species rather than African ways of life). But there was also an 'appropriation' of the environment involved: this time not of local landscapes by those who occupied them, but of distant African nature by observers in the West. The mixture can be seen as a further example of the 'stories' which Phythian-Adams tells us every generation needs in order to make sense of its environment. Present anxieties about ecological change spring from some of the same origins; and it is salutary to reflect that future generations may find our perceptions, our stories about the environment, as partial and as rooted in a particular historical moment as those which preceded them.

The long chronological sweep of the final chapter in this volume prompts historical reflections of this kind. It also draws together many of the topics considered by the other contributors. The aboriginal clans and bands of northern Australia, described by Howard Morphy, were aware of cultural boundaries between their ranges and territories. They had suffered and adjusted to both short- and long-term changes in climate, to drought and oscillations in rainfall, to the rise and fall of sea levels since the Ice Age. They had methods of land-management which enabled resources to be utilized over thousands of years, as opposed to the voracious and immediate deforestation brought by European colonists and miners. And they had stories to tell which are at last being listened to. As Morphy says, their experience of the interactions between environments and historical change has something to teach us about the value of 'the long-term attachment of people to place'.

REFERENCES

Ambrosoli, M. (1997). *The Wild and the Sown: Botany and Agriculture in Western Europe, 1350–1850*. Cambridge: Cambridge University Press.
Bailey, M. (1998). 'Peasant welfare in England, 1290–1348'. *Economic History Review*, 51: 223–51.

Baillie, M. G. L. (1991). 'Marking in marker dates: towards an archaeology with historical precision'. *World Archaeology*, 23: 233–43.

Baillie, M. G. L. (1995). *A Slice Through Time: Dendrochronology and Precision Dating*. London: Routledge.

Beinart, W. and Coates, P. (1995). *Environment and History: The Taming of Nature in the USA and South Africa*. London: Routledge.

Bennassar, B. (ed.) (1996). *Les Catastrophes naturelles dans l'Europe médiévale et moderne*. Toulouse: Presses Universitaires du Mirail.

Clube, V. and Napier, B. (1990). *The Cosmic Winter*. Oxford: Blackwell.

Crosby, A. W. (1986). *Ecological Imperialism: The Biological Expansion of Europe, 900–1900*. Cambridge: Cambridge University Press.

Delumeau, J. (1989). *Rassurer et protéger*. Paris: Fayard.

De Vries, J. (1980). 'Measuring the impact of climate on history: the search for appropriate methodologies'. *Journal of Interdisciplinary History*, 10: 599–630.

Flint, K. and Morphy, H. (eds) (2000). *Culture and Environment*. Oxford: Oxford University Press (forthcoming).

Goody, J. (1993). *The Culture of Flowers*. Cambridge: Cambridge University Press.

Grove, R. H. (1995). *Green Imperialism: Colonial Expansion, Tropical Island Edens and the Origins of Environmentalism, 1600–1860*. Cambridge: Cambridge University Press.

Grove, R. H. (1997). *Ecology, Climate and Empire: Colonialism and Global Environmental History, 1400–1940*. London: White Horse Press.

Horden, P. (1992). 'Disease, dragons and saints: the management of epidemics in the Dark Ages', in T. Ranger and P. Slack (eds), *Epidemics and Ideas: Essays on the Historical Perception of Pestilence*. Cambridge: Cambridge University Press, 45–76.

Hoskins, W. G. (1955). *The Making of the English Landscape*. London: Hodder and Stoughton.

Hoskins, W. G. and Taylor, C. (1988). *The Making of the English Landscape*. Revised edition. London: Hodder and Stoughton.

Jordan, W. C. (1996). *The Great Famine: Northern Europe in the Early Fourteenth Century*. Princeton NJ: Princeton University Press.

Kjaergaard, T. (1994). *The Danish Revolution 1500–1800: An Ecohistorical Interpretation*. Cambridge: Cambridge University Press.

Lamb, H. H. (1966). *The Changing Climate: Selected Papers*. London: Methuen.

Landes, D. S. (1998). *The Wealth and Poverty of Nations: Why Some are So Rich and Some So Poor*. New York: Norton.

Macfarlane, A. (1997). *The Savage Wars of Peace: England, Japan and the Malthusian Trap*. Oxford: Blackwell.

McNeill, W. H. (1977). *Plagues and Peoples*. Oxford: Blackwell.

Phythian-Adams, C. (1993). 'Introduction: an agenda for English local history', in C. Phythian-Adams (ed.), *Societies, Cultures and Kinship 1580–1850: Cultural Provinces and English Local History*. Leicester: Leicester University Press.

Post, J. D. (1977). *The Last Great Subsistence Crisis in the Western World*. Baltimore: Johns Hopkins University Press.

Post, J. D. (1985). *Food Shortage, Climatic Variability, and Epidemic Disease in Preindustrial Europe: The Mortality Peak in the Early 1740s*. Ithaca NY: Cornell University Press.

Schama, S. (1995). *Landscape and Memory*. London: Fontana Press.

Sherratt, A. (1997). 'Climatic cycles and behavioural revolutions: the emergence of modern humans and the beginning of farming'. *Antiquity*, 71: 271–87.

Thirsk, J. (1997). *Alternative Agriculture: A History From the Black Death to the Present Day*. Oxford: Oxford University Press.

Thomas, K. (1971). *Religion and the Decline of Magic*. London: Weidenfeld and Nicolson.

Thomas, K. (1983). *Man and the Natural World: Changing Attitudes in England 1500–1800*. London: Allen Lane.

Wigley, T. M. L., Ingram, M. J., and Farmer, G. (eds) (1981). 'Introduction', in *Climate and History. Studies in Past Climates and their Impact on Man*. Cambridge: Cambridge University Press.

Wrigley, E. A. (1988). *Continuity, Chance and Change: The Character of the Industrial Revolution in England*. Cambridge: Cambridge University Press.

1

The Ice Age in the Tropics and Its Human Implications

Andrew S. Goudie

INTRODUCTION: THE EARLY HISTORY

LOUIS Agassiz, the Swiss natural historian, was a young man in a hurry. In 1836 he was guided around Switzerland by two colleagues, Venetz and de Charpentier, and as a result of their inspiration became an enthusiast for the idea that, in the past, glaciers had been much more extensive than now—the so-called Glacial Theory. As G. L. Davies has pointed out (1969: 265):

in his unbounded enthusiasm, he elaborated the theory far too rapidly for the liking of the theory's two pioneers. Understandably they resented what they regarded as Agassiz's forceful intrusion into glacial affairs, and the cavalier manner in which he seemed to have taken the glacial theory over as his own.

Agassiz wrote it up in just one night in July 1837 as his famous 'Discours de Neuchâtel'. The Glacial Theory had an impact on the earth sciences in the 1830s which was as striking as the impact that Leg Theory was to have on cricket a century later. Part of this impact arose from Agassiz's vigorous prose:

The development of these ice-sheets must have led to the destruction of all organic life at the Earth's surface. The ground of Europe, previously covered with tropical vegetation and inhabited by herds of great elephants, enormous hippopotami, and gigantic carnivora, became suddenly buried under a vast expanse of ice, covering plains, lakes, seas and plateaux alike. The silence of death followed . . . springs dried up, streams ceased to flow, and sunrays rising over that frozen shore . . . were met only by the whistling of northern winds and the rumbling of the crevasses as they opened across the surface of that huge ocean of ice. (Agassiz, cited in Imbrie and Imbrie, 1979: 33)

Another part of the impact arose from his cavalier exuberance, for, in his enthusiasm for *Die Eizeit* (the Ice Age), he threw scientific caution to the winds and boldly claimed that the entire northern hemisphere, from the North Pole down to the latitude of the Mediterranean and Caspian seas, had, until recently, been shrouded beneath great ice-caps.

Agassiz maintained this tendency for unbounded and, it has to be said, unjustified Ice Age fever until late in life. Indeed, in the late 1860s he visited Brazil, and on his arrival in Rio de Janeiro his attention was 'immediately attracted by a very peculiar formation consisting of an ochraceous, highly ferruginous, sand clay' (Agassiz 1869: 398–9). Thereafter, he found similar deposits 'spreading over the surface of the country from north to south and from east to west' (400). The deposits were not glacial, but were the product of deep tropical weathering, and although this possibility crossed Agassiz's mind, he none the less believed that the geological winter had afflicted the equatorial regions, and that Brazil had been covered by great ice-sheets.

In the 1860s Agassiz's extreme views met a frosty reception, but it was in this decade that a spectrum of observers from many different parts of the world began to recognize that Ice Age climatic changes (the main dates of which are shown in table 1.1), while not causing Amazonian glaciation, had their counterparts in lower latitudes.

John Strong Newberry, one of the greatest explorers of the Colorado Plateaus in the 1850s, recognized these classic landscapes as having been 'formerly much better watered than they are today' (1861: 47). Lake basins, of the type that abound in the Basin and Range Province of the American West, gave particularly clear evidence of hydrological change and in 1863 T. F. Jamieson proposed that during glaciations in higher latitudes the arid regions would be moister and their lakes would expand. In 1865 L. Lartet noted the present shrunken size of the Dead Sea and Hull (1865: 182) used the term 'pluvial' to describe the period when the Dead Sea had been a fuller water body. However, perhaps the greatest

TABLE 1.1 *Some major events of the Quaternary*

	Years before present
Start of the Holocene (post-glacial)	10,000
Younger Dryas	10,000–11,000
Late Glacial Maximum	18,000–20,000
Last Interglacial Maximum	120,000
Start of Pleistocene	1.64 million
Initiation of mid-latitude glaciation	2.4 million

advances were made in the American West by two intellectual heirs to Newberry—G. K. Gilbert, who had worked for Newberry in the Ohio Survey (Pyne 1980), and I. C. Russell who was appointed by Gilbert when the latter was working for the United States Geological Survey. Russell (1885) worked on pluvial Lake Lahontan and Gilbert (1890) worked on pluvial Lake Bonneville. Both postulated arid lake expansion as being synchronous with glacial advance. As Russell (1885: 106 and 111) wrote:

During the time of great climatic changes that witnessed the birth, growth, and decadence of the great lakes of the Laurentian and Winnepeg basins, equally important fluctuations occurred in the lakes of the Arid region. Many of the valleys of Utah and Nevada, and of adjacent areas both north and south, that are now parched and desert-like throughout the year, were then flooded, and in some instances filled to the brim so as to overflow. All of the enclosed lakes west of the Rocky Mountains were then of greater size that at present and underwent marked changes in sympathy with the advance and retreat of glaciers on neigh-bouring mountains, and had their oscillations controlled by the same causes, viz., variations in precipitation, evaporation, and temperature.

Of these numerous water bodies there were two of broad extent which may be taken as types of their class and will serve to give an epitome of the history of their time. The two ancient lakes referred to are Bonneville and Lahontan. . . .

Every island and rocky crag that rose in Lake Lahontan became a centre of accumulation for tufa deposits and was transformed into strange and frequently fantastic shapes by the material precipitated upon it. Now that the waters of the ancient sea have disappeared, these structures stand in the desert valleys like the crumbling ruins of towers, castles, domes, and various other shapes, in keeping with the desolation surrounding them.

Thus in the south-west of the United States we have one of the germs of the idea that low latitude pluvials are synchronous with high latitude glacials. A corollary of this view is that post-glacial times will have been characterized by desiccation (Goudie 1972). The concept of post-glacial progressive desiccation spread like a contagion through many parts of the world. A particularly notable focus in the early years of this century was Central Asia, particularly after the great explorations of the Tarim Basin, Lop Nor, and Tibet promoted by Russia territorial ambitions on the one hand, and the imperial ambitions of George Nathaniel Curzon, Viceroy of India, on the other. It was perhaps fortunate that Curzon was himself, amongst all his remarkable accomplishments, a geographer and scientific explorer of considerable ability, an enthusiast for ancient monu-ments, and an acknowledged supporter of Sir Aurel Stein and Francis Younghusband, both of whom undertook major surveys in Central Asia.

However, some of the most important work in Central Asia was neither of Russian nor of British origin, for in 1903 Andrew Carnegie financed an expedition to Turkestan and Persia of which, among others, Raphael Pumpelly, W. M. Davis and E. Huntington were members. In 1905–6 Huntington was able to go a second time to Asia, and was this time financed by a classmate, R. L. Barrett; the expedition went to India and Tibet via Russia and Siberia.

Huntington was rather unpromising material as an explorer. As a child he had been very slight of build and his mother had great trouble buying him underwear and gloves that would fit (Martin 1973: 8). He also fell out with Barrett, who felt that Huntington had claimed the credit for the expedition of which Barrett was leader. Barrett was certainly less than flattering about Huntington's conduct on the roof of the world (quoted in Dunbar 1996: 140–3):

I find that H is very well behaved in camp aside from his eccentricities such as wearing starched collars and using a bed and chair. These last two get on my nerves so that I have a mind to offer him a hundred rupees if he will throw them away. They do clutter up the tent and are such eyesores anyway. . . . H's behaviour outside camp is more open to question. I gave him a very loose rein at the start, spoke of the expedition as 'ours,' etc. I had him do a good deal of correspondence with people we have to deal with. I have been somewhat startled lately with the replies to these letters. One would gather from them that H was running the expedition, Barrett being mentioned only casually, or not at all. More than this, a notice recently appeared in the Royal Geographical Journal, that H was setting out for Central Asia accompanied by R.L.B. This is going it a little strong.

On these journeys, Huntington noted the evidence for ruined cities and abandoned settlements, and recognized after the Pumpelly Expedition that lake terraces indicated a 'gradual desiccation of the country from early historical times down to the present'. After the Barrett Expedition, which took him to the famed Tarim basin, he wrote his *Pulse of Asia* and moved away from any simple idea of progressive desiccation to a view embracing multiple large fluctuations. He believed that the pulsations of climate had served as a driving force in the history of Eurasia, forcing nomadic invaders to overrun their more civilized neighbours whenever the climatic cycle reached a trough of aridity.

At much the same time as Huntington put forward his views, Prince Kropotkin, the anarchist-geologist-explorer-evolutionist, who travelled widely in the wastes of Central Asia with the unfashionable Mounted Cossack Regiment, put forward a simple view of progressive desiccation (1904: 722):

Recent exploration in central Asia has yielded a considerable body of evidence, all tending to prove that the whole of that wide region is now, and has been since the beginning of the historic period, in a state of rapid desiccation. . . . It must have been the rapid desiccation of this region which compelled its inhabitants . . . pushing before them the former inhabitants of the lowlands to produce those great migrations and invasions of Europe which took place during the first centuries of our era.

He went on to write that 'It is a geological epoch of desiccation that we are living in . . . nor is the phenomenon of desiccation limited to a small portion of the continent' (ibid.).

Like Huntington, Kropotkin was not an obvious role model as an explorer. He was short, slight, had unusually small feet, was bald on top, and had a luxuriant beard which decorated a short neck and a large head. Born to a life of privilege as a page of the Russian Tsar, he became an anarchist and had to flee Russia. He fled to Hull, one of the few places in the world where the secret police might not think to search for him (Stoddart 1986: 136).

The evidence for such progressive desiccation and the effects that it was held to have were not universally accepted. Sven Hedin, the Swedish explorer, thought that much of the evidence for desiccation resulted from the shifting of river courses (Hedin 1940). Sometimes dubbed 'Hun Swedin', because of his pro-German stand in both world wars, he received honorary degrees from both Oxford and Cambridge. Although bookish, bespectacled, and small in stature, he was one of the world's most tenacious explorers (Hopkirk 1980: 54).

Other workers, notably Sir Aurel Stein (1938), believed that the melting of relict Pleistocene glaciers and ice caps in the Himalayas would provide progressively less discharge to rivers during the course of the Holocene and so would promote the drying up of rivers and lakes without the direct reduction of precipitation envisaged by Kropotkin.

Although these various points of view have weakened the simple Kropotkin hypothesis, and in spite of evidence to the contrary produced in the 1870s by Blanford (1877) and by Heron (1917), the concept of post-glacial desiccation into historical times (even to the present) was much favoured in Indian literature of the 1950s and 1960s. In particular, fears were expressed that the Great Indian Sand Desert was on the move eastwards into eastern Rajasthan, Haryana, the Punjab, and Uttar Pradesh, and plans were formulated for the amelioration of the Rajasthan Desert (National Institute of Sciences 1952). D. N. Wadia, one of the most distinguished of Indian geologists, wrote that in many parts of Asia 'the same sequence of events has happened, increasing dryness, migration of the indigenous fauna and flora, erosion of the soil-cover by wind and undisciplined rush of water across the fields during the few occasional rain storms and the loss of vegetation cover. These ravages of nature have been supplemented by the acts of man' (1960: 1).

The concept of post-glacial progressive desiccation was also espoused in West Africa, though it came under attack by Jones (1938). It was also a widespread cause of fear in Southern Africa and there were grandiose schemes to promote rainfall by flooding the Kalahari with waters diverted from the north (Schwarz 1923). Archaeologists adopted the concept also, with Childe (1936) seeing it as the stimulus for domestication.

ANCIENT ERGS

In the 1950s we see the development of an increasing uneasiness about correlations between glacial events in high latitudes and pluvial events in low. This change of attitude was prompted by a combination of new dating technologies and by new types of evidence for environmental reconstruction (see table 1.2) and is well represented in the work of Zeuner, the German-born Professor of Environmental Archaeology in the University of London (Zeuner 1959). Of especial importance was the recognition that some tropical areas, far from being highly desiccated at the present time, had experienced far more severe desiccation at some point or points in the past. Instrumental in this was the identification of ancient sand seas (ergs) in areas that are now relatively moist, most notably on the south side of the Sahara (Grove 1958).

The study of ancient ergs did not begin with Grove and there had been a series of sporadic discussions of them prior to the 1950s, most notably by Armstrong Price in Texas (Price 1944). None the less, Grove and his pupils, using air photos and field surveys, did much to establish the extent of ancient sand deserts in the Sudan (Grove and Warren 1968), in the Kalahari (Grove 1969) and in India (Goudie *et al.* 1973). More recently, considerably expanded ranges of dunes have been established for South America (Clapperton 1993), North America (Wells 1992), and Australia (Wasson *et al.* 1988). There are many indicators that show dunes to be relict and these are listed in table 1.3. The global extent of dunes during the Late Pleistocene was plotted by Sarnthein, who argued that:

Today about 10 per cent of the land area between 30°N and 30°S is covered by active sand deserts . . . Sand dunes and associated deserts were much more widespread 18,000 years ago than they are today. They characterised almost 50 per cent of the land area between 30°N and 30°S forming two vast belts. In between,

TABLE 1.2 *Evidence of climate change in deserts*

Evidence	Inference
1. Geomorphological	
Fossil dune systems	Past aridity
Breaching of dunes by rivers	Increased humidity
Discordant dune trends	Changed wind direction
Lake shorelines	Balance of hydrological inputs and outputs
Old drainage lines	Integrated hydrological network
Fluvial aggradation and siltation	Desiccation
Colluvial deposition	Reduced vegetation cover and stream flushing
Karstic (e.g. cave) phenomena	Increased hydrological activity
Frost screes	Palaeotemperature
2. Sedimentological	
Lake floor sediments	Degree of salinity, etc.
Lee dune (lunette) stratigraphy	Hydrological status of lake basin
Spring deposits and tufas	Groundwater activity
Duricrusts and palaeosols	Chemical weathering under humid conditions
Dust and river sediments in ocean cores	Amount of aeolian and fluvial transport
Loess profiles and palaeosols	Aridity and stability
3. Biological and miscellaneous	
Macro-plant remains, including charcoal (e.g. in Packrat middens)	Vegetation cover
Pollen analysis of sediments	Vegetation cover
Faunal remains	Biomes
Disjunct faunas	Biomes
Isotopic composition of groundwater and speleothems	Palaeotemperatures and recharge rates
Distribution of archaeological sites	Availability of water
Drought and famine record	Aridity

tropical rainforests and adjacent savannahs were reduced to a narrow corridor, in places only a few degrees of latitude wide. (1978: 43)

However, not all ancient ergs have been securely dated to the Late Pleistocene, and so this may be an exaggeration. There has also been some latitude in views about the humid limits to widespread dune formation and in recent years it has become more apparent that sand movement is controlled by factors other than vegetation cover, including wind velocity (which may have changed in the past), and sand supply (which could

TABLE 1.3 *Indicators that dunes are relict*

Geomorphological
  Degraded slopes
  Gully development
  Mantled in colluvium
  Flooded by lakes
  Submerged in alluvium
Pedological
  Calcification
  Development of clay and silt
  Soil horizons
Biological
  Mantled in vegetation
Archaeological
  Covered in artefacts of known age

be augmented from actively flowing seasonal sand-bed rivers, from lake shorelines, or from marine sources). Moreover, recent research has demonstrated how some dune types develop even when there is a certain vegetation cover, that some may be rendered active by fire, and that others may be mobilized by short-lived droughts or windy phases (Bullard 1994). As a result of these caveats, care has to be taken with the use of dunes as palaeoclimatic indicators. That said, the presence of dunes over wide areas in regions that have a humid climate and a dense vegetation cover today leaves little doubt as to the very substantial degree of change that their existence implies.

One of the great problems with dunes is that, until recently, they proved very difficult to date. They were nearly always dated indirectly by means of their stratigraphic association with sediments that were thought (sometimes optimistically in the case of calcretes and the like) to be susceptible to radiocarbon dating. There were no means to date them directly. The picture has changed since the early 1980s because of the availability of thermoluminescent (TL) and optical dating techniques which can be applied to the grains (feldspar, quartz, etc.) which make up the dunes themselves. Moreover, such dates, many of which have been produced by Oxford-trained palaeomagicians, enable one to date dunes over longer time spans than the range covered by radiocarbon (see, for example, Stokes *et al.* 1997).

The application of TL and optical dates has had some important consequences: they have increased the sheer volume of dates available to a marked degree; they have expanded the range over which dates for dune

formation have been available; and they have demonstrated the rather frequent changes from dune formation to dune stabilization that have taken
place not only in the Late Pleistocene but also in the Holocene (Thomas
et al. 1997).

DUST DEPOSITION IN THE OCEANS

In the oceans the evidence for past fluctuations in aeolian activity is provided by the record of dust accumulation preserved in ocean cores.

At the present time, areas like the Sahara Desert, Arabia, Australia, and
north-west India generate large quantities of atmospheric dust derived
from the deflation of desert surfaces (Goudie 1978). This dust can be
transported over large distances and much of it falls out into the oceans.
It accumulates on the ocean floor, and is distinguishable on the basis of
its grain size, mineralogy and the presence of terrestrially derived pollen
and diatoms. Investigation of the Pleistocene sediments retrieved from
deep sea cores (de Menocal *et al.* 1993) therefore gives an indication
of the amounts of dust that have accumulated at different phases of the
Quaternary and of changes that have taken place in its geographical
spread.

There are now large numbers of studies that address this issue in many
tropical areas, including off the Sahara (Sarnthein and Koopman 1980),
Arabia (Sirocko *et al.* 1991), India (Kolla and Biscaye 1977), and
Australia (Thiede 1979). These studies suggest that in general there were
greatly increased fluxes of dust from drylands into the oceans at around
the last glacial maximum and that dust plumes had a greater geographical extent than at the present time. This serves to confirm the picture provided by the study of the history of ancient ergs, and is indicative of
heightened tropical aridity in glacial times. However, as Ruddiman (1997)
has pointed out, changes in aridity may not have been the only control
of heightened dust generation rates. Also of significance may have been
changes in velocity in the trade winds.

LAKES

Lakes like the oceans, can preserve a long record of sedimentation. Arid
regions have more than their fair share of closed lake depressions (sometimes referred to rather unromantically as 'terminal sumps'), and these
lake basins, as Gilbert and Russell noted over a century ago, are rich
depositories of palaeoenvironmental information. Ancient shorelines
demonstrate that, at times, what are now shrunken, salty relicts were once

fine, large, fresh-water bodies. In addition, lake basins, if they have not been deflated out, can provide a long sequence of information from the sediments that occur within them.

Since the late 1960s at least two main developments have taken place in the study of tropical lake basins. The first of these has been the dating of former high stands of lake level using radiocarbon methods. The remarkable result of such work was the recognition that in low latitudes glacial and pluvial were not synchronous and that, if anything, the Late Glacial Maximum could be equated with aridity and the Early Holocene interglacial with humidity. This was pointed out for tropical Africa by Grove and Goudie (1971) and shortly thereafter by Butzer *et al.* (1972).

The second development, which builds upon the first, has been the construction of a global database of lake status that permits interregional comparisons to be made (Street and Grove 1979). This work showed conclusively that while the mid-latitude lakes of the American southwest (studied by Gilbert and Russell) may have been high at the time of the last glacial maximum, those of the tropics and monsoonal lands (e.g. West Africa, East Africa, Southern Arabia, Northwest India, and tropical Australia) were low at that time and reached very high levels in the Early Holocene (around 8,000–9,000 years ago). These discoveries, combined with the evidence of ancient ergs, put the final nail in the coffin of post-glacial desiccation.

Recently, such databases have been developed for more parts of the world (see, for example, Fang 1991, on China). Their temporal resolution has also improved as more dates have become available, and this has enabled some investigators to suggest correlations between tropical lake fluctuations and short-lived events like the Younger Dryas of the Late Glacial (Gasse *et al.* 1990; Sirocko *et al.* 1996; Roberts *et al.* 1993).

This is important because palaeoclimatologists have in recent years become increasingly aware that climate can and does change suddenly. This is probably because the oceanic circulation can flip from one state to another, thereby modifying climate on a global basis. If this is the case, the human implications are great. Substantial evidence for such flips has been detected in ice-cores retrieved from polar ice-caps, but it is also now being detected in carefully dated and analysed sediment sequences from lakes in the equatorial regions. For example, Beuning *et al.* (1997), who studied cores from Lake Albert in East Africa, found that a very dramatic change in catchment vegetation occurred between 11400 and 9900 BP. Both before ~11400 BP and after 9900 BP arboreal pollen constituted over 60 per cent of the pollen sum and non-arboreal <20 per cent. Within this interval a complete shift occurs, with arboreal pollen falling to <20 per cent and non-arboreal components, primarily grasses and sedges, rising to almost 60 per cent of the total pollen sum.

GLACIERS IN THE TROPICS

One cannot talk of the Ice Age in the tropics without saying something about what happened to glaciers and ice-caps. Let us consider, first of all, Africa, a continent that is more noted for its coral strands than for its icy mountains, and where, under present conditions, glaciers are of limited extent and area. However, in the Pleistocene some of the higher areas were glaciated, though the chronology is insecure and fragmentary, and there remains controversy in some locations as to whether or not the evidence for past glaciers is reliable.

The greatest development of glaciation was in the East African mountains (Mahaney 1989), where an abundance of sound geomorphological and sedimentological evidence points to a much larger ice extent than now and to a temperature depression of as much as 6–8°C. The presently glaciated mountains, Kilimanjaro, Mount Kenya, and Ruwenzori, have a total ice cover of around 10 km², but the same mountains, together with the currently unglaciated Aberdares and Mount Elgon, had a maximum combined extent in the Pleistocene of 800 km² of glacier ice (Hastenrath 1984). These mountains probably experienced multiple phases of glaciation and Mahaney *et al.* (1991) have identified five Pleistocene and two Holocene glacial advance phases on Mount Kenya. Further north there was extensive glaciation in the mountains of Ethiopia, with ice covering 10 km² in the Simen Mountains, possibly more than 600 km² in the Bale Mountains, and 140 km² on Mount Badda (Messerli *et al.* 1980).

It is also possible that there was limited glaciation in the Saharan mountains (e.g. Tibesti), but the extent of glaciation (if any) in Southern Africa is a matter of speculation. Whereas there is evidence for periglacial activity, most workers reject the notion of glaciation in the Drakensbergs, but there is a possibility of glaciation in the mountains of the western Cape (Gellert 1991).

Glaciers were also considerably expanded in the Andes of South America. A Pliocene till has been identified in the altiplano of Bolivia, and other tills have been dated to the Pleistocene and the Holocene. At present the snowline in the Northern Andes lies at around 5,000 m, so that only peaks rising above that level currently show glaciers. During the last glacial maximum the regional snowline fell, so that terrain rising above about 4,000 m became ice-covered. Full details of the Andean tropical glaciations are given in Clapperton (1993).

A third tropical area where glaciation has left an impressive record of cirques, arêtes and moraines is in Southeast Asia. At the present time, New Guinea has an ice-covered area that amounts to only 8 km², yet during the last glaciation the total area was around 2,000 km². The snowline depression was of the order of 1,000–1,100 m, indicating a temperature depression that would have been at least 5–6°C (Brown 1990).

The shifts in glacier levels and snowlines is reflected in the down mountain displacement of vegetation belts, many of which were depressed by 1,000–1,500 m (Flenley 1979). It is likely that these belts were depressed not only because of the cold; it is also probable that high altitude plants were particularly highly stressed by low atmospheric carbon dioxide levels during glacials (Street-Perrott *et al.* 1997). So, for example, Jolly *et al.* (1997) have recently analysed pollen sequences from Burundi, Rwanda, and Western Uganda, and have found that areas now characterized by Afromontane forests were, at the time of the last glacial maximum at around 18,000 years ago, characterized by relatively xerophytic ericaceous scrub and grassland, only found at much higher altitudes. Montane forest was only re-established as recently as 11,000 to 10,000 years ago.

THE CLIMATOLOGICAL CONTEXT

Pluvials were not in phase in all areas and in both hemispheres (Spaulding 1991), and the effect of climate on the local occurrence of pluvials and interpluvials is a major question for research.

In a mid-latitude situation like the south-west of the United States, as recognized early on by Russell and Gilbert and more recently by Smith and Street-Perrott (1983), there was greatly increased effective moisture at the time of the Last Glacial Maximum. This was partly caused by decreased rates of evaporation, but also by the intensified zonal circulation and equatorward displacement of mid-latitude westerlies and associated rain-bearing depressions, particularly in the winter months.

Lower latitudes were less under the influence of the displaced westerlies during the full glacial. They experienced relatively dry conditions at that time and underwent a major pluvial in early to mid-Holocene times. Under warmer conditions monsoonal circulation was intensified, and in the northern hemisphere the Intertropical Convergence Zone would have shifted northwards, bringing rainfall into areas like West Africa, Ethiopia, Arabia, and Northwest India. The basis for this change may have been increased summer insolation, for at around 9000 years BP Milankovitch-forcing (i.e. the orbital position of the Earth) led to northern hemisphere summers that received almost 8 per cent more insolation than today (Kutzbach and Street-Perrott 1985).

This simple model only gives a first-order explanation of reality, and certain complexities need to be added. For example, as Wells (1983) has pointed out, the situation in an area like North America should not be viewed in a slavish latitudinal manner, for the trajectories of the great Rossby Waves in the westerly circulation of the atmosphere mean that the situation in, say, Florida, might be very different from that in California. Likewise, changes in insolation receipts at 9000 BP are applicable to the northern hemisphere low latitude pluvial, but have less direct relevance to the southern hemisphere. Also important in determining the spatial and temporal patterning of precipitation change are sea surface temperature conditions associated with the build-up and disintegration of the great ice-sheets. For example, the presence of a vigorous cold current off the Canary Islands and Northwest Africa, related to glacial meltwater and iceberg discharge into the North Atlantic, might account for arid conditions in the Late Glacial Maximum at a time when the presence of westerly winds might have been expected to produce moister conditions (Rognon and Coudé-Gaussen 1996). Also important may have been the effects that changes in snow and ice cover over Asia, including Tibet and the Himalyas, could have had on monsoon circulation in Asia (Zonneveld *et al.* 1997).

It is also apparent that the Holocene may have experienced a series of abrupt and relatively short-lived climatic episodes, which have caused, for example, dune mobilization in the American high plains (Arbogast 1996) and alternations of pluvials and intense arid phases in tropical Africa (Gasse and Van Campo 1994). The Holocene in low latitudes was far from stable and benign and it is not inconceivable that a climatic deterioration around 4,000 years ago could be involved in the mysterious collapse or eclipse of advanced civilization in Egypt, Mesopotamia, and Northwest India (Dalfes *et al.* 1997). These events cannot readily be accounted for by solar radiation changes, so other mechanisms need to be considered, including changes in the thermohaline (temperature and salinity driven) circulation in the oceans, or in land surface conditions. To that end, Gasse and Van Campo (1994: 453) proposed a model of the way in which the dynamics of land surface processes could bring about abrupt reversals in the amounts of monsoon rainfall:

(1) The establishment of monsoon rains under insolation forcing initiates the development of vegetation cover, expansion of wetlands and lake filling, and an increase in soil moisture. The subsequent decrease in surface albedo and increase in methane production provides a significant positive feedback enhancing the direct effects of insolation forcing.

(2) When the lakes reach their greatest extent, methane production falls. Sun energy efficiency reaches a minimum when evapotranspiration and evaporation are high. The subsequent cooling of tropical continents may explain the switching off of the monsoon.

(3) The land dries and warms again, and the ocean–land pressure gradient

increases. Moist oceanic air is once again forced to penetrate inland, and precipitation takes place once more.

What is apparent, therefore, is that the mechanisms causing changes in tropical circulations have been numerous and complex, and that there will have been lagged responses to change (e.g. slow decay of ice-masses, etc.). It is also apparent that there will have been differing hemispheric and regional responses to change (de Menocal and Rind 1993). For example, Arabia and Northeast Africa may have been especially sensitive to changes in Fennoscandian ice volumes and albedo (reflectivity of the surface), Northwest Africa may have been especially sensitive to changes in North Atlantic sea surface temperature conditions, while monsoonal Asia may have been especially affected by snow and ice conditions in its high mountain and plateau terrains.

THE DEGREE OF CHANGE

Whatever the driving forces may have been, the degree of environmental change during the Pleistocene and Holocene in low latitudes was immense. Even today's driest deserts show evidence for change. Indeed, the driest parts of the Sahara appear to have been habitable at certain times, not least in the Holocene. At the Kharga Oasis there are immense deposits of lime-rich spring tufas and lake beds around or in which Neolithic tools have been found in great numbers. This indicates higher groundwater levels and a considerable population. The Neolithic was a time particularly favourable for human activities in the Sahara. This has been known for a long time not least because of the collaboration of that wonderful Cambridge/Oxford duo of determined ladies, Gertrude Caton-Thompson and her long-time companion Elenor Gardner (see Caton-Thompson 1952).

A good example of mid-Holocene humidity in the dry heart of the eastern Sahara is provided by a study undertaken at Oyo by Ritchie and Haynes (1987). Their pollen spectra dating from 8500 BP until around 6000 BP show that there were strong Sudanian elements in the vegetation, and they identified pollen of tropical taxa such as *Hibiscus*. During this phase Oyo must have been a stratified lake surrounded by savannah vegetation similar to that now found 500 km to the south. After 6000 BP the lake became shallower, and *Acacia* thorn and then scrub grassland replaced the sub-humid savannah vegetation. At around 4500 BP the lake appears to have dried out, aeolian activity returned and vegetation disappeared except in wadis and oases. Roberts (1989) suggests that, in effect, the Sahara did not exist during most of the early Holocene. This is a point of view that is supported by the work of Petit-Maire (1989) in the western Sahara: 'Biogeographical factors implicate total disappearance of the hyperarid belt at least for one or two millenniums before 7000 BP . . . The Sahel northern limit shifted abut 1,000 km to the north between 18000 and 8000 BP and about 600 km to the south between 6000 BP and the present' (1989: 652). This contrasts with the situation in the Late Pleistocene, when, as Wendorf *et al.* (1976: 113) remark, 'There are no traces anywhere in the Nubian Desert of any occupation, spring, or lacustrine deposits that are between the Aterian sites and the terminal Palaeolithic in age. For this period of more than 30,000 years duration the Western Desert of Egypt was apparently devoid of surface water and of any sign of life.'

The remarkable blossoming of archaeological sites and lake deposits in the Sahara at 8000 BP is shown in figure 1.1. This work is the result of explorations by Petit-Maire and Kröpelin (1991). There is an abundance of mortars and grinders (indicating grass cover) and of bone hooks and harpoons (indicating lakes and fishing therein). Sites became less common after 6000 BP, as climate deteriorated (Petit-Maire *et al.* 1997).

Conversely, elsewhere in the tropics there is abundant evidence for sharply drier climatic conditions in the Pleistocene in some areas that are now quite moist. Not even the rainforests were immune. For example, pollen analysis in Amazonia has shown that the world's greatest rainfor-

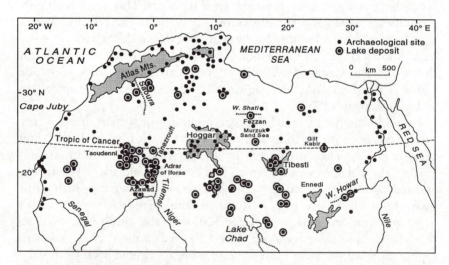

F I G. 1.1   Distribution of lake deposits and archaeological sites in Northern Africa at around 8000–9000 BP (modified from Petit-Maire and Kröpelin 1991).

est retreated into isolated pockets of vegetation (*Refugia*) and that its mean annual rainfall was 500–1,000 mm less than today (a reduction of 25–40 per cent) (Van der Hammen and Adsy 1994). The extent to which severe fragmentation of the Amazonian rainforest occurred is still debated, for some pollen analysts believe that although the composition of the forest changed as a result of temperature depression, the forests themselves persisted (Colinvaux *et al.* 1996). More clearly established is that the rainforest of the Congo Basin was greatly diminished in size, as deserts expanded from the Sahara in the north and the Kalahari in the south. Likewise, as figure 1.2, based on the work of Lezine (1989), shows, the extent of Guinean forest in West Africa has expanded and contracted by as much as 10° of latitude over the last 20,000 years. Similarly, figures 1.3a and b, based on the work of Yan and Petit-Maire (1994), show the changes that have taken place in monsoon extent over the same period.

The degree of temperature change that took place during the cold phases in the tropics has been the subject of some debate. As recounted earlier, the degree of temperature depression suggested by the depression of snowlines and expansion of glaciation on tropical mountains is of the order of 5–8°C. Recent work also suggests that the tropical oceans may have cooled substantially, which could have had considerable implications for the health of coral reefs. Cool oceans could have absorbed more carbon dioxide from the atmosphere, reducing the greenhouse effect and contributing to global cooling (Patrick and Thunell 1997). The oceans probably cooled by 3–5°C (Webb *et al.* 1997).

CONCLUSION

While the Pleistocene Ice Age may not have had quite the impact envisaged by Agassiz, there is no doubt that low latitudes have witnessed frequent events of considerable magnitude over the last few millions of years. Neither the centres of the world's tropical deserts nor the hearts of the great tropical rainforests have remained unscathed. While we may no longer accept some of the rather crude attempts to relate low latitude climatic changes to events in history and prehistory, which were developed by the environmental determinists in the era of Kropotkin and Huntington, we now have a range of techniques for both dating and for environmental reconstruction about which they could only have dreamed. We need to revisit many great themes (some of which are discussed by Vrba *et al.* 1995), in the light of these new developments, including the emergence of hominids in Africa, the diffusion of humans

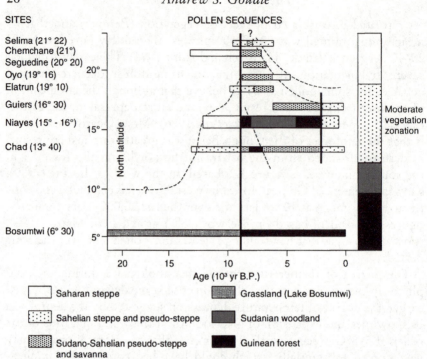

F I G. 1.2 Late Quaternary vegetational changes in North Tropical Africa from pollen analysis, showing the latitudinal locations of sites, pollen sequences according to the chronology with their phystogeographical significance, and the modern vegetation zonation. The heavy lines at 9000 and 2000 BP underline the contemporaneity of the vegetation changes in each site (modified from Lezine 1989).

from Africa, hiatuses in the prehistory of drylands, and the origin and timing of domestication. As Andrew Sherratt (1997: 283) has recently pointed out:

Environmental change is not simply a backdrop to evolution: it is a principal reason for major episodes of biological change. It is no coincidence that successive species of hominid made their appearance during the Quaternary Period, with its rapid pace and massive scale of environmental alteration. Over 90% of this period has been cooler and dryer than the Holocene, so contemporary conditions are unrepresentative. Although colloquially termed the (high latitude) 'Ice Age', it could equally appropriately be called the (low latitude) 'Desert Age', especially—from a human point of view—since increasing and cyclically enforced desiccation has been the principal driving force of hominid evolution.

Perhaps Huntington wasn't so wide of the mark after all.

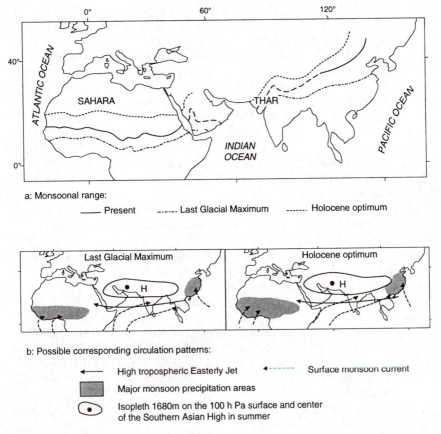

a: Monsoonal range:

——— Present   ‐‐‐‐‐ Last Glacial Maximum   ‐‐‐‐‐‐‐ Holocene optimum

b: Possible corresponding circulation patterns:

◄——— High tropospheric Easterly Jet   ◄‐‐‐‐‐‐ Surface monsoon current

▩ Major monsoon precipitation areas

⬮ Isopleth 1680m on the 100 h Pa surface and center of the Southern Asian High in summer

FIG. 1.3   (a) Comparison of climate changes along the Afro-Asian transitional zone between the Last Glacial Maximum and the Holocene. (b) Possible corresponding circulation patterns (after Yan and Petit-Maire 1994).

REFERENCES

Agassiz, L. (1840). *Etudes sur les glaciers.* Neuchâtel, privately published. 346pp.
——(1869). *A Journey in Brazil.* Boston: Ticknor and Field.
Arbogast, A. F. (1996). 'Stratigraphic evidence for late-Holocene aeolian sand mobilization and soil formation in south-central Kansas, USA'. *Journal of Arid Environments*, 34: 403–14.
Blanford, W. T. (1877). 'Geological notes on the Great Indian Desert Between Sind and Rajputana'. *Records, Geological Survey of India*, 10 (1): 10–21.
Brown, I. M. (1990). 'Quaternary Glaciations of New Guinea'. *Quaternary Science Reviews*, 9: 273–80.

Buening, K. R. M., Talbot, M. R., and Kelts, K. (1997). 'A revised 30,000 year palaeoclimatic and paleohydrological history of Lake Albert, East Africa'. *Palaeogeography, Palaeoclimatology, Palaeoecology*, 136: 259–79.

Bullard, J. E. (1994). 'An analysis of the morphological variation of linear sand dunes and of their relationship with environmental parameters in the Southwest Kalahari'. Unpublished PhD thesis, University of Sheffield.

Butzer, K. W., Isaac, G. L., Richardson, J. L., and Washbourne-Kamau, C. (1972). 'Radiocarbon dating of East African lake levels'. *Science*, 175: 1069–75.

Caton-Thompson, G. (1952). *Kharga Oasis in Prehistory*. London: Athlone Press.

Childe, V. G. (1936). *Man Makes Himself*. London: Watts.

Clapperton, C. (1993). *Quaternary Geology and Geomorphology of South America*. Amsterdam: Elsevier.

Colinvaux, P. A., De Oliveira, P. E., Moreno, J. E., Miller, M. C., and Bush, M. B. (1996). 'A long pollen record from lowland Amazonia: forest and cooling in glacial times'. *Science*, 274: 85–9.

Dalfes, H. N., Kukla, G., and Weiss, H. (eds) (1997). *Third Millennium BC Climate Change and Old World Collapse*. Berlin: Springer Verlag.

Davies, G. L. (1969). *The Earth in Decay*. London: Macdonald.

de Menocal, P. B. and Rind, D. (1993). 'Sensitivity of Asian and African climate to variations in seasonal insolation, glacial ice cover, sea surface temperature and Asian Orography'. *Journal of Geophysical Research*, 98, D4: 7265–87.

de Menocal, P. B., Ruddiman, W. F., and Pokras, E. M. (1993). 'Influences of high- and low-latitude processes on African terrestrial cimate: Pleistocene aeolian records from equatorial Atlantic Ocean Drilling Program Site 663'. *Palaeoceanography*, 8: 209–42.

Dunbar, G. S. (1996). *The History of Geography*. Cooperstown (NY): Dodge-Graphic Press.

Fang, J. Q. (1991). 'Lake evolution during the past 30,000 years in China, and its implications for environmental change'. *Quaternary Research*, 36: 37–60.

Flenley, J. R. (1979). 'The late Quaternary vegetational history of the equatorial mountains'. *Progress in Physical Geography*, 3: 488–509.

Gasse, F. and Van Campo, E. (1994). 'Abrupt post-glacial climate events in West Africa and North Africa monsoon domains'. *Earth and Planetary Science Letters*, 126: 435–56.

Gasse, F., Tehet, R., Durand, A., Gilbert, E., and Fontes, J. C. (1990). 'The arid–humid transition in the Sahara and the Sahel during the last deglaciation'. *Nature*, 346: 141–6.

Gellert, J. F. (1991). 'Pleistozän-Kalfzeitliche Vergletscherungen im Hochland von Tibert und im Sudafrikanischen Kapgebirge'. *Eiszeitalter und Gegenwart*, 41: 141–5.

Gilbert, G. K. (1890). Lake Bonneville. *U.S. Geological Survey Monography 1*, 438pp.

Goudie, A. S. (1972). 'The concept of post-glacial progressive desiccation'. *Research Papers, School of Geography, University of Oxford*, 4–48.

Goudie, A. S. (1978). 'Dust storms and their geomorphological implications'. *Journal of Arid Environments*, 1: 291–310.

Goudie, A. S., Allchin, B., and Hegde, K. T. M. (1973). 'The former extensions of the Great Indian Sand Desert'. *Geographical Journal*, 139: 243–57.

Grove, A. T. (1958). 'The ancient Erg of Hausaland, and similar formations on the southside of the Sahara'. *Geographical Journal*, 124: 528–33.

Grove, A. T. (1969). 'Landforms and climate change in the Kalahari and Ngamiland'. *Geographical Journal*, 135: 192–212.

Grove, A. T. and Goudie, A. S. (1971). 'Late Quaternary lake levels in the Rift Valley of southern Ethiopia and elsewhere in tropical Africa'. *Nature*, 234: 403–5.

Grove, A. T. and Warren, A. (1968). 'Quaternary landforms and climate on the south side of the Sahara'. *Geographical Journal*, 134: 194–208.

Hastenrath, S. (1984). *The Glaciers of Equatorial East Africa.* Dordrecht: Kluwer.

Hedin, S. (1940). *The Wandering Lake.* London: G. Routledge and Sons.

Heron, A. M. (1917). 'The geology of north-eastern Rajputana and adjacent districts'. *Memoirs, Geological Survey of India*, 45 (1): 1–128.

Hopkirk, P. (1980). *Foreign Devils on the Silk Road.* London: John Murray.

Hull, E. (1865). *Mount Seir, Sinai and Western Palestine.* London: Bentley.

Huntington, E. (1907). *The Pulse of Asia.* London: Constable.

Imbrie, J. and Imbrie, K. P. (1979). *Ice Ages: Solving the Mystery.* London: Macmillan.

Jamieson, T. F. (1863). 'On the parallel roads of Glen Roy, and their place in the history of the glacial period'. *Quarterly Journal of the Geological Society of London*, 19: 235–59.

Jolly, D., Taylor, D., Marchant, R., Hamilton, A., Bonnefille, R., Buchet, G., and Riollet, G. (1997). 'Vegetation dynamics in central Africa since 18000 BP: pollen record from the interlacustrine highlands of Burundi, Rwanda and western Uganda'. *Journal of Biogeography*, 24: 495–512.

Jones, B. (1938). 'Desiccation and the West African colonies'. *Geographical Journal*, 91: 4–23.

Kolla, V. and Biscaye, P. E. (1977). 'Distribution and origin of quartz in the sediments of the Indian Ocean'. *Journal of Sedimentary Petrology*, 47: 642–9.

Kropotkin, Prince, P. (1904). 'The desiccation of Eur-Asia'. *Geographical Journal*, 23: 722–41.

Kutzbach, J. and Street-Perrott, F. A. (1985). 'Milankovitch forcing of fluctuations in the level of tropical lakes from 18 to 0 kyr BP'. *Nature*, 317: 130–4.

Lartet, L. (1865). 'Sur la formation du bassin de la mer morte ou lac asphaltite, et sur les changements survenus dans le niveau de ce lac'. *Comptes Rendus Academie des Sciences (Paris)*, 60: 796–800.

Lezine, A.-M. (1989). 'Late Quaternary vegetation and climate of the Sahel'. *Quaternary Research*, 32: 317–34.

Mahaney, W. C. (ed.) (1989). *Quaternary and Environmental Research on East African Mountains.* Rotterdam: Balkema.

Mahaney, W. C., Harmsen, R., and Spence, J. R. (1991). 'Glacial and interglacial cycles and development of the Afroalpine ecosystem on East African Mountains. Glacial and postglacial geological record and paleoclimate of Mount Kenya'. *Journal of African Earth Science*, 12: 505–12.

Martin, G. J. (1973). *Ellsworth Huntington. His Life and Thought.* Hamden, CT: Archon Books.

Messerli, B., Winninger, M., and Rognon, P. (1980). 'The Saharan and East African uplands during the Quaternary', in M. A. J. Williams and H. Faure (eds), *The Sahara and the Nile.* Rotterdam: Balkema, 87–118.

National Institute of Sciences (1952). *Proceedings of the Symposium on the Rajputana Desert.* Delhi.

Newberry, J. S. (1861). *Report Upon the Colorado River of the West*, part III, Geological Report, Washington DC.

Patrick, A. and Thunell, R. C. (1997). 'Tropical Pacific sea surface temperatures and upper water column thermal structure during the last glacial maximum'. *Palaeoceanography*, 12: 649–57.

Petit-Maire, N. (1989). 'Interglacial environments in presently Hyperarid Sahara: palaeoclimatic implications', in M. Leinen and M. Sarnthein (eds), *Palaeoclimatology and Palaeometerology: Modern and Past Patterns of Global Atmospheric Transport.* Dordrecht: Kluwer, 637–61.

Petit-Maire, N. and Kröpelin, S. (1991). 'Les Climats Holocènes du Sahara le long du Tropique du Cancer', in N. Petit-Maire (ed.), *Paléoenvironments du Sahara.* Paris: CNRS, 205–11.

Petit-Maire, N., Benfort, L., and Page, N. (1997). 'Holocene climate change and man in the present day Sahara Desert', in H. N. Dalfes, G. Kukla, and H. Weiss (eds), *Third Millennium BC Climate Change and the Old World Collapse.* Berlin: Springer Verlag, 297–308.

Price, W. A. (1944). 'Greater American deserts'. *Texas Academy of Science Proceedings and Transactions*, 27: 163–70.

Pyne, S. J. (1980). *Grove Karl Gilbert: A Great Engine of Research.* Austin: University of Texas Press.

Richie, W. and Haynes, C. V. (1987). 'Holocene vegetation zonation in the Eastern Sahara'. *Nature*, 330: 645–7.

Roberts, N. (1989). *The Holocene.* Oxford: Blackwell.

Roberts, N., Taieb, M., Barker, P., Damnati, B., Icole, M., and Williamson, D. (1993). 'Timing of the Younger Dryas event in East Africa from lake-level changes'. *Nature*, 366: 146–8.

Rognon, P. and Coudé-Gaussen, G. (1996). 'Paleoclimates off Northwest Africa (28°–35°N) about 18000 BP based on continental eolian deposits'. *Quaternary Research*, 46: 118–26.

Ruddiman, W. F. (1997). 'Tropical Atlantic terrigenous fluxes since 25000 BP'. *Marine Geology*, 136: 189–207.

Russell, I. C. (1885). *Quaternary History of Lake Lahontan.* United States Geological Survey Monograph, No. 11.

Russell, I. C. (1895). *Lakes of North America*. Boston: Ginn.

Sarnthein, M. (1978). 'Sand deserts during Glacial Maximum and Climatic Optimum'. *Nature*, 272: 43–6.

Sarnthein, M. and Koopman, B. (1980). 'Late Quaternary deep-sea record of north-west African dust supply and wind circulation'. *Palaeoecology of Africa*, 12: 238–53.

Schwarz, E. H. L. (1923). *The Kalahari or Thirstland Redemption*. Cape Town: Oxford University Press.

Sherratt, A. (1997). 'Climatic cycles and behavioural revolutions: the emergence of modern humans and the beginning of farming'. *Antiquity*, 71: 271–87.

Sirocko, F., Sarnthein, M., Lange, H., and Erlenkeuser, H. (1991). 'Atmospheric summer circulation and coastal upwelling in the Arabian Sea during the Holocene and the Last Glaciation'. *Quaternary Research*, 36: 72–93.

Sirocko, F., Garbe-Schönberg, D., McIntyre, A., and Molfino, B. (1996). 'Teleconnections between the subtropical monsoons and high-latitude climates during the last deglaciation'. *Science*, 272: 526–9.

Smith, G. I. and Street-Perrott, F. A. (1983). 'Pluvial lakes of the western United States', in S. C. Porter (ed.), *Late-Quaternary Environments of the United States*. London: Longman, 190–212.

Spaulding, W. G. (1991). 'Pluvial climatic episodes in North America and North Africa: types and correlation with global climate'. *Palaeogeography, Palaeoclimatology and Palaeoecology*, 84: 217–27.

Stein, A. (1938). 'Desiccation in Asia: a geographical question in the light of history'. *Hungarian Quarterly*.

Stoddart, D. R. (1986). *On Geography*. Oxford: Blackwell.

Stokes, S., Thomas, D. S. G., and Washington, R. (1997). 'Multiple episodes of aridity in southern Africa since the last interglacial period'. *Nature*, 338: 154–8.

Street, F. A. and Grove, A. T. (1979). 'Global maps of lake-level fluctuations since 30,000 yr BP'. *Quaternary Research*, 12: 83–118.

Street-Perrott, F. A., Huang, Y., Perrott, R. A., Eglinton, G., Barker, P., Ben Khalifa, L., Harkness, D. D., and Olago, D. O. (1997). 'Impact of Lower Atmospheric CO_2 on Tropical Mountain Ecosystems'. *Science*, 278: 1422–6.

Thiede, J. (1979). 'Wind regimes over the late Quaternary Southwest Pacific Ocean'. *Geology*, 7: 259–62.

Thomas, D. S. G., Stokes, S., and Shaw, P. A. (1997). 'Holocene aeolian activity in the south western Kalahari Desert, southern Africa: significance and relationship to late-Pleistocene dune-building events'. *The Holocene*, 7: 273–81.

Van der Hammen, T. and Adsy, M. L. (1994). 'Amazonia during the last Glacial'. *Palaeogeography, Palaeoclimatology and Palaeoecology*, 109: 261–97.

Vrba, E. S., Denton, G. H., Partridge, T. C., and Burckle, L. H. (eds) (1995). *Paleoclimate and Evolution with Emphasis on Human Origins*. New Haven: Yale University Press.

Wadia, D. N. (1960). 'The post-glacial desiccation of Central Asia'. *Monograph, National Institute of Sciences of India*, 1–26.

Wasson, R. J., Fitchett, K., Mackey, B., and Hyde, R. (1988). 'Large-scale patterns of dune type, spacing and orientation in the Australian continental dunefield'. *Australian Geographer*, 19: 80–104.

Webb, R. S., Rind, D. H., Lehman, S. J., Healy, R. J., and Sigman, D. (1997). 'Influence of ocean heat transport on the climate of the Last Glacial Maximum'. *Nature*, 385: 695–9.

Wells, G. L. (1983). 'Late glacial circulation over North America revealed by aeolian features', in F. A. Street-Perrott, M. Beran, and R. Radcliffe (eds), *Variation in the Global Water Budget*. Dordrecht: Kluwer, 317–30.

Wells, G. L. (1992). 'The aeolian landscape of Central North America from the Late Pleistocene'. Unpublished DPhil thesis, University of Oxford, 3 vols.

Wendorf, F., Schild, R., Said, R., Haynes, C. V., Gautier, A., and Kobusiewicz, P. (1976). 'The prehistory of the Egyptian Sahara'. *Science*, 193: 103–16.

Yan, Z. and Petit-Maire, N. (1994). 'The last 140 ka in the Afro-Asian arid/semi-arid transitional zone'. *Palaeogeography, Paleoclimatology and Palaeoecology*, 110: 217–33.

Zeuner, F. E. (1959). *The Pleistocene Period: Its Climate, Chronology and Faunal Successions* (2nd edn). London: Hutchinson.

Zonneveld, K. A. F., Ganssen, G., Troelsma, S., Versteegh, G. J. M., and Visser, H. (1997). 'Mechanisms forcing abrupt fluctuations of the Indian Ocean Summer Monsoon during the last deglaciation'. *Quaternary Science Reviews*, 16: 187–201.

2

Climate and History in the Old and New Worlds

Claudio Vita-Finzi

He had been eight years upon a project for extracting sun-beams out
of cucumbers, which were to be put into vials hermetically sealed,
and let out to warm the air in raw inclement summers.

Jonathan Swift, *Gulliver's Travels (Voyage to Laputa)*

SWIFT was mocking science with the insouciance of the ignorant—for
what is a pickled cucumber but a bunch of sunbeams trapped by photosynthesis? But his quip conveniently convolves the key themes of this
chapter: time, the sun, and agriculture, the linking threads being (a) the
parallels in a major component of the landscape during historical times
in large parts of the Americas and Eurasia, (b) the impact these changes
had on agriculture, and therefore social history, in later times, and (c) the
evidence for a solar role in changing the topography.

The history of attempts to uncover the links between climate and
human affairs is long and often unedifying. The protagonists include
Friedrich Nietzsche, who argued that anyone who had great duties to
perform was limited in the choice of climates in which to dwell, and
Hegel, who saw the temperate zone as 'the true theatre of history'. Huntington (1922) claimed a close match between human progress and what
he termed climatic energy, just as Charles Darwin (1888) argued that
progress up the scale of civilization was favoured by a cool climate
because it led to 'industry and the various arts'. The climatic determinism of Arnold Toynbee (1946) was in the velvet glove of challenge-
and-response. Ease, he argued, is inimical to civilization; the most
stimulating challenge lies between insufficient and excessive environmental severity.

Throughout, an equation is being sought which seeks to balance such
items as mean annual temperature against bellicosity or artistic sensibil-
ity: 'In the cold of Europe, under prudish northern fogs, except where

slaughter is afoot, you only glimpse the crawling cruelty of your fellow men. But their rottenness rises to the surface as soon as they are tickled by the hideous fevers of the tropics' (L.-F. Celine). Of course an equation can be drafted where the impact of climate is catastrophic. Many epidemics appear to have been triggered by unusual weather (Ladurie 1967). Famine in France in 1660–1 was preceded by cold winters and a wet and cold spring and summer. Even today, and in developed communities, many illnesses have a marked seasonal incidence (Cliff and Haggett 1988). Yet famine and pestilence, like earthquakes, may weaken but rarely eradicate societies. In any case, to view the weather in isolation from social and economic conditions is to traduce economic history. The spread of the blight that led to the potato famine in Ireland was favoured by the autumns of 1845 and 1846; but more important were the emergence of a new, virulent pathogen, and a dense population relying on monoculture (Burroughs 1997).

Even so, the hunt for climatic explanations is harmless enough and even beneficial if it displaces ethnic or cultural stereotypes or if a change in climate provides a plausible alternative to political machinations or human foibles. The danger lies in the recycling of such conjectures in the reconstruction of past climates. Historians have plotted valuable charts which show how severe winter, floods, and glacial advances can sometimes be traced right across Europe; for earlier centuries they have drawn on such delicate indicators as the date of the wine harvest and the incidence of appeals for assistance to God (Ladurie 1967). These historical conjectures in due course are transmuted to hard data by which to test and refine climatic theories and models.

CLIMATE AND HISTORY

The fact remains that, however confidently particular climates may be linked to the dynamism or personality of the peoples they envelop, the contribution of climatic change to the human record remains elusive, even in marginal settings. Consider the suggestion by Weiss *et al.* (1993) that the Akkadian empire, which stretched some 1,300 kilometres from the Persian Gulf to the upper Euphrates, was (in the words of Kerr (1998: 325)) laid low in about 2200 BC not by 'leaders who overreached, armies that faltered, farmers who degraded the land' but by prolonged drought. The same drought 'toppled' other civilizations in Greece, Old Kingdom Egypt, and the Indus valley. 'Many archaeologists' (we are told) 'were skeptical because the timing of these collapses was imprecise, and purely social and political explanations seemed to suffice' (Kerr 1998: 325). But a few years later the theory appeared to receive independent support from a sediment core taken from the bottom of the Gulf of Oman, which indicated that the worst dry spell in the region during the last 10,000 years began about 2200 BC, just when the Akkadians were abandoning their northern stronghold of Tell Leilan, a major city in northern Mesopotamia whose farmers depended on rainfall rather than on irrigation waters from the Tigris and Euphrates. The drought lasted 300 years, after which Tell Leilan was reoccupied.

The dry spell was inferred from a rise in the volume of windblown dust derived from Mesopotamia in about 2000 ± 100 BC to its highest levels in the last 10,000 years. The dust was traced to Mesopotamia 1,800 km away by its content of dolomite, calcite, and quartz. This composition characterizes most dust in the region, and dust is hardly an unambiguous indictor of a lethal level of aridity; indeed, other cultures—including that of Ur III—apparently persisted in the region for decades or even centuries after the postulated drought had peaked. The crucial difficulty evidently lies more with the question than with the proposed explanation. What is it that calls for explanation, and how will we know when our proposed explanation is satisfactory? Is the abandonment of a city synonymous with the end of an entire civilization?

The difficulty is not eliminated by focusing on agriculture rather than urban life, as any climatic impact may be difficult to isolate from other sources of change. On the Bolivian altiplano around Lake Titicaca, according to Binford *et al.* (1997), aridity inhibited agriculture until about 1500 BC, when wetter conditions favoured specialized agricultural methods including (after about AD 600) raised-field cultivation on wetlands in the core area of the Tiwanaku civilization. The decline in available moisture in AD 1100–1400 was less drastic, but its impact was profound because the dense population made possible by the raised-field system could not be sustained in drier times. Land abandonment led to cultural collapse.

Most of the explanations put forward for the collapse of Classic Maya civilization in about AD 800–900 blame it on a 'disequilibrium between different parts of the system' (Renfrew and Bahn 1991). In the account by Hosler *et al.* (1977), for example, the disequilibrium was between agriculture and monument construction: population growth put pressure on food production, which prompted more monument construction by part of the agricultural labour force and thus a further decline in productivity.

The puzzle is compounded by difficulties in documenting the collapse, which is generally defined by the end of Lowland Maya elite class culture and especially the production of carved monuments, platform temples, and certain kinds of artefact, a process which was 'apparently accompanied by a rapid and large-scale depopulation of the commoner class' (Sidrys and Berger 1979).

The publication in 1966 of a 3500-year climatic sequence from Punta Laguna showed that the collapse took place at a time dominated by drought. An earlier such spell coincided with the Maya Hiatus between Early and late Classic Periods in about AD 600 (Curtis *et al.* 1996). On the other hand, the Classic Period appears to have begun (in ~AD 250) at a time of increasingly dry conditions, so that the investigators were led to consider whether Maya culture evolved in response to climatic drying—or whether it was its success that led to a reduction in rainfall as a consequence of deforestation (Curtis *et al.* 1996).

There is, of course, nothing new in trying to account for the flamboyant collapse of Maya civilization by invoking a shift in the local climate: for many of the ruins are in regions of heavy rainfall, dense forest, and malignant fevers, and much of the surrounding land does not favour cultivation, although it is a mere hundred miles away from the drier, densely populated areas of the Yucatan coast (Huntington and Visher 1922). The novelty lay in the reliance on climatic evidence which was independent of the events it was supposed to illuminate.

The renewed enthusiasm for climatic explanations that is found in current analyses of Andean, Mayan, and other agricultural societies also characterizes recent studies of the beginnings of farming. According to Sherratt (1997), the mood owes much to widespread acceptance of discontinuous biological evolution coupled with growing evidence for rapidly changing climatic conditions during the Pleistocene. The notion of an economic revolution which had been hastened, if not dictated, by climatic vicissitudes was favoured a few decades ago and was later found unacceptably deterministic or naive. The thesis is now revived by some prehistorians as the product of a specific climatic event, the close of the Younger Dryas stadial that brought the last glacial period to a close. But, as Sherratt (1997) notes, the need then arises to define farming. There is no point in having a precise chronology if the events it records are nebulous. As Mortimer Wheeler (1954) put it, we need trains as well as timetables.

CLIMATE AND SOIL

Agriculture clearly provides a convenient link between climatic prompt and social reaction. Voltaire advocated broadening the scope of history to include social and economic activities—always provided they represented the peaks of human achievement (Berlin 1981). Agriculture admittedly tends to be set in the valley bottoms; yet without agriculture the peaks could not have been scaled: no bread, no circuses. More important in the present context, agriculture depends on soil; and soil is tangible, often datable, and (especially if alluvial in origin) very sensitive to minor climatic perturbations.

Since the 1930s geologists have chronicled the filling and destruction of alluvial valley floors in the course of recent millennia in various parts of the USA. The extent to which the events operated synchronously in separate valleys or even the same drainage system has proved controversial, a pivotal component of the dispute between those who champion climatic controls and those who emphasize human activity or, more recently, the spontaneous occurrence of cutting and filling in basins with high sediment loads.

In a review of the topic for the last ten millennia throughout the conterminous USA, Knox (1983) concluded that, although the major alluvial episodes did not begin or end everywhere at precisely the same time, they represent intervals when similar types of fluvial activity were dominant within large regions. In many valleys in the American Southwest the last unit is a fill for which radiocarbon ages range from AD 460 to AD 1750 (identified as Fill 3; Deposition E, in Haynes 1968). In the upper San Pedro, in Arizona, entrenchment into the fill (which here began to accumulate as late as AD 1450) can be traced from written accounts, Indian irrigation practice, and photographs, and affected 32 km of the channel in less than 18 years (Hereford 1993).

A similar deposit is found in central and northern Mexico, and, to judge from radiocarbon ages and archaeological evidence, it dates from approximately AD 500–1700. Here too there is wide disagreement over the contribution of climatic factors to its genesis. Heine (1976), for example, links soil erosion in central Mexico to human influence, with a lull during about AD 100–650 due to a reduction in the cultivated area. But the nature of the sediments shows that they were laid down by stream discharges less flashy than those of the present, a fact which is not consistent with the accelerated run off that often accompanies soil erosion. If we combine the Mexican and western USA records, the New World zone—for which there is evidence for aggradation roughly between AD 450 and 1750—extends over 25 degrees of latitude and 15 of longitude.

In parts of the Old World there is evidence for an extensive phase of silting at about the same time (Leopold and Vita-Finzi 1998). The phenomenon was first identified in Italy and Libya, and later traced within an area framed by latitudes 25–45°N and longitudes 10°W–60°E to other parts of the Mediterranean and Southwest Asia (fig. 2.1). At first, dating was based on the age of ruins covered by the sediments (see figure 2.2)

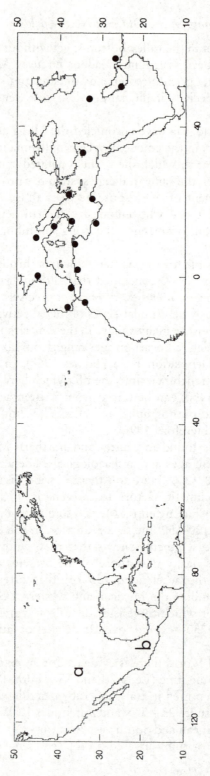

FIG. 2.1 Principal areas discussed: (a) southwest USA; (b) central Mexico. The filled circles indicate locations in Eurasia on which the radiocarbon alluvial chronology of Vita-Finzi (1995) is based.

F I G. 2.2   Ruins of Olympia (Greece). The surface of the alluvial fill may be seen at centre.

and of sherds and coins within it; as the number of radiocarbon dates for the silts grew, so did the impression that the process, which began about AD 500 in the north of the zone surveyed, was delayed by about 1,000 years in the south. The nature of the sediments indicated that silting here, too, had been performed by streams less flashy or seasonal than those occupying the valleys today.

The crucial step towards an explanation was taken by Leopold (1951), who showed that changes in the annual distribution of rainfall without necessarily any change in annual total could determine whether a drainage system was cutting or filling its beds. If rainfall events are more intense, channels erode. If the climatic trend is towards light but frequent rains, then vegetation prospers and sediment is supplied by slow but effective sheet erosion from the hillsides (Leopold 1997).

Kirk Bryan (1941), who was perhaps the first to identify synchronous alluvial phases in the American West, argued that in Colorado, Arizona, and New Mexico channel incision led to the loss of fields which had previously been watered by the Puebloans (or Anazazi) using flood irrigation, and thence prompted the great migrations of about AD 1300.

As he noted, floodwater farming was especially favoured by broad valley floors over which the runoff could spread widely. A slight change in climate was sufficient to convert ephemeral streams from alluviation to erosion. The change was often signalled by an unusually violent flood, as in 1881 in the San Pedro valley (Hereford 1993), whereupon the new channel cut its way upstream rendering field after field useless for stream irrigation.

An intriguing passage in Herodotus illustrates that there may be a price to pay for aggradation. At the time of King Moeris, Herodotus writes, a rise of 8 cubits (about 4 metres) in the level of the Nile was sufficient to flood the land to the north of Memphis; by his day it needed 15 or 16 cubits to achieve the same result. If the trend were to persist, he comments, the Egyptians will become as dependent on rainfall as the Greeks, and will need to till the soil and carry out all the other tasks that burden the farmer instead of letting the river do most of the work. Although the observed change could stem from river downcutting, it is more probably the product of silt accumulation by successive nilotic floods. If, as the translator suggests, Moeris was Amenemhet III, he was on the throne 1,400 and not (as Herodotus thought) less than 900 years before the time of Herodotus. The resulting rate of silt accumulation averages out at a little under 3 mm per year, well within the long-term aggradation rate of ~9 mm per year for the Nile near Karnak and Memphis calculated in 1906 (Leopold *et al.* 1964).

As various commentators have observed, Herodotus made light of the work required to exploit the Nile silts, however obliging the river, but he was right to sing the praises of flood irrigation. In semi-arid areas the process also leads to a gradual gain not only in the area of cultivable land but also in its depth and hence in access by wells to water stored in the alluvium.

In wetter areas, however, the benefits of aggradation often had to await drainage by natural stream incision or by human intervention. A notable example is the fertile Arta plain of Greece, which was not rendered productive until the present century. In Italy the plains between Ferrara, Bologna, Ravenna, and the mouth of the river Po were repeatedly built up and drained. According to Veggiani (1991), a major phase of flooding and silting in AD 400–750 saw areas which had been well drained in Roman times turn into swamps. The 'climatic optimum' of AD 1000–1200 that has been identified throughout northern Europe (Lamb 1965) led to a temporary hydrological reprieve during which reclamation was helped by stream incision, locally by as much as 8 m; the ensuing climatic relapse lasted until about AD 1400, when reclamation was again favoured by downcutting. There followed a second major phase of silting which Veggiani equates with the cold conditions that prevailed in Europe in

AD 1550–1850. The twofold (or threefold) division of the post-Roman channel fill is echoed in other parts of Europe, and may await identification in the fills here described as unitary.

Besides illuminating the rural implications of fluvial history the detailed studies of Veggiani starkly demonstrate that urban life was not immune. First, there was the risk of famine (as in AD 568 and 1619–22) which might encourage the spread of bubonic plague (as in AD 571 and 1630–2). Second, many cities were undermined and buried by the floods: Roman Modena, for example, lies under 4–6 metres of alluvium, Imola under 8 metres. Undermined by the floodwaters and choked with mud, the latter easily succumbed in AD 568–70 to the Longobard invaders. It was in the midst of this environmental decay, Veggiani comments, that the Ancient World came to an end.

THE SOLAR FACTOR

The parallels between the recent alluvial histories of the Old and New Worlds are difficult to accommodate within anthropogenic explanations, both chronologically and as regards the geometry and nature of the deposits. The universality of evidence for a change in the rainfall pattern would seem to present even greater problems, given the wide range of environments at issue. Yet seasonality can vary surprisingly little over large areas. In Mexico, for instance, the percentage of the total annual rain that falls in winter is currently 10.2 or less over much of the country (García 1969). Changes in seasonality over time at all but equatorial and polar latitudes are linked to the circumpolar vortex, which blows W–E round the globe over the middle latitudes at an altitude of 2–20 kilometres. The two key circulation patterns are zonal, when the vortex meanders little, and meridional, when it displays large waves or loops (Lamb 1995).

In Mexico the instrumental data suggest that climatic oscillations propagate northwards in response to movement of the subtropical high-pressure cells (Wallén 1955). In the 1950s and 1960s there was a northward shift in the Intertropical Convergence Zone and the east South Pacific anticyclone, which led to the highest precipitations ever recorded at Mexico City and, more important, to a greater concentration of precipitation in the summer months in comparison with dry years, possibly due to mid-latitude depressions tracking far south (Metcalfe 1987). The return of a meridional circulation brought back dry conditions.

In the American Southwest an early Holocene zonal circulation was replaced by prevalently meridional circulation, with a corresponding increase in frontal activity (Knox 1983). In the Old World a plausible explanation for the observed changes could be a temporary increase in the incidence of cyclonic rains brought about by a southward shift of the Eurasian depression belts (Vita-Finzi 1995). The same mechanism had been put forward by Lamb (1964) to account for the climatic conditions in Europe between AD 1200–1300 and 1600–1700, the displacement he proposed amounting to 5–10° of latitude.

There is a high degree of correlation between global temperatures from the mid-seventeenth to the mid-nineteenth centuries and solar irradiance (Mann *et al.* 1998), which, for the period before artificial satellites made direct measurement possible, is derived from sunspot numbers. The Maunder minimum, a period between AD 1645 and 1715 when sunspots were almost absent, coincided with the European cold spell mentioned earlier, while there was a sunspot maximum at the time of the Medieval Optimum (Hoyt and Schatten 1997).

More important in the present context, however, is the observation that at low sunspot levels ('quiet sun') a strong circumpolar vortex—a zonal pattern—is favoured. Conversely, a strong sun means that the solar wind penetrates the geomagnetic shield and the upper atmosphere, and locally leads to heating of the atmosphere so that the zonal pattern breaks up into a cellular blocking pattern (Willett 1987). In addition, at times of high solar activity the northern mid-latitude cyclones are displaced south, whereas more southerly tracks, such as those crossing the Mediterranean, are shifted polewards (Brown and John 1979); in the north Atlantic the equatorward shift of storm tracks may be as much as 6° at solar maximum (Tinsley 1988). The number of cyclonic storms, on the other hand, increases at solar minimum (Herman and Goldberg 1985).

Other sunspot minima are the Spörer (1420–1530), the Dalton (1795–1830), the Wolf (1280–1340), the Oort (1010–50), and two unnamed ones in 1790–1830 and 1880–1915. Using the radiocarbon content of dated tree-rings as an inverse measure of solar activity, it can be shown that these century-scale oscillations are superimposed on others on a thousand-year scale; moreover, they represent short-lived departures from a decrease in the radiocarbon content of the atmosphere since 22,000 years ago, which is at least partly due to increased solar activity (Vita-Finzi 1995). In other words, if our alluvial episode is linked to solar activity, it suggests that other such episodes are likely to occur and should eventually be predictable; the longer-term data of solar irradiance imply that even more profound hydrological events have stemmed, and will stem, from the sun's inconstancy.

Huntington (1922) was an early champion of explanations for historical changes in climate which were similar in Western Asia and the western USA and which hinged on the relative importance of cyclonic storms. In his analysis storms are beneficial to human energy by providing stimulating challenges to mind and body; and they favour agriculture by supplying abundant, reliable rain at all seasons. Huntington (1945) also showed that there was a close parallelism between the 11-year sunspot cycle for 1880–1940 and the relative number of storm tracks for large parts of Canada and Siberia. A close match between sunspot number and the position of the main depression tracks has been demonstrated for Europe since 1920 (Tinsley and Heelis 1993).

Toynbee (1946) tells how Stanley Jevons began by suggesting that trade cycles 'might be the effects of fluctuations of the radioactivity of the Sun, as advertised by the appearance and disappearance of sun-spots', but by 1909 'agreed' (presumably with Toynbee) that periodic collapses of trade were 'really mental in their nature, depending on variations of despondency, hopefulness, excitement, disappointment, and panic'. The evidence on the ground—*of* the ground—suggests that Jevons's original assessment was, if anything, too conservative.

REFERENCES

Berlin, I. (1981). 'The divorce between the sciences and the humanities', reprinted in *Against the current*. Oxford: Oxford University Press, 80–110.

Binford, M. W., Kolata, A. L., Brenner, M., Janusek, J. W., Seddon, M. T., Abbott, M., and Curtis, J. H. (1997). 'Climate variation and the rise and fall of an Andean civilization'. *Quaternary Research*. 47: 235–48.

Brown, G. M. and John, J. I. (1979). 'Solar cycle influences in tropospheric circulation'. *J. Atmos. Terrestr. Phys.* 41: 43–52.

Bryan, K. (1941). 'Pre-Columbian agriculture in the south-west, as conditioned by periods of alluviation'. *Annals Ass. Amer. Geog.* 31: 219–42.

Burroughs, W. J. (1997). *Does the Weather Really Matter?* Cambridge: Cambridge University Press.

Cliff, A. D. and Haggett, P. (1988). *Atlas of Disease Distributions*. Oxford: Blackwell.

Curtis, J. H., Hodell, D. A., and Brenner, M. (1996). 'Climate variability on the Yucatan peninsula (Mexico) during the past 3,500 years, and implications for Mayan cultural evolution'. *Quaternary Research*. 46: 37–47.

Darwin, C. (1888). *The Descent of Man* (2nd edn). London: Murray.

García, E. (1969). 'Distribución de la precipitación en la República Mexicana'. *Bol. Inst. Geog., Univ. Autón. Mex.* 1: 2–30.

Haynes, C. V., Jr. (1968). 'Geochronology of Late Quaternary alluvium', in R. B. Morrison and H. E. Wright, Jr. (eds), *Means of Correlation of Quaternary Successions*. Salt Lake City, UT: University of Utah Press, 591–631.

Heine, K. (1976). 'Schneegrenzdepressionen, Klimaentwicklung, Bodenerosion und Mensch im zentralmexikanischen Hochland im jüngeren Pleistozän und Holozän', *Z. Geomorph., Suppl. Bd.* 24: 160–76.

Hereford, R. (1993). 'Entrenchment and widening of the Upper San Pedro River, Arizona'. *Geol. Soc. Amer., Spec. Pap.* 282: 1–46.

Herodotus (1998). *The Histories* (tr. R. Waterfield). Oxford: Oxford University Press.

Herman, J. R. and Goldberg, R. A. (1985). *Sun, Weather, and Climate* (orig. pub. 1978). New York, NY: Dover.

Hosler, D. H., Sabloff, J. A., and Runge, D. (1977). 'Simulation model development: a case study of the Classic Maya collapse', in N. Hammond (ed.), *Social Processes in Maya Prehistory.* New York: Academic Press, 533–90.

Hoyt, D. V. and Schatten, K. H. (1997). *The Role of the Sun in Climate Change.* Oxford: Oxford University Press.

Huntington, E. (1922). *Civilization and Climate* (2nd edn). Yale, NH: Yale University Press.

Huntington, E. (1945). *Mainsprings of Civilization.* New York: Wiley.

Huntington, E. and Visher, S. S. (1992). *Climatic Changes.* New Haven: Yale University Press.

Kerr, R. A. (1998). 'Sea-floor dust shows drought felled Akkadian empire', *Science,* 279: 325–6.

Knox, J. C. (1983). 'Responses of river systems to Holocene climates', in H. E. Wright (ed.), *The Holocene.* Minneapolis, MN: University of Minnesota Press, 26–41.

Ladurie, E. Le Roy (1967). *Histoire du climat depuis l'an mil.* Paris: Flammarion.

Lamb, H. H. (1964). 'Climatic changes and variations in the atmospheric and ocean circulations'. *Geol. Rdsch.* 54: 486–504.

Lamb, H. H. (1965). 'The early medieval warm epoch and its sequel'. *Palaeogeogr., Palaeoclimatol., Palaeoecol.* 1: 13–37.

Lamb, H. H. (1995). *Climate, History and the Modern World* (2nd edn). London: Routledge.

Leopold, L. B. (1951). 'Rainfall frequency: an aspect of climatic variation'. *Trans. Amer. Geophys. Un.* 32: 347–57.

Leopold, L. B. (1997). *Water, Rivers and Creeks.* Sausalito, CA: University Science Books.

Leopold, L. B. and Vita-Finzi, C. (1998). 'Valley changes in the Mediterranean and America and their effects on humans'. *Proc. Amer. Philos. Soc.* 142: 1–17.

Leopold, L. B., Wolman, M. G., and Miller, J. P. (1964). *Fluvial Processes in Geomorphology.* San Francisco: Freeman.

Mann, M. E., Bradley, R. S., and Hughes, M. K. (1998). 'Global-scale temperature patterns and climate forcing over the past six centuries'. *Nature,* 392: 779–87.

Metcalfe, S. E. (1987). 'Historical data and climatic change in Mexico—a review'. *Geog. Jour.* 153: 211–22.

Renfrew, C. and Bahn, P. (1991). *Archaeology.* London: Thames and Hudson.

Sherratt, A. (1997). 'Climatic cycles and behavioural revolutions: the emergence of modern humans and the beginning of farming'. *Antiquity*, 71: 271–87.

Sidrys, R. and Berger, R. (1979). 'Lowland Maya radiocarbon dates and the classic Maya collapse'. *Nature*, 277, 269–74.

Tinsley, B. A. (1988). The solar cycle and the QBO influences on the latitude of storm tracks in the North Atlantic', *Geophys. Res. Lett.* 15: 409–12.

Tinsley, B. A. and Heelis, R. A. (1993). 'Correlations of atmospheric dynamics with solar activity: evidence for a connection via the solar wind, atmospheric electricity, and cloud microphysics.' *J. Geophys. Res.* 98: 10,375–84.

Toynbee, A. (1946). *A Study of History*, abr. by D. C. Somervell. Oxford: Oxford University Press.

Veggiani, A. (1991). 'Fluttuazioni climatiche e trasformazioni ambientali nel territorio imolese dall'alto medioevo all'età moderna', in *Imola nel medioevo*. Imola: Galeati, 41–102.

Vita-Finzi, C. (1995). 'Solar history and paleohydrology during the last two millennia'. *Geophys. Res. Lett.* 22: 699–702.

Wallén, C. C. (1955). 'Some characteristics of precipitation in Mexico'. *Geogr. Annlr.* 37: 52–8.

Weiss, H., Courty, M.-A., Wetterstrom, W, Guichard, F., Senior, L., Meadow, R., and Curnow, W. (1993). 'The genesis and collapse of third millennium North Mesopotamian civilization'. *Science*, 261: 995–1004.

Wheeler, M. (1954). *Archaeology from the Earth*. Oxford: Clarendon Press.

Willett, H. C. (1987). 'Climate responses to variable solar activity—past, present, and predicted', in M. R. Rampino, J. E. Sanders, W. S. Newman, and L. K. Königsson (eds), *Climate: History , Periodicity and Predictability*. New York, NY: Van Nostrand Reinhold, 404–14.

3

Putting Abrupt Environmental Change Back into Human History

M. G. L. Baillie

INTRODUCTION

LET us start with two propositions:

1) the history that has come down to us is notoriously light in its recording of past environmental conditions;
2) in most palaeo-environmental research poor chronological control results in abrupt change being essentially invisible.

The contention in this essay is that these propositions are true, and that, as a result, scholars of the past have, since Lyell and Darwin, and the victory of uniformity over catastrophism, laboured under the false doctrine that sudden, catastrophic, environmental change does not happen on any large scale. This is well exemplified in the belief that widespread collapses of civilization, such as that which overtook the Mycenaean world in or around the twelfth century BC, were due principally to human agency. The development of better swords (Drews 1993) is more acceptable as a vector for the wholesale destruction of cities than the catastrophic environmental effects of altered wind patterns, or massive tectonic effects, quite possibly involving volcanism, or even visitations by debris from space.

The reason for this somewhat radical view is that the increasing avail-

Acknowledgements. The author is grateful to numerous colleagues for supplying unpublished European oak data of the last two millennia, namely Ian Tyers, Cathy Groves, Jennifer Hillam, Esther Jansma, Niels Bonde, Thomas Bartholin, Dieter Eckstein, Hubert Leuschner, and Tomasz Wazny. For the unpublished world data sets I am particularly indebted to Ed Cook (Tasmanian Huon pine), Keith Briffa (Fennoscandian and Polar Urals pine), Peter Kuniholm (Aegean oak and pine), and Xiong Limin (New Zealand cedar). The data collection relevant to this article was funded under EU grant ENV4-CT95-1027, Climatology and Natural Hazards 10K.

ability of long year-by-year tree-ring chronologies has allowed European dendrochronologists to interrogate for the first time the reaction of ancient trees to their growth conditions. Dendrochronologists in SW North America have been in the enviable position of being able to do this since the 1930s. Not only can they date the actual timbers from Amerindian sites exactly, to the calendar year, they can also infer environmental factors such as droughts from the tree-ring patterns themselves. So, for example:

In the arid Southwest one cultural group of prehistoric agriculturists were the Anasazi. These people colonised canyons which today are mostly very inhospitable. They built some huge multi-roomed, indeed multi-storey, pueblos and they developed irrigation systems for their agriculture. Dan Larson and Joel Michaelsen (1990) have studied one group, the Virgin Branch Anasazi in the South-western Great Basin where the states of California, Arizona and Utah meet. From the tree-rings they found that the population had suffered from two significant droughts. During the first, between AD 1000 and 1015, with relatively low population density, deduced from the size of the dated buildings, they appear to have survived by concentrating more on agriculture and storage as reliance on hunting and gathering became too risky a strategy—they needed an assured food supply. Following this first drought it became wetter and the population expanded for about a century. The second drought, between AD 1120 and 1150, although not as severe as the first, saw an expanded population fully reliant on agriculture. What seems to have happened is that at some point in this second drought they ran into several consecutive failed harvests and simply had to abandon the area. Having come to rely totally on farming, their population had become too large to fall back on hunting and gathering when crops failed (Baillie 1999: 20–1).

TREE-RING CHRONOLOGIES AND HUMAN TRAUMA

Now that long tree-ring chronologies are available outside America, it has been possible to point out that several widespread growth downturns recorded in tree-ring chronologies appear to 'coincide' with traumatic events in human affairs (Baillie and Munro 1988; Baillie 1994; 1995; 1999). In other words the occurrence of events in robust tree-ring chronologies, at around the time of documented dynastic changes and/or collapses of civilization, raises the question of whether human trauma might have been caused by the same environmental events that affected the trees. These apparent coincidences do not in themselves prove cases; however, they do serve to raise the issue of abrupt environmental change and human response.

In a relatively uniformitarian world such a suggestion does not find easy acceptance, even as a basis for discussion. An example of the consequence of this conservative approach is provided by Renfrew (1996). In considering evidence presented by Kuniholm *et al.* (1996), which showed that a dramatic, positive, growth anomaly in Anatolian trees tended to support the contention that Santorini might have erupted in 1628 BC, Renfrew states:

to adopt the date of 1628 BC proposed by Kuniholm *et al.* would imply very substantial changes to the historical chronology of Ancient Egypt. That cannot be ruled out, but such changes would need to be based upon more than a supposititious correlation between the Thera eruption and the 1628 BC event seen in Northern Hemisphere tree-rings and ice cores. (1996: 734)

In other words, even though the new evidence, from trees some 800 kilometres downwind of Santorini, points quite strongly towards a seventeenth-century BC dating for the eruption, Renfrew feels that it is not appropriate to act on the information until the case is more comprehensively proven. These comments tell us that there is a climate of considerable resistance to the introduction of extreme events into pre-existing human records, be they ancient historical or archaeological. This can be viewed in another way by asking the following question: in the history and prehistory of the British Isles spanning, say, the last six thousand years, is there a single instance of major human change having been brought about by abrupt environmental change? The current answer tends towards 'no'. All the major changes—arrival of agriculture, arrival of metal use, construction of hill-forts, arrival of the Romans, departure of the Romans, arrival of the Saxons, the Vikings, the Normans— are induced by human agency. If we turn to plagues—those of the sixth century AD, the Black Death, and the Plague of London—were they environmentally induced? Apparently not. There may have been disturbed climate in the early fourteenth century, but this is considered to have contributed merely to the weakening of the population so that the bubonic plague was so much more effective when it *arrived*. Obviously, not everyone subscribes to the relatively uniformitarian scenario of history as portrayed here; there are catastrophists out there, such as Burgess (1985), Nur and Hagai (1997), and Clube and Napier (1990). However, it is fair to say that currently the main thrust in history, ancient history, and archaeology is to ignore catastrophism, until proof positive is presented.

CATASTROPHES AND THEIR EFFECTS

This is the curious situation with which the dendrochronologist, looking at the records in the tree-ring chronologies, is confronted. We live, it would seem, in a non-catastrophic world. But, patently, that is not true.

We know that the environment can have catastrophic effects. Indeed, it has had catastrophic effects on human populations in recent times. For example, as recently as 27 July 1976 the earthquake in Tangshan, China, killed somewhere between 240,000 and 750,000 people, depending on which report is believed. It is accepted that the quake in AD 1556, which affected Shaanxi, Shanxi, and Henan provinces, again in China, killed around 830,000 people. Are non-catastrophists content to assume that the 'worst', the most severe, earthquakes in the last 5,000 years have both taken place in the last 440 years? To make such an assumption would be naive in the extreme. It is easy to envisage that in a period of time more than ten times as long we might expect an earthquake an order of magnitude more effective than either of those just mentioned. It is not difficult to imagine that once in 5,000 years we might have had not just a bigger or more widespread single earthquake, but a major crustal readjustment involving widespread tectonic activity. The reader's first response is likely to be that such a thing has not happened or cannot have happened. The sobering truth is that we would not know whether such a thing had happened or not—almost no one has looked for evidence.

Exactly the same line of thinking can be applied to several other possibly catastrophic vectors. Large explosive volcanic eruptions have tended to occur singly in recent times, for example, Pinatubo in 1991, Agung in 1963, Katmai in 1912, Krakatoa in 1883, and Tambora in 1815. We might ask what the environmental effects would be if several large explosive eruptions took place in a single year or within a small number of years. The effects, with respect to loading of the atmosphere, might well be cumulative and much more severe environmentally than any single eruption. Has such a multiple event taken place in the last 5,000 years? The conventional answer is 'no'. The real answer is that *we do not know*. Because ancient volcanoes cannot be dated to anything like calendrical resolution, it is impossible to answer the question. However, it is worth noting that Chester (1988), reviewing the role of volcanoes in climate change, quoted Budyko's view that,

if four large eruptions are taken as representative of the past 100 years and this frequency of occurrence is assumed to coincide with the overall frequency in the Quaternary [the last 2 million years] and, in addition, eruptions are considered to be independent events and subject to purely random variations in frequency, then . . . 40 large eruptions occur [in a] century, once every 10,000 years.

This line of scientific thinking suggests that some clusters of eruptions should have occurred during the 5,000 years since the development of civilization; yet no good record of a significant cluster exists. Thus we have to ask whether it is the scientific logic which is at fault, or the quality of human recording.

Most people are aware of the general nature of earthquakes and volcanoes. However, the same cannot be assumed for some of the other hazards which face species inhabiting this planet in this solar system. Let us briefly elaborate on four other potential hazards.

Impacts

In July 1994 some twenty, approximately kilometer-sized fragments of the comet Shoemaker-Levy 9 ploughed into the giant planet Jupiter. Astronomers were able to view the exact consequences of such impacts. Suffice it to say that Jupiter is 300 times the size of the Earth and the most energetic impacts left 'scars on Jupiter four to five times the diameter of our own planet' (Steel 1995). Estimates of the energy released in some of these impacts were of the order of 100,000 megatons up to 10 million megatons of TNT equivalent. Astronomers are also aware that the Earth is hit each year by numerous small objects in the 2–6 metre range; that in any 50–300-year period we are hit by objects around 40 metres in diameter. The Tunguska impact over Siberia on 30 June 1908 yielded energy equivalent to a 15–20 megaton airburst and flattened some 2000 square kilometres of forest (Clube and Napier 1990). Astronomers know that there are estimated to be around 2,000 objects more than a kilometre in diameter which are in 'Earth-crossing orbits' and therefore pose the threat of eventual impact (Steel 1995: 30). These particular objects are big enough, if we run into one of them, to collapse our current civilization. It should be noted that the estimated number of Earth-crossing asteroids larger than 100 metres in diameter (which would produce impacts considerably larger than Tunguska) lies in the range of 150,000 to 1 million (Steel 1995). Since the late 1980s several objects in the 5–20 metre size-range have passed within 200,000 kilometres of Earth—in astronomical terms, a hair's breadth. It is worth noting one particular fly-by:

The object 1989FC, or Asclepius as it is now called, passed just beyond the moon's orbit, which sounds like a nice, safe distance. But it missed by only 6 hours, which sounds very close. No one is quite sure how large it was (about 300 meters across) and the impact would have produced a blast of between 1,000 and 20,000 megatons, the uncertainty related to not knowing just what 1989FC was made of . . . it was firmly in a size category for objects capable of creating a global catastrophe. (Verschuur 1996: 116)

These statements are not conjecture, and serious astrophysicists are asking why no good historical or archaeological records exist for impact-related events in the last five millennia (Bailey 1995).

Tsunami

A tsunami is a giant sea-wave which can be caused by tectonic movement or impact. The most recent significant example occurred on 17 July 1998, when three waves, the largest measuring up to 15 metres, came ashore in northern New Guinea and killed many thousands of people living in coastal villages (Koshimura *et al.* 1998). The problem with tsunami is that they may not appear to be all that big out in the deep ocean; however, when they run up onto a shelving shoreline, they amplify by a factor of up to 40 (Lewis 1996). Thus, a 5-metre sea-wave can become a 200-metre wall of water. To get a feel for the possible consequences of a small asteroid striking the Atlantic ocean one cannot do better than quote the following comment, again relating to asteroid 1989FC:

> we can figure out what would have happened if asteroid 1989FC had struck the Atlantic ocean 1000 kilometers from the coast of the United States. If it was an iron asteroid (which would get right through the atmosphere), the deep-water wave would have been 20 meters at the coast. The tsunami it would have produced would have been about 0.8 kilometers high. The notion of such a high wave breaking along the east coast of the United States is a stunning one. (Verschuur 1996: 154)

Ignoring the latter scenario, which almost certainly has a long return time (i.e. has *probably* not happened recently), has even a modest tsunami arrived at the coast of Ireland or Britain in the last 5,000 years? As usual, we do not know. Almost the only good evidence for a significant tsunami affecting the coast of Britain relates to the Storegga event of around 7,200 radiocarbon years ago, when masses of unstable submarine sediment from the Norwegian Margin slid along the continental shelf and appear to have given rise to tsunami deposits on the Scottish coast (Dawson *et al.* 1988). There is currently no good evidence for a major impact or tectonically induced tsunami in the north Atlantic during the period of human civilization.

The Gulf Stream

It is widely accepted that the cause of the cold snap termed the Younger Dryas between *c.* 12,700 and 11,500 BP was the shutting off of the Gulf Stream. The problem with shutting off this warm current is that it exposes the fact that Northwest Europe lies at the same latitude as Alaska, and is only kept from extremes of cold by the warm water which flows up from the Caribbean. Can the Gulf Stream falter or temporarily turn off? Indeed, has it ever, during the last 5,000 years, faltered or turned off temporarily? We do not know for certain, but it is an increasing source of concern for some scientists, who worry that human interference with the climate, particularly the warming of the north Atlantic, may lead to a reduction of the 'deep cold water formation' which powers the world ocean circulation (Rahmstorf 1995). As we will see below, Irish oaks seem to record some extreme cold events very clearly; this may give a hint that Ireland and Britain have found themselves at the receiving end of ocean changes in recent millennia.

Ocean Outgassing

Outgassing is something which can happen. It is a necessary consequence of the existence, in many deep seabed deposits, of what are commonly called clathrates or gas hydrates (Sloan *et al.* 1994). Put simply, at certain conditions of temperature and pressure (cold conditions coupled with high pressures) water molecules form themselves into a ice 'mesh', within which methane gas, or other equivalently sized small molecules, can be fitted (methane, CH_4, is natural gas as burnt in millions of homes; other molecules would be hydrogen sulphide, H_2S, and ammonia, NH_3). It turns out that, for example, one cubic centimetre of gas hydrate can contain 180 cubic centimetres of methane gas.

Geologists have now noted that it is commonplace for a layer of gas hydrate to be present beneath some hundreds of metres of ocean deposit, where temperature and pressure conditions suit its formation. It is estimated by some workers that there may be up to 10,000 gigatons (ten thousand billion tons) of methane gas stored in this form in the ocean beds. In addition, there may be enormous quantities of free methane and hydrogen sulphide gas trapped (as gas) in pockets beneath the clathrate layers. These clathrate layers show up on seismic survey traces where the hydrate layer acts as a bottom-simulating reflector, or BSR (the layer shows as a surface below and parallel to the seabed); it is these traces which suggest that free gas also exists below the BSR, waiting to 'get out'. It would seem that there is real potential for release into the atmosphere of large quantities of gas from the ocean floor; all that may be needed is some suitable tectonic movement as a trigger. Once the possibility of ocean outgassing is raised, a logical step is to ask if there is any evidence of such an outgassing affecting a populated coast in the past. The usual answer is 'no', although a better answer, albeit circumstantial, might be 'probably'.

A DOOMSDAY SCENARIO

Ignoring for the present the idea of the Gulf Stream faltering, it is safe to say that there is no good evidence for significant catastrophes in the form of impacts, tsunami, or outgassings in the last 5,000 years. We can take this as one extreme case—in agreement with conventional wisdom—that nothing catastrophic has happened (nor will it). Let us, for the sake of discussion, define the other extreme case. In other words, let us accumulate these catastrophes in order to define a worst-case scenario. Let us imagine a 'doomsday' scenario where a salvo of impacts from space trigger a tectonic reaction resulting in volcanism, ocean outgassing, and tsunami. We can envisage the symptoms. There would be a dust-veil from the loading of the atmosphere by both extra-terrestrial and volcanic debris; the sun and moon would be dimmed. Atmospheric detonations would cause earthquakes, as witnessed at the time of the solitary Tunguska detonation on 30 June 1908; those in the ocean would cause tsunami, and the whole package could induce the release of gas from the ocean floor. Indeed, even if gas were not released from, or from beneath, the clathrate deposits in the ocean bed, gas loading of the atmosphere might well be an accompaniment to the impacting space debris (given the high organic component of some recent comets). Has such a thing happened during the Holocene? The answer, again, is *not* 'no'; it is that 'we do not know'. We can obviously conceive of the possibility, but all the direct evidence, or lack of it, suggests that the doomsday scenario has not (yet) occurred. However, while we may take comfort from this lack of direct evidence for such a scenario, various important ancient traditions are remarkably explicit in their descriptions of 'the end of the world'. Ragnarök, the Norse myth of the end of the world, is surely based on something unpleasant which had happened before. A brief survey of its main elements reveals remarkable parallels to the doomsday scenario painted above.

At Ragnarök, the sun and the moon are swallowed by wolves. The 'stars turn from their steadings in heaven', as the heavens split asunder and a tide of the sons of Muspell gallop through, while the Fenris Wolf, which has flames coming from his eyes and nostrils, rakes the earth. Other symptoms are earthquakes—'the earth and the mountains shake'—and the destruction of forests—'woods are torn up by the roots', while 'a great bore of waters inundates the land'. To round off the proceedings, the World Serpent comes bucking and boiling up out of the sea blowing 'clouds of poison' over the earth and sky. With very little stretch of the imagination, we can paraphrase the Ragnarök scenario as fireballs in the sky, tumult in the oceans, earthquakes, the sun and moon dimmed, and outgassing of some description. If this bears even the faintest resemblance to reality, then the memory which the Norse carried with them, of the worst happenings they could imagine, must reflect real events. The only question is when, or, indeed, how often these things happened. Of course, Norse mythology does not sit in isolation. Biblical Revelation describes a similar scenario in even more colourful language; in this case with the star Wormwood falling and poisoning the waters, the sun and moon being dimmed, etc. The Celts, who surprised the Romans by claiming that 'they feared nothing save the sky falling on their heads', had an oath which included the following elements: they would not move from where they stood 'unless the stars fall from the sky, the earth shakes and the sea comes over the land' (Sayers 1986). It appears that it is not hard to find past populations which had the conception of the stars falling in association with earthquake and tsunami.

It would be possible to go on in this vein, but there seems little need. Catastrophists can conceive of some pretty unpleasant configurations of natural catastrophe, most of them involving abrupt change, and can see no reason why such configurations should not have occurred within the timespan of human civilization. Conventional wisdom, based mostly on recent experience, says they have not occurred, while mythology, presumably based on ancient experiences, suggests really quite strongly that they have. Moreover, archaeologists and ancient historians admit to the existence of Dark Ages, population movements, and abandonments in their records; civilizations have undoubtedly collapsed in the past. Few seem willing to allow for the possibility that the contents of the myths might relate directly to the evidence on the ground; catastrophism has been expunged, or so one might think. The rest of this essay will seek to demonstrate that within the last two millennia there are signs that approximations to the doomsday scenario, or at least some of its components, have indeed been worked out in the form of abrupt environmental changes affecting human populations.

THE TREE-RING CHRONOLOGIES

Dendrochronologists have constructed long, year-by-year records of tree growth in numerous areas. To take only northern Europe in the first instance, oak chronologies spanning seven millennia or more have been constructed in Ireland (Pilcher *et al.* 1984), England (Brown and Baillie 1992), and both North and South Germany (Leuschner and Delorme 1988; Becker and Schmidt 1990). These central European chronologies allow the dating of major timber groupings from Switzerland (Orcel *et al.* 1992). Chronologies of similar length are almost complete for both Finland (Zetterberg *et al.* 1994) and Fennoscandia (Briffa *et al.* 1992). Chronologies spanning most of the last two millennia are available for a transect from Ireland, through Scotland, England, France, the Netherlands, Denmark, Germany, to Poland. Although most of the chronologies are regional, there is extensive evidence for cross-dating between these chronologies. Thus, the oak chronologies for the last two millennia are precisely dated and replicated and direct comparisons can be made between growth features within the various data sets. The rapid progress towards this situation was largely the product of intensive chronology construction during the 1970s and 1980s. Thus, it is only in the 1990s that it has become possible to interrogate these data sets.

Although the temperature-sensitive records from Fennoscandia have allowed the reconstruction of summer temperatures for the last two millennia (Briffa *et al.* 1992), and in a very provisional way for several millennia BC (Briffa 1994), the first tentative environmental deductions from the long oak chronologies centred round the recognition of several 'narrowest ring' events in Irish sub-fossil (or bog) oaks which grew between 5200 BC and AD 1000. The events can be listed as follows:

4370 BC
3195 BC
2345 BC
1628 BC
1159 BC
207 BC
AD 540

These tree-ring events coincided with significant acid layers in various Greenland ice-core records, within the limits of the ice-core dating (Baillie and Munro 1988). From 1988 the assumption was that major volcanic dust-veil events had given rise to notable environmental downturns, evidenced by the reduced growth in the Irish trees. So much additional information flowed in to support the hypothesis that these severe environmental events were widespread, possibly hemispheric or global, that by 1991 these had been christened 'marker dates', that is, dates which were likely to show up in records of various sorts in the future (Baillie 1991).

From the list above, one in particular—that at AD 540—stood out as being very widely observed (Baillie 1994, 1995). Thus, as more regional chronologies became available across Europe, it was deemed sensible to construct a European master chronology for oaks from Ireland to Poland in an attempt to gauge the worst tree-ring events in the last two millennia and provide a context for the AD 540 event. Preliminary results of this approach, spanning AD 500 to the present, were published in 1996. It is simplest to quote those preliminary results:

For Northern Europe we have year-by-year records of mean oak growth for up to fifteen reasonably dispersed site or regional chronologies. It is thus possible to look at something that approximates mean oak growth for northern Europe. We have made up such a chronology from AD 500 to 1980 (first equalising each chronology by fitting a loose polynomial to the data, a process called indexing, which removes long-term trends but leaves an accurate record on short and medium term variations). Surprisingly, two of the four most extreme narrow-growth departures are for the years AD 540–541 and AD 1741–1742. So, by employing a straightforward dendrochronological procedure, namely the production of a multi-site index master chronology, the dates of two major human crises drop out of a study of oak tree-rings. With respect to the other extreme growth departures we can point to a major growth reduction from AD 1163 to 1189, with a minimum value at AD 1177, and another from AD 1318 to 1353, with its minimum at 1325. (Baillie 1996: 107)

Thus, an initial 'quick and dirty' survey of the oak chronologies of northern Europe yielded four 'minimum' dates, namely 540, 1177, 1325, and 1740, which will be discussed below. While that pilot exercise relied on published or available master chronologies, in differing formats and from various regions, in the last five years serious moves have been made to centralize most of the European oak data so that detailed study of the most basic raw material—the individual tree-ring patterns—can begin. The specific aim of this collaboration is the reconstruction of aspects of past environmental changes in northern Europe. Figure 3.1 shows a more robust record from AD 440 to AD 1900, wherein each individual ring pattern from each of eight laboratories from Ireland to Poland has been treated in an identical manner. Each ring pattern has a 30-year spline fitted to the raw tree-ring width data to remove growth trend. Eight regional master chronologies were produced from the resulting standardized tree-ring indices. These were averaged to produce a grand mean chronology for northern European oak, and this data set was smoothed with a standard five-point running mean to show the overall growth trend most clearly. It is evident that in this more objectively derived data set the negative growth events at AD 540 and 1740 still stand out, as does the negative departure in the 1320s; the 1170s event is reduced in significance in this analysis, and several other events appear (interestingly, several centuries have events in the '40s of each century).

The observation that the 540 event survived a more rigorous analysis was pleasing, because in the 500-year overlap with the original narrowest-ring Irish survey, AD 540 had already shown up as the most extreme narrowest-ring event in the first millennium. It was notable that AD 540 fell just before the outbreak of the Justinian plague in 542—indeed the Justinian plague appears to break out during the environmental event reflected in the tree-rings. The AD 1325 event lies in the run-up to the Black Death, while AD 1740 marks the 'last great demographic crisis of

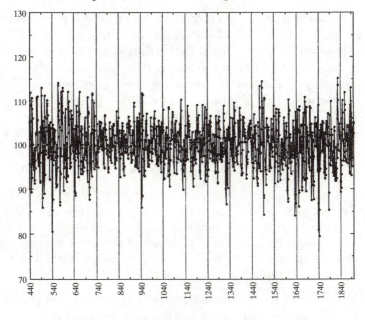

Date AD

FIG. 3.1 Eight standardized regional master chronologies were constructed from raw tree-ring data, supplied by tree-ring laboratories in Ireland, England, Netherlands, Denmark, Germany, and Poland (see acknowledgments). The grand mean presented here has been 5-point smoothed for clarity. The strong negative growth departures in northern European oaks at AD 540s, 940s, 1320s, and 1740s are evident.

the pre-industrial era' in Ireland (Post 1977; Drake 1968). Asking a very simple question of European oaks—what were the worst growth conditions in your collective 'memories'?—yielded several dates close to traumatic episodes for human populations in Europe. Thus we have an apparently clear statement that the environment had a significant role in key periods of human history.

What was also interesting was that that other date, AD 1177, because it was more muted in the rigorous tree-ring analysis, might appear to be without significance. But it turns out that the period around that time may have some Doomsday significance after all. It has been noted by several authors that Gervase of Canterbury records a most amazing description of what must have been, if true, a major impact on the moon on 18 June 1178. Apparently, several men reported that they had seen the horn of the new moon split and writhe, pouring out sparks and hot coals.

Subsequently, the moon turned black. If true, it is possible that they witnessed the formation of the Giordano Bruno crater at 36°N and 105°E (Clube and Napier 1990). If the Earth/Moon system was passing through an annulus of cometary debris at that time, and if there was a major impact on the moon, the Earth may have been affected by related dust and lesser debris. Emilio Spedicato (1997) has now accumulated information for this episode and provides plausible arguments that the Earth/Moon system was affected around the 1170s. In case anyone thinks this is fanciful, I would draw attention to a completely independent reference in the Irish Annals of the Four Masters, which record for 10 February 1173

the dark night became bright from dusk till morning, and it appeared to the inhabitants that the adjacent parts of the globe were illuminated; and a large body of fire moved over the town [Londonderry] and remained in the south east; and all the people rose from their beds, for they thought it was the day; and it continued so eastwards along the sea (Britton 1937).

This sighting has traditionally been assumed to be an aurora. However, it could just as easily (and exactly as it states) be explained as a major fireball impact. One symptom of the Tunguska atmospheric impact of 1908 was the anomalously bright nights witnessed in northern Europe. Taking this package of information at face value, it would appear that these narrow growth rings across northern Europe might be consistent with the loading of the Earth's atmosphere by dust or debris from space associated with material from a dead comet. This is exactly the scenario which Bailey, Clube, and Napier (1990) have suggested poses the greatest risk to this planet: namely, that in running through the orbit of a dead comet, the Earth intersects sizeable fragments as it crosses the annulus of dust which marks the original orbit of the comet. Interestingly, they proposed two windows of risk, namely 400–600 AD and 1000–1200 AD (Bailey *et al.* 1990). Perhaps the AD 1170s need to be looked at more closely.

The close juxtaposition of reduced growth events in oaks, signifying the trees' negative response to some environmental factors, with evidence for trauma for human populations, raises the issue of the impact of abrupt environmental change on human affairs. In recent papers I have attempted to raise the profile of abrupt environmental events during the Holocene (Baillie 1991, 1994, 1995). The latter two publications looked in some detail at the widespread nature of the AD 540 tree-ring event which appears from tree-ring records to start in AD 536 and last to possibly AD 545. This period represents a notable downturn in human affairs in Europe and beyond; as we have seen, the Justinian plague (normally assumed to be bubonic plague) broke out in AD 542. Tree-rings from temperature-sensitive areas of the northern hemisphere give us some quite specific information relevant to this event. In a temperature reconstruction from Fennoscandian pine-ring widths and densities, Briffa *et al.* (1992) note that AD 536 was the second coldest summer in the last 1,500 years, with a 2.0 degree Celsius negative departure. Independent evidence from foxtail pines in the Sierra Nevada finds AD 536 to have been the third coldest year in the last 2,000 years (Scuderi 1993), with a similar negative departure. Both records also single out AD 541 as a notably cold year. These are the only extreme years to agree in both records, implying that AD 536 was easily the most significant cold year in the last 1,500 years, with AD 541 close behind. These two independent observations, on Scots pine in Fennoscandia and foxtail pines in the USA, when coupled with the clear indications from European oak that the period around AD 540 was exceptionally bad for growth, suggest that something quite exceptional happened at that time and that cold was a principal factor (interestingly, the happenings indicated in the European oak tree-rings at AD 1740 coincide with the coldest year in the whole of Manley's (1974) Central England temperature record which extends back to AD 1659).

The initial supposition was that the AD 536 environmental event, as recorded in the tree-rings and human history, was caused by a large volcanic eruption. Two lines of evidence supported this supposition. First, Stothers and Rampino (1983; Stothers 1984) showed that there were several descriptions of a severe 'dry fog' in AD 536/7. The records suggested to them that the most likely interpretation for this dry fog was a major volcanic dust veil. This linked with the second line of evidence which was a significant acid layer in the Dye 3 ice-core from Greenland, dated initially to AD 540+/−10 (Hammer *et al.* 1980). Unfortunately for this 'volcano' theory, subsequent redating of the Dye 3 acid signal to AD 516+/−4 (Hammer 1984), coupled with the loss of a 14-metre section of the new American GISP2 core relating to the sixth century AD (Baillie 1994; Alley *et al.* 1997), meant that there was no good evidence for an exceptional, large, sulphur-producing volcano at or around AD 536–45. The more recent, detailed acidity records of the GRIP and Dye 3 cores also fail to indicate any exceptional volcanic activity at this time (Clausen *et al.* 1997). Since the tree-ring and human evidence still showed a dramatic environmental event, or series of events, at AD 536–45, the absence of direct volcanic evidence meant that other causal mechanisms could be entertained (Baillie 1994, 1995). From a scientific viewpoint, the next most likely cause of an abrupt, widespread, environmental downturn, associated with descriptions of a dim sun and atmospheric aerosol, should be related to an impact of some kind, with cometary dust or debris being the most likely culprits. However, other events such as solar changes, interstellar dust and even *undersea outgassing* could not be ruled out.

Events such as that at AD 540 underline the difficulties faced by researchers attempting to link cause and effect in the case of abrupt environmental changes in the past. Outside tree-ring studies, ice-cores, and history, little evidence is sufficiently well constrained in time to contribute usefully to the debate. Other than tree-rings and ice-cores there are few well-dated 'encapsulating' records which might have trapped evidence for analysis. Most environmental studies involving palynology or volcanic effects suffer from being based on radiocarbon chronology. This situation means, in simple terms, that almost no abrupt environmental downturns in the Holocene have a defined cause.

Interestingly, it is possible to demonstrate a powerful circumstantial case for extra-terrestrial bombardment around AD 540, based on mythology (Baillie 1999). Suffice it to say that the Arthurian legends abound with fireball imagery, while tradition places the death of Arthur (an Apollo figure) variously at AD 537 and 542, quite remarkably within the confines of the tree-ring downturn. Similarly, it is possible to find allusions to the death of Merlin, with associations to the Celtic god Lugh—who is described as a 'red fiery wooshing dragon'—in AD 536. Similarly, the Anglo-Saxon poem *Beowulf* has its hero wrestling with a fiery dragon at some date after, in the view of some serious scholars of the subject, AD 535 (Klaeber 1950). But such evidence remains circumstantial. If we look at events such as AD 540 or 1740, or the decades running up to the Black Death in 1347, the one common factor is the lack of a defined *cause*. It is into this information vacuum that I wish to inject a discussion of one possible, but hitherto unconsidered, vector for abrupt environmental change. I wish to lay down the challenge that the Black Death may have involved, quite possibly alongside real bubonic plague, elements of undersea outgassing.

UNDERSEA OUTGASSING AND THE BLACK DEATH OF AD 1347

It is only in the last decade or so, with the advent of ice-cores and tree-rings, that high resolution environmental information, compatible with historical records, has started to become available for the first time. Previously, the generally poor chronological resolution of most environmental information meant that abrupt environmental changes could not be discerned; environmental change does not normally figure largely in discussions of either the Justinian plague or the Black Death. Thus, when we do come to consider the likely driving forces behind the observed changes in the tree-ring records, almost anything is possible at the outset. Any vector might be responsible. I wish in the remainder of this essay to present a circumstantial case that ocean outgassing was somehow involved in the happenings of the mid-fourteenth century. The question to be addressed is as follows: did large quantities of methane and/or hydrogen sulphide have significant effects on the global environment or on local human populations during the Black Death? The question could be recouched more generally as: has there been even one catastrophic out-gassing event during the last 5,000 years?

Possible Outgassing Events

The geochemist Richard McIver has suggested undersea outgassing as a possible explaination for the sudden disappearance of ships and aero-planes from certain ocean regions. In a sudden outgassing, massive quan-tities of gas coming to the surface would radically alter the buoyancy of any passing vessel. With methane as a significant component, it is pos-sible to imagine associated 'lights', and, after combustion, carbon dioxide rising as an invisible cloud into the atmosphere could easily bring down an aircraft which was unlucky enough to fly into the plume. At least one incident in historic times suggests that the outgassing phenomenon has indeed been observed.

The earthquake associated by name with the city of Lisbon took place in the morning of All Saints' Day, 1 November 1755. It is recorded that the effects were felt from North Africa around northern Europe to Scan-dinavia, with lakes and wells affected in Ireland, Britain, Germany, and Norway (Niddrie 1961). This was a major tectonic readjustment, with tsunami arriving later in the day in the West Indies. Of relevance to the gas hydrate debate are the observations of a British sea captain made while sailing off the Azores at what appears to be the time of the Lisbon earthquake. The record comes from *The Gentleman's Magazine* for 1755:

The captain felt a strange agitation as if the ship had been jerked and suspended by a string from the masthead. He dashed up on deck and observed within a league three craggy pointed rocks throwing up water of various colours resem-bling liquid fire. This phenomenon ended in about two minutes with a black cloud which ascended very quickly.

This appears to be a direct eye-witness account of gas surfacing from the seabed due to tectonic disturbance; the ship in this case had a lucky escape. At face value, it appears that the gas was ignited. The importance of this record is that it raises as an issue whether outgassing can happen near inhabited coasts. Is there any evidence? There may be. It has been known for many years that numerous Late Minoan (LM1B) sites on the island of Crete were destroyed and abandoned in the context of massive conflagration. No evidence has been forthcoming for the hand of hostile invaders, and the hallmark of many of the sites is the evidence of sudden abandonment. Remains of meals, cooking utensils, and tools of all kinds 'lay where they were being used on that day' (Platon 1971). Similarly, at the end of the Mycenaean period numerous cities are recorded as 'totally destroyed and totally burned' (Drews 1993). Everywhere, there was evidence of intense burning. Earthquake activity is also involved. The question has to be whether the fires were simply due to overturned lamps and spilled oil, or whether they may have been due to the island being overcome with a wave of burning gas. How could we tell?

The simple answer is that at present it is not possible to make a definitive case for gas hydrate involvement in the LM1B or Mycenaean conflagrations. For one thing, the evidence is not well enough constrained chronologically. It is not known for certain that the burnt sites were all burned at the same instant in time. Even if the conflagrations were simultaneous, the exact calendar age of the Minoan demise is not known more precisely than to within half a century. As a result, it is impossible to interrogate the ice-core or tree-ring records for supporting evidence. What is certain is that a perfectly reasonable question about the hazards of gas hydrates can be asked in the context of these Bronze Age happenings. By comparison, the Black Death is the one major human trauma in the present era where good chronological control, combining tree-ring information and documentary evidence, allows a plausible case to be made for the involvement of gas hydrates.

The Search for Causes

We have already seen that European oaks pick out the decades before the Black Death as poor for growth. We are not, however, restricted to European oaks. Although much global tree-ring data is unpublished in numerical form, it is widely available to the peer group. So, with the kind collaboration of colleagues, acknowledged above, it was possible to check pine chronologies from the Polar Urals and Fennoscandia, American bristlecone pines, Aegean oak and pine, Tasmanian Huon pine, and New Zealand cedar. In figure 3.2 I show five-point smoothed tree-ring curves from these seven regions (smoothing is applied simply because of the sheer amount of noise in the annual resolution data). It is clear that the

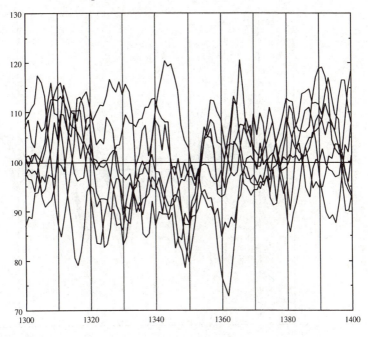

FIG. 3.2 Five-point smoothed growth indices/temperature reconstructions for large-scale chronologies from the Polar Urals, Fennoscandia, European, Aegean, Western America, Tasmania, and New Zealand (see acknowledgments). Although noisy, the general decline in growth towards AD 1350 is evident; 100 per cent can be regarded as normality.

situation is noisy, as would be expected with tree-ring chronologies from all over the globe, which are not expected to be doing the same things. However it is interesting that in every case, with the exception of the Aegean chronologies, all the chronologies show below normal growth in the 1340s; by 1352 all the chronologies are below 100 per cent. In order to demonstrate more clearly what is going on I have meaned seven different random combinations of five from the seven chronologies (see figure 3.3). This indicates that the same global picture is obtained irrespective of which chronologies were constructed. It also demonstrates most graphically the 'tree-growth context' of the Black Death—the Black Death sits in a tree-ring trough and is not a solely human affair.

Since a very widespread growth reduction in trees is almost certainly due to overall cooler conditions (which might be consistent with wider

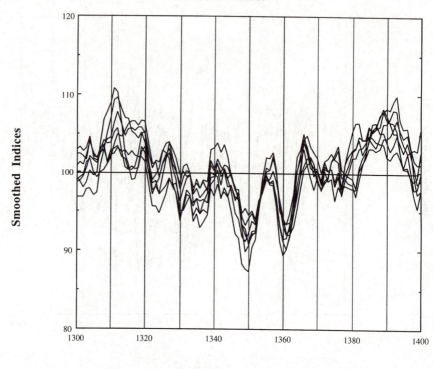

FIG. 3.3 The seven smoothed chronologies in Figure 3.2 have been binned into means of five chronologies. This indicates that the general pattern of growth across the fourteenth century is preserved irrespective of which chronologies were available. The significant decline in the later 1340s provides a clear environmental context for the Black Death, as does the secondary decline into 1361, which marks the second wave of the plague.

growth in the drought-sensitive Aegean), it appears that the decade of the Black Death is marked as a significant global downturn for trees as well as humans. Since our primary interest is in what caused the Black Death, and since we can now see the Black Death in an environmental context, the next obvious question must relate to the *cause of the environmental downturn*. This question is not quite what it seems. Most readers would assume that we want to know if conditions were 'cold' or 'dry' or 'stormy' or whatever. In a sense these are secondary issues. Rather than wanting to know the nature of the global downturn, we really want to know what caused the downturn—we want the prime mover. It is the prime movers that are missing from Holocene studies. If we see major environmental downturns at 540 or 1340 or 1740, we need to know the physical causes; at present we do not know the fundamental causes of any of these events. Were the downturns caused by (i) chaotic weather anomalies, (ii) solar variations, (iii) volcanoes, (iv) impacts, (v) extra-terrestrial dust, (vi) giant forest fires, or (vii) undersea outgassing (or indeed something else)?

This takes us to the main point of this essay. If we accept that there was an environmental downturn in the run up to the Black Death in 1347, can we take the debate on cause any further? Apart from tree-rings, there are three principal sources of information we can call on at this prelimi-nary stage. We can look at historical records, we can look at the radio-carbon records, and we can look at essentially annual, encapsulating, ice-core records. It is easiest to treat these in reverse order. The ice-cores have the potential to provide essentially year-by-year records of such things as dust, acid, and stable isotope records in the atmosphere. So, for example, we can see that there is a small acid spike, presumably indicat-ing a volcanic eruption, at AD 1345+/−2 in the Crete ice-core (Hammer *et al.* 1980) and two, at 1328+/−2 and 1344+/−2 in the GISP2 core (Zielin-ski *et al.* 1994). These ice-acid levels are unremarkable, as is also the case in the Dye 3 and GRIP cores (Clausen *et al.* 1997), and there is no reason to see the environmental downturn of the 1340s as being initiated by a volcanic dust veil. At the present time, therefore, the ice records do not provide any definitive solutions.

The Evidence from Radiocarbon

If we move to radiocarbon measurements, a more immediate picture emerges. Part of the driving force behind the construction of at least some of the European oak chronologies was calibration of the radiocarbon timescale. This work was necessary because of the limitations of Libby's original theory, which had to assume that radiocarbon concentrations in the atmosphere had always been the same, and because of the observed divergence between historical dates and radiocarbon dates in the BC era; it was observed that radiocarbon dates were many centuries *too young* by 3000 BC when compared with historically dated objects. Thus, various laboratories supplied precisely dated wood samples for radiocarbon cal-ibration purposes. This resulted in several calibration curves, principally those of Suess (1970), Pearson *et al.* (1986), and Stuiver and Becker (1993). For the purposes of this discussion of the fourteenth century we will restrict ourselves to the high-precision radiocarbon measurements made by Pearson on Irish oak and Stuiver on American conifers.

These radiocarbon calibration results are of interest because they reflect the amount of radiocarbon in the atmosphere through time. Radiocarbon is produced in the upper atmosphere by the interaction of cosmic radiation with nitrogen atoms. Although the cosmic ray flux from deep space is presumed to be constant, there is no doubt that it is affected by both the Earth's magnetic field and the solar wind, and as a result there are both short-term and long, secular variations in the amount of radioactive Carbon-14 in the atmosphere. The amount of carbon in the atmosphere, in the form of CO_2, also varies with time due to exchange with the biosphere and the oceans. Thus, measurements of the past record of radiocarbon in the atmosphere may contain information relating to past solar variations, past ocean and biosphere variations, past variations in the atmosphere, and past alterations in the Earth's magnetic field strength. The basic work has been done, and the calibration measurements are available; the only snag is that the results were not produced at annual resolution—for practical reasons, blocks of ten and twenty dated growth-rings were measured. Taken overall, this sounds too complex a set of variables to make any easy deductions about radiocarbon. However, we are helped in one principal way. Radiocarbon production is a one-way valve—you can have zero or positive radiocarbon production; you cannot have negative radiocarbon production. Thus, when we look at the calibration curve, it is possible to see periods of enrichment, when radiocarbon ages on consecutive wood samples become rapidly younger and the calibration curve becomes 'steep', indicating that more radiocarbon is being produced. It is also possible to see periods of depletion, when radiocarbon ages become older on consecutive samples and the calibration curve 'turns back'; where it turns back steeply, something is depleting the amount of Carbon-14.

Our interest is in anything which might give a clue as to the cause of the environmental downturn in the 1340s. Figure 3.4 shows all the Pearson and Stuiver results relevant to the fourteenth century AD. It is obvious that there is a notable *enrichment* between 1260 and 1335, then around 1335–60 the radiocarbon ages become noticeably older, that is there is a *depletion* in radiocarbon. A preliminary interpretation of this overall section could be that from 1260 to 1335 more cosmic radiation reached the atmosphere and more radiocarbon was produced (possibly due to the sun being quiet and the solar wind being weaker). However, when we come to consider the period 1335–60 it is not enough simply to reverse the process. Turning up the solar wind and lessening the production of radiocarbon would not cause the observed radiocarbon reversal. In order to 'get rid of' radiocarbon from the atmosphere, the amount of radioactive Carbon-14 in the atmosphere has to have been *diluted*. To dilute the amount of radiocarbon, some mechanism has to inject large

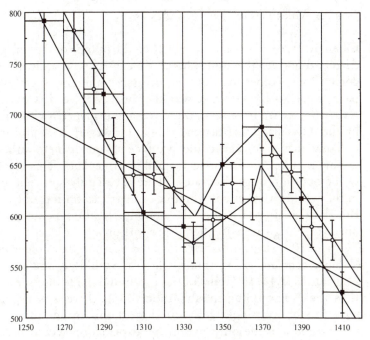

FIG. 3.4 All the high-precision radiocarbon determinations obtained by Pearson *et al.* (1986) and Stuiver and Becker (1993) relevant to the fourteenth century. The straight line indicates Libby's theoretical relationship between radiocarbon age and real age. The enrichment in radiocarbon concentration in the atmosphere, where radiocarbon ages become rapidly younger, is evident from 1260 to 1335, as is the depletion between 1335 and 1360. The question is whether this coarse resolution depletion hides an abrupt dilution of the atmospheric concentration of radiocarbon due to an outgassing event in 1347.

amounts of inert Carbon-12 (or carbon deficient in Carbon-14) into the atmosphere. Conventional wisdom suggests that the dilution is brought about by older CO_2 from ocean water exchanging with the atmosphere. However, this would take place over time. The question I wish to ask is what would happen if the injection was sudden, within a year. This is where the decadal wood samples used in the calibration curve represent a limiting factor; is it possible that somewhere between 1335 and 1360 there is an abrupt dilution disguised by the coarse resolution of the calibration? What mechanisms exist which could inject large amounts of ancient carbon abruptly into the atmosphere?

Comets, Volcanoes or Gas Hydrates

Of these three phenomena, which could pump, or dump, gigatons of dead carbon into the atmosphere? We can rule out a direct impact by a comet; for a comet to inject the necessary amount of carbon it would have to be so large that it would probably have destroyed most life on Earth. As we have seen, there is some evidence for a volcano signal in the Greenland ice around 1345. However, it seems intrinsically unlikely that a volcano could produce so much inert carbon without leaving a more significant acid signal in Greenland. This brings us back to the question of gas hydrates. There is certainly sufficient gas hydrate in the world to inject any amount of inert carbon into the atmosphere. Rough calculations based on the amount of carbon dioxide in the atmosphere (2,400 gigatons) and the proportion of radioactive ^{14}C to inert ^{12}C (1 in 10^{12}) suggest that to move radiocarbon dates older by 80 years (a 1 per cent depletion) in a single year would require an injection of 24 gigatons (2.4×10^{10} tons) of inert carbon dioxide into the atmosphere. If in the Pearson/Stuiver calibration results there is a disguised short-term (possibly a single year) dilution of this magnitude, or even half this magnitude, the only reasonable explanation would be an episode of undersea outgassing (forest fires simply would not be adequate, because the carbon being burnt in the case of contemporary forests is not sufficiently old). It is at this point that it is worth referring back to Figure 3.3. What is almost more striking than the tree-ring decline into the 1340s is the universal recovery immediately after 1350. This synchronous recovery, given the widespread grid of chronologies involved, has to be interesting. Is it, one could ask, that something has reversed the cooling trend? Might it represent a small pulse of greenhouse warming, or a hint of fertilization effect; is it what might be expected if a large amount of methane or carbon dioxide were suddenly injected into the atmosphere?

It is at this juncture that we have to turn to history, though one preliminary point needs to be made. A recent paper by Rogers and Yevi (1996) on Lake Nyos, Cameroon, has shown pretty conclusively that masses of hydrogen sulphide came out of the crater lake in 1986 as an energetic ground-hugging poisonous cloud, killing thousands of people and animals. Local witnesses were not originally believed when they reported the characteristic smell of rotten eggs at the time of the outgassing; it is now obvious that they were correct. In order to set the scene for the history of the 1340s, it is worth noting that Ziegler (1970) makes almost exactly the same point about witnesses; to paraphrase his comments, he says you cannot really believe these medieval writers who were trying to wrestle with something they did not understand. He chides the Medical Faculty of the University of Paris for citing a planetary conjunction as a possible cause (though see below) and tells us that modern science has sorted out 'as a fact the main elements of the Black Death'. This is the modern standpoint: ignore contemporary witnesses because we know better.

From the evidence of the tree-ring downturn, and the radiocarbon enrichment/depletion turning-point, we can undoubtedly suggest an environmental event, and we can construct an hypothesis involving a possible outgassing event in or around the 1340s. With that in mind we can look at what people writing in the late 1340s and 1350s—exactly contemporary with the Black Death—thought of as the cause of the pestilence which was literally at their door. The comments are interesting, because several are really quite specific.

THE BLACK DEATH REVISITED

Conventional wisdom suggests that the plague started in the East, perhaps after 1333, when drought and famine were followed by flood and pestilence. There seem to have been earthquakes in China in 1334 and earthquakes and floods from 1337 to 1345. In this scenario the plague had emerged and was on its way a decade before it reached Europe in 1347 (Ziegler 1970). Ziegler uses some extreme imagery to suggest that things had, in fact, been going badly wrong in the East from the 1330s, though, as noted, he essentially dismisses most of the rhetoric as retrospective attempts by medieval writers to discover some signs that might have anticipated the plague.

While Ziegler knew that there had been some extremes of climate in the period before the Black Death, he could have had no knowledge that trees would point a clear environmental finger at the 1340s, nor could he have known that radiocarbon calibration measurements would point to some significant change around the same period. We can now be fairly sure that there was more depleted carbon in the atmosphere and we can contemplate concepts such as gas hydrates which would have been unimagined back in the late 1960s. So, with a more open mind, what can we glean from contemporary writers from the mid-fourteenth century? The following quotations come from Horrox's 1994 tabulation of contemporary fourteenth-century documents. These include the report of the Paris Medical Faculty from October 1348, which, although it talks of planetary conjunctions and eclipses, also refers to 'a deadly corruption of the air around us':

We believe that the present epidemic or plague has arisen from air corrupt in its substance . . .

Also the sky has looked yellow and the air reddish because of the burnt vapours . . . and in particular the powerful earthquakes, have done universal harm and left a trail of corruption. There have been masses of dead fish, animals and other things along the sea shore, and in many places trees covered in dust . . . and all these things seem to have come from the corruption of the air and earth. (Horrox 1994: 162)

From a later fourteenth-century German treatise we hear a quite specific, and obviously well-considered suggestion. This source is particularly interesting because the author dismisses acts of God, planetary conjunctions and foul odours from corpses, and then says this:

There is a fourth opinion, which I consider more likely than the others, which is that insofar as the mortality arose from natural causes its immediate cause was a corrupt and poisonous earthy exhalation. . . . I say that it is the vapour and corrupted air which has been vented . . . in the earthquake which occurred on St Paul's day, 1347, along with the corrupted air vented in other earthquakes and eruptions, which has infected the air about the earth. (Horrox 1994: 177)

Such a specific statement is rendered even more authoritative, because the author lists eight points to support his decision; he then lists six areas of doubt about his opinion, and, in turn, replies to each of these. Such a scientific approach would put many a modern researcher to shame, and suggests that there is nothing hysterical about the statements he makes. Since he is writing after the 1340s, it is of even more interest that he says the following: 'there was a lot of that earthy smoke which affected the length and breadth of the earth . . . [and] . . . although it is steadily dispersing, it is doing so over a long period, and it is not possible to know when it will disperse entirely' (Horrox 1994: 181).

And from Ziegler we have reference to happenings on Cyprus, where in 1347 (apparently):

While the plague was just beginning a particularly severe earthquake came to complete the work of destruction. A tidal wave swept over large parts of the island . . . A pestiferous wind spread so poisonous an odour that many . . . fell down suddenly and expired in dreadful agonies. (Ziegler 1970: 113)

Here, there is a clear differentiation between the plague, which is just beginning, and the pestiferous wind, which is associated with what appears to be a tsunami. One of the most telling throw-away lines can again be found in Ziegler. He refers to an observation in Italy: 'The wine in the casks had become turbid [muddy] "a statement which" as the nineteenth-century German historian Hecker hopefully remarked "may be considered as furnishing proof that changes causing a decomposition of the atmosphere had taken place"' (Ziegler 1970: 43).

What Ziegler seems not to have recognized, but which Hecker may have, is that for wine in casks to go turbid, a gas would have to be involved which could travel through the cask walls. It can be argued quite convincingly that the small hydrogen sulphide molecule would exactly fit the bill. What is not in doubt is Ziegler's paraphrase of the whole situation 'This concept of a corrupted atmosphere, visible in the form of mist or smoke, drifting across the world and overwhelming all whom it encountered was one of the main (contemporary) assumptions' (Ziegler 1970: 14).

All these observations—earthquakes, fire from heaven, dead fish, corrupted atmosphere, sky yellow/reddish with burnt vapours, and people dying very rapidly—could be reasonable attempts by contemporary observers to describe the aftermath of outgassing events. In particular, there is no doubt that appropriate sources of methane and hydrogen sulphide exist; and that Cyprus is a likely candidate for such an event, since there are massive sources of gas in the eastern Mediterranean. Our only difficulty may be in deciding whether mud-volcanoes or actual hydrate deposits were to blame. One could even ask whether the acid layer in Greenland at 1345 +/− 2 might reflect this source rather than the activity of a more conventional volcano. However, it has to be stressed that this argument is not an attempt to replace bubonic plague. It is not being suggested that the Black Death was solely due to an outgassing event; rather, that the worst plague in 1,500 years may have been multi-causal, and that outgassing may have played a part. It should be noted that one side-effect of exposure to hydrogen sulphide gas would be skin blotches caused by the gas turning to sulphuric acid on the damp skin of victims. In a plague situation who would care to differentiate between acid burns and the black or livid spots of *Yersinia pestis*?

So, do we have enough to go on? Currently, no. Our problem is that the radiocarbon measurements were made only at decadal and bi-decadal resolution. As we see from Figure 3.4, this coarse resolution could obscure very rapid changes at annual resolution. Thus, at least, we do have a very specific target for research. In the case of tree-rings we can look at annual resolution within the growth rings at the relative amounts of radioactive Carbon-14 and stable Carbon-13. Although we can ask ice-core workers to take a fresh look at the relevant well-dated layers in several of their ice records, they unfortunately suffer from the following problem: atmospheric gasses are not taken up in the ice on a year-to-year basis, rather the upper 50–100 metres of ice are porous and in balance with the atmosphere. Thus, trapped air bubbles have a mean age which can be considerably younger than the ice in which they occur. Irrespective of that complication, it should be possible to ascertain whether or not a massive dose of relatively inert carbon was injected into the atmosphere in or around AD 1347. If it was, it is virtually certain that the source would have been the mud volcanoes and/or gas hydrate deposits which occur in exactly the right areas to verify the historical accounts.

CONCLUSION

The increasing availability of a whole new spectrum of high resolution environmental information is bound to change our existing view of the past. As with the contemporary documents relating to the Black Death, we may be forced to look again at many eyewitness accounts which have hitherto been largely dismissed by modern scholars. New balances may have to be struck. The Great Famine of AD 1315–22, which has received much attention (Jordan 1996), does not show up as a global tree-ring downturn, whereas the Black Death has a clear environmental context, as indeed does the second wave of 1361.

Irrespective of the mechanisms involved in the environmental events, the tree-ring evidence already tells us that there were strong environmental components associated with some key events in recent human history. As we have seen, almost all the events seem to have a relatively abrupt component. The limiting case would be impacts, or outgassings, or eruptions which might take place in a single day. There is, however, no reason to limit our considerations to such abrupt happenings. Implicit in Clube and Napier's bombardment scenarios would be *episodes* of bombardment. Volcanoes could be additive; even outgassing could be brought on by an episode of tectonic activity rather than a single earthquake. It is now necessary to study the ice-core and tree-ring records in more detail and to work out strategies for separating the effects of the different possible environmental factors which may have been involved. Even if the scenario presented in this essay is completely wrong, disproving it will significantly narrow the range of possibilities.

REFERENCES

Alley, R. B., Shuman, C. A., Meese, A. A., Gow, A. J., Taylor, K. C., Cuffey, K. M., Fitzpatrik, J. J., Grootes, P. M., Zielinski, G. A., Ram, M., Spinelli, G., and Elder, B. (1997). 'Visual stratigraphic dating of the GISP2 ice core: basis, reproducibility, and application'. *Journal of Geophysical Research*, 102 (C12): 26,411–23.

Bailey, M. E. (1995). 'Recent results in cometary astronomy: implications for the ancient sky'. *Vistas in Astronomy*, 39 (4): 647–71.

Bailey, M. E., Clube, S. V. M., and Napier, W. M. (1990). *The Origin of Comets*. London: Pergamon Press.

Baillie, M. G. L. (1991). 'Marking in marker dates—towards an archaeology with historical precision'. *World Archaeology*, 23: 233–43.

Baillie, M. G. L. (1994). 'Dendrochronology raises questions about the nature of the AD 536 dust-veil event'. *The Holocene*, 4: 212–17.

Baillie, M. G. L. (1995). *A Slice Through Time: Dendrochronology and Precision Dating*. London: Routledge.

Baillie, M. G. L. (1996). 'Dendrochronology provides an independent background for studies of the human past', in D. Cavaciocchi (ed.), *L'UOMO E YLA FORESTA SECC. XIII–XVIII* Atti della 'Ventisettesima Settimana di Studi', 8–13 maggio 1995, Istituto Internazionale di Storia Economica 'F. Datini': 99–119.

Baillie, M. G. L. (1999). *Exodus to Arthur: Catastrophic Encounters With Comets*. London: Batsford.

Baillie, M. G. L. and Munro, M. A. R. (1988). 'Irish tree-rings, Santorini and volcanic dust veils'. *Nature*, 332: 344–6.

Becker, B. and Schmidt, B. (1990). 'Extension of the European Oak Chronology to 9224 years'. *PACT*, 29 (ESF) Strasbourg: 37–50.

Briffa, K. R. (1994). 'Mid and late Holocene climate change: evidence from tree-growth in northern Fennoscandia', in B. M. Funnell and R. L. F. Kay (eds), *Palaeoclimate of the Last Glacial/Interglacial Cycle*. Special Publication, no 94/2, London: NERC, 61–5.

Briffa, K. R., Jones, P. D., Bartholin, T. S., Eckstein, D., Schweingruber, F. H., Karlen, W., Zetterberg, P., and Eronen, M. (1992). 'Fennoscandian summers from AD 500: temperature changes on short and long timescales'. *Climate Dynamics*, 7: 111–19.

Britton, C. E. (1937). *A Meteorological Chronology to AD 1450*. Geophysical Memoirs, no. 70, London: HMSO.

Brown, D. M. and Baillie, M. G. L. (1992). 'Construction and dating of a 5000-year English bog oak tree-ring chronology'. *Lundqua*, Report 34: 72–5.

Burgess, C. (1985). 'Population, climate and upland settlement', *British Archaeological Reports* (British Series), 143: 195–22.

Chester, D. K. (1988). 'Volcanoes and climate: recent volcanological perspectives'. *Progress in Physical Geography*, 12 (4): 1–35.

Clausen, H. B., Hammer, C. U., Hvidberg, C. S., Dahl-Jensen, D., and Steffensen, J. P. (1997). 'A comparison of the volcanic records over the past 4,000 years from the Greenland Ice Core Project and Dye 3 Greenland ice cores'. *Journal of Geophysical Research*, 102 (C12): 26,707–23.

Clube, S. V. M. and Napier, B. (1990). *The Cosmic Winter*. Oxford: Blackwell.

Dawson, A. G., Long, D., and Smith, D. E. (1988). 'The Storegga Slides: evidence from eastern Scotland for a possible tsunami'. *Marine Geology*, 82: 271–6.

Drews, R. (1993). *The End of the Bronze Age: Changes in Warfare and the Catastrophe c. 1200 BC*. Princeton, NJ: Princeton University Press.

Drake, M. (1968). 'The Irish demographic crisis of 1740–41', in T. Moody (ed.), *Historical Studies VI* (Dublin, June 1965), London: Routledge and Kegan Paul, 101–24.

Hammer, C. U. (1984). 'Traces of Icelandic eruptions in the Greenland ice sheet'. *Jökull*, 34: 51–65.

Hammer, C. U., Clausen, H. B., and Dansgaard, W. (1980). 'Greenland ice sheet evidence of post-glacial volcanism and its climatic impact'. *Nature*, 288: 230–5.

Horrox, R. (1994). *The Black Death*. Manchester: Manchester University Press.

Jordan, W. C. (1996). *The Great Famine: Northern Europe in the Early 14th Century*. Princeton, NJ: Princeton University Press.

Klaeber, Fr. (1950). *Beowulf and the Fight at Finnsburg*. Boston, MA: Heath and Co.

Koshimura, S., Hamzah, L., and Imamura, F. (1998). *The earthquake and tsunami of 17 July 1998. Papua New Guinea*. Preliminary Report from Disaster Control Research Center, Tohoku University, 18pp.

Kuniholm, P. I., Kromer, B., Manning, S. M., Newton, M., Latini, C. E., and Bruce, M. J. (1996). 'Anatolian tree rings and the absolute chronology of the eastern Mediterranean, 2220–718 BC'. *Nature*, 381: 780–3.

Larson, D. O. and Michaelsen, J. (1990). 'Impacts of climatic variability and population growth on virgin branch Anasazi cultural'. *American Antiquity*, 55: 227–49.

Leuschner, von H. H. and Delorme, A. (1988). 'Tree-ring work in Göttingen—absolute oak chronologies back to 6255 BC', *PACT II.5 Wood and Archaeology*: 123–32.

Lewis, J. S. (1996). *Rain of Iron and Ice: The Very Real Threat of Comet and Asteroid Bombardment*. Massachusetts: Helix Books.

Manley, G. (1974). 'Central England temperatures: monthly means 1659 to 1973', *Quarterly Journal of the Royal Meteorological Society*, 100: 389–405.

Niddrie, D. (1961). *When the Earth Shook*. London: The Scientific Book Club.

Nur, A. and Hagai, R. (1997). 'Armageddon's Earthquakes'. *International Geology Review*, 39: 532–41.

Orcel, A., Orcel, C., Danérol, A., and Ramseyer, D. (1992). 'Contribution to the study of the Neolithic forest dynamic. The example of Delley/Portalban II (CH)'. *Lundqua*, 34: 242–6.

Pearson, G. W., Pilcher, J. R., Baillie, M. G. L., Corbett, D. M., and Qua, F. (1986). 'High-Precision 14-C measurement of Irish oaks to show the natural 14-C variations from AD 1840 to 5210 BC'. *Radiocarbon*, 28: 911–34.

Pilcher, J. R., Baillie, M. G. L., Schmidt, B., and Becker, B. (1984). 'A 7272-year tree-ring chronology for Western Europe'. *Nature*, 312: 150–2.

Platon, N. (1971). *Zakros. The Discovery of a Lost Palace of Ancient Crete*. New York: Charles Scribner.

Post, J. (1977). *The Last Great Subsistence Crisis in the Western World*. Baltimore: Johns Hopkins University Press.

Rahmstorf, S. (1995). 'Bifurcations of the Atlantic thermohaline circulation in response to changes in the hydrological cycle, *Nature*, 378: 145–9.

Renfrew, C. (1996). 'Kings, tree rings and the Old World'. *Nature*, 381: 733–4.

Rogers, R. and Yevi, G. (1996). 'Hydrate theory explains Lake Nyos disaster'. *2nd International Conference on Natural Gas Hydrates*, 2–6 June 1996 Toulouse, France.

Sayers, W. (1986). 'Mani, Maidi an Nem . . . : ringing changes on a cosmic motif'. *Erin*, 37: 99–117.

Scuderi, L. A. (1993). 'A 2000-year tree-ring record of annual temperatures in the Sierra Nevada Mountains'. *Science*, 259: 1433–6.

Sloan, E. D., Happel, J., and Hnatow, M. (eds) (1994). '1st International Conference on Natural Gas Hydrates'. *New York Academy of Sciences*, Vol. 715.

Spedicato, E. (1997). 'Evidence for Tunguska-type impacts over the Pacific basin around the year 1178 AD'. Abstract P-3 of the Second SIS Cambridge Conference, 'Natural catastrophes during Bronze Age Civilizations', 11–13 July 1997.

Steel, D. (1995). *Rogue Asteroids and Doomsday Comets*. New York: John Wiley and Sons.

Stothers, R. B. (1984). 'Mystery Cloud of AD 536', *Nature*, 307: 344–5.

Stothers, R. B. and Rampino, M. R. (1983). 'Volcanic eruptions in the Mediterranean before AD 630 from written and archaeological sources'. *Journal of Geophysical Research*, 88: 6357–71.

Stuiver, M. and Becker, B. (1993). 'High-precision decadal calibration of the radiocarbon time scale, AD 1950–6000 BC'. *Radiocarbon*, 35: 35–65.

Suess, H. E. (1970). 'Bristlecone pine calibration of the radiocarbon timescale from 5200 BC to the present', in I. U. Olsson (ed.), *Radiocarbon Variations and Absolute Chronology*. New York: John Wiley and Sons, 303–9.

Verschuur, G. L. (1996). *Impact! The Threat of Comets and Asteroids*. Oxford: Oxford University Press.

Ziegler, P. (1970). *The Black Death*. Harmondsworth: Penguin Books.

Zetterberg, P., Eronen, M., and Briffa, K. R. (1994). 'Evidence on climatic variability and prehistoric human activities between 165 BC and AD 1400 derived from subfossil scots pines (*Pinus sylvestris L.*) found in a lake in Utsjoki, northernmost Finland'. *Bulletin of the Geological Society of Finland*, 66: 107–24.

Zielinski, G. A., Mayewski, P. A., Meeker, L. D., Whitlow, S., Twickler, M. S., Morrison, M., Meese, D. A., Gow, A. J., and Alley, R. B. (1994). 'Record of volcanism since 7000 BC from the GISP2 Greenland ice core and implications for the volcano-climate system'. *Science*, 264: 948–52.

4

Meeting Human Energy Needs: Constraints, Opportunities, and Effects

E. A. Wrigley

INTRODUCTION

IT IS often said that the two most significant breakpoints in the material circumstances of mankind in recent millennia have been the Neolithic food revolution and the industrial revolution. This essay is set in that framework. All major changes affecting the way in which the material needs of men and women are met are bound to be complex both in their effects and in their causation. Constraints of space will prevent a sophisticated discussion and I must use this as my excuse if parts of the following seem oversimplified. However, viewing these fundamental changes in social and economic organization from the standpoint of energy needs and energy supplies provides a perspective which should be illuminating in its own right and has the added attraction of throwing light on many other aspects of historical change.

Food is to animal life what fuel is to engines. In their absence both animals and engines cease to function, and, in the case of animals, once this has happened they cannot be restarted in the way that engines can. The life of animals is therefore perforce constantly shaped by the need to secure food in order to survive. In many species the great bulk of their waking hours is spent in feeding or seeking food. But to *secure* food all animals must *consume* food, since energy must be expended in the process. The balance between the energy expended in seeking food and the energy gained from securing it is critical to survival. The brilliant immediacy of nature films has made us all aware of this. Each time a cheetah attempts to make a kill but fails, it uses up a part of the store of energy it has acquired from previous kills. If poor judgement, inexperience, increasing age, or sheer bad luck causes it to fail in several successive charges, it will prove increasingly difficult for the cheetah to reach maximum speed, or to maintain that speed for as long as normal, and as a result its chance of making a kill will decline, ultimately to the point at which its fate is sealed, and it will die directly or indirectly for lack of energy. The nature of the problem is particularly clear in the case of predator animals such as the cheetah, but *mutatis mutandis* something similar is true of all animals.

As human society has developed, the relationship between energy availability and welfare has changed, but the importance of energy, whether as food or in other forms, in shaping human welfare has not changed. Almost all energy accessible on the surface of the earth originates in the sun. There is a very large inflow of such energy each year in the form of insolation. Even a small island in northern latitudes such as Britain receives in this way a quantity of energy which has been estimated as the equivalent of 22,000 million tons of coal in the course of a year. The great bulk of this energy, however, brings no direct benefit to living creatures. Until very recently, when human ingenuity has started to change the picture, they could gain access to the sun's energy only through the intermediate process of photosynthesis, a process which is able to capture only between 1 and 4 parts in 1,000 of the energy streaming in from the sun (White and Plaskett 1981: 2, 12). Tiny though this fraction is, the vegetable growth sustained in this way is, in turn, the base on which all animal, bird, and insect life on earth is pyramided.

People living in hunter-gatherer societies were in the same fundamental relationship to the energy made available through photosynthesis as other animals. Their activities were directed towards garnering for human use a proportion of naturally occurring fruits, grains, nuts, and other edible vegetable growth, and towards killing animals and fish for food. Successive technical innovations gradually increased their efficiency in securing such supplies. A man with a bow and arrow is a more successful predator than a man with a club or spear. But the stock of edible food, whether vegetable or animal, was not increased by such changes. Indeed, any increase in the efficiency with which prey is caught may affect predators no less than their prey, since any reduction in the available annual 'crop' of prey through 'overfishing' must lead to a reduction in the number of predators also.

The environment was not left untouched by changes in the range of the technical accomplishments of hunter-gatherer societies. The extinction of a particular species by man or the effects of activities such as the periodic burning of the original vegetation complex might lead to substantial and sometimes irreversible changes in the ecology of an area. But the basic environmental constraints experienced by hunter-gatherer societies did not alter. Their food base remained very limited and populations were therefore extremely sparse. As with animal species, moreover, there were often major seasonal fluctuations in the quantity and type of food available for consumption, and the size of the population which could be sustained was further limited by such factors.

THE NEOLITHIC FOOD REVOLUTION

The circumstances of life changed dramatically in the wake of the Neolithic food revolution, which resulted for the first time in sedentary, agricultural populations tilling the land. The substitution of plants which were directly of use for food or as raw materials for the original vegetation cover over huge areas and the domestication of animals both increased vastly the carrying capacity of the land. A much greater proportion of available energy was being reserved for man. In an area of irrigated rice cultivation in one of the great riverine deltas of Southeast Asia, for example, a very high proportion of the whole product of photosynthesis during the annual cycle of insolation was routinely annexed for human use by the nature and intensity of the agriculture. Population densities could easily rise as much as a hundred fold with the advent of agriculture.

Although the Neolithic food revolution secured far more of the products of photosynthesis for human use, the scale of the total annual capture of energy through plant growth over the surface of the earth did not greatly change. The implications of the revolution for nutrition and living standards for the mass of the population were ambiguous. In an initial phase, as land of high fertility was taken into cultivation for the first time, population might rise without producing any tension between overall population growth and individual prosperity. But if, after an early halcyon period, the total of individuals had increased in the same ratio as the increase in the proportion of the annual inflow of energy captured for human use, it was plainly possible that the material circumstances of the average individual might be little improved; indeed, that in other respects his circumstances might worsen. Boserup identified this possibility in a forceful fashion in the 1960s, when, in her book *The Conditions of Agricultural Growth*, she made much of the point that output per hour under slash and burn cultivation was often much higher than in, say, paddy rice cultivation, and suggested that the successive shifts to steadily more intensive forms of cultivation involving a more 'advanced' agriculture were normally made only under the duress of having to provide for steadily rising numbers (Boserup 1965: 41). The disadvantage of adopting more intensive forms of agriculture was, in Boserup's view, that it was characteristically necessary to work longer and longer hours to secure the same quantity of food. A peasant in a rice delta might toil for 10 hours a day to secure the same quantity of food that a slash and burn cultivator could gain by working 2 hours a day (Boserup 1965: ch. 5).

While Boserup's work proved instrumental in engendering a lively and instructive debate, it is possible to take a very different view of the range of possibilities made available to societies in the wake of the Neolithic food revolution, and in this context energy supply issues are of central importance. A first point to note is that the scale of output per head of material products is heavily conditioned by the scale of energy inputs. Anyone who has dug over a vegetable plot by hand and has also had experience of turning the soil with a gang plough drawn by a powerful tractor will have a clear appreciation of the extent to which the scale of the energy applied to a task determines how quickly it can be completed.

Consider first the most basic instance of the phenomenon. There is a wide range of levels of food intake over which ability to perform work is linearly related to nutrition. Thus a man who is regularly receiving 3,500 calories of food a day can perform far more useful work than he could if he were regularly receiving only 2,500 calories a day. If a contrast of this sort persists thoughout whole communities over a long period of time, the result, in an economic and technological setting in which personal effort and personal output are closely linked, may well be a stark and stable contrast in living standards and physical well-being. Poor nutrition implies low output per head, which in turn means inadequate nutrition, thus forming a vicious circle of relationships. One should note, incidentally, that relatively small differences in calorie intake can imply big differences in ability to perform useful work. A diet providing 2,500 calories a day represents a food intake 71 per cent as large as a diet consisting of 3,500 calories. But if food intake among a working population were permanently reduced from 3,500 to 2,500 calories on average, ability to carry out useful work would fall not by 29 per cent but by 50 per cent, because the first 1,500 calories of a daily diet are needed to meet basic metabolic needs. It is possible to remain alive but not to carry out any signficant physical exertion on a diet of 1,500 calories a day. Only above this level can work be sustained. The quantum of energy available for work is therefore halved from 2,000 to 1,000 calories if daily calorie intake falls from 3,500 to 2,500 calories. Hence, the substantial leverage represented by a comparatively modest increase in overall food intake above the basic level when ability to perform work is at issue. It is a well-advised labour camp commandant who raises the food available to inmates from, say, 2,000 to 2,500 calories a day. A 25 per cent increase in food intake in such circumstances should result in a 100 per cent rise in work performed.

This account is far too simple-minded to satisfy those who have studied these issues in detail. Prolonged poor nutrition will affect average height and weight and cause the basic metabolic need to be less and the amount of work performed consequently greater for any given level of nutrition. And an extended treatment of this topic would require many other refinements.[1] But one basic point is clear. In agricultural societies, in which productive labour involves a large expenditure of personal energy by the individuals who take part in the production process, energy intake in the form of food will play a major role in determining levels of output per head, and it is possible for substantial and relatively stable differences in the living standards of different communities to be linked to this factor.

DRAUGHT ANIMALS AND MECHANICAL ENERGY

In agricultural societies, however, the interlinkage between energy availability per head and output per head extends well beyond the question of average individual nutrition, important though this may be. The domestication of animals radically increased the quantity of mechanical energy per head available in favourable circumstances. In the absence of animal assistance, the amount of work performed by a man was chiefly a function of his personal physical strength. If, miraculously, each man had awoken one morning to find that he could perform twice as much work in a day for a given level of food intake as had previously been possible, output per head and, consequently, the living standards of the community would have risen substantially, *ceteris paribus*. But the muscular strength of men is dwarfed by that of draught animals. A horse is on average about ten times stronger than a man. For tasks that are suitable to be tackled by horses, therefore, a man who benefits from the harnessed strength of a horse or of another draught animal will accomplish far more in a given interval of time than a man without such assistance. Comparative data collected in Mexico in the 1940s, for example, showed that when oxen were used only a third as many man-hours of work were needed to produce a crop of maize in a given area as when cultivation was undertaken entirely by hand (Wrigley 1988: 39; Pimentel 1984: 5–6).

---

[1] For a discussion of the complexity of interrelationships between economic circumstances, nutrition, and human physiology, see Fogel (1994).

Draught animals introduced a new element into the energy equation. In many agricultural tasks, in most types of pre-industrial transport, and in some aspects of industrial production also, a horse-rich community was a mechanical energy-rich community, which would consequently probably also be rich in the conventional sense, at least in comparison with other communities lacking such support.

Agricultural societies, therefore, were, in principle, capable of becoming substantially differentiated from one another in rough accordance with their success in supplementing human muscle power with animal energy. This may introduce great complexity into the description and analysis of such economies. For example, although enjoying the assistance of a horse in many energy-intensive tasks is a major boon, the advantage is offset by the fact that for a large output of energy there must be a balancing input of energy in the form of fodder. It required approximately five acres of land to support a working horse, and land that was used for fodder could not at the same time also be used to produce food for people. In a country in which human population totals were restrained to the point where there existed a surplus of land available for raising oxen and horses as beasts of burden, the two demands could be reconciled. In effect, in such a country the population was preferring a relatively high standard of living associated with a high level of mechanical energy per worker to a large population total living less well. But if numbers increased for any reason, a conflict between man and beast for land was unavoidable. A decline in livestock to accommodate human food needs would limit the extent to which the most energy-intensive tasks could be offloaded onto draught animals. It will be recalled that one of the most striking differences between England and the continent at the beginning of the nineteenth century was the radically smaller proportion of the English labour force engaged in agriculture, even though the country remained very largely self-sufficient in food. Though many other factors played a part in bringing about this situation, one element was the significantly higher ratio of draught animals to arable acreage which obtained in England compared with France and, no doubt, most other countries (Wrigley 1988: 39–42; 1991).

In advanced agricultural societies there were other elements in the overall energy situation which might lead to certain areas enjoying greater benefits and a potentially higher standard of living than others. The water-wheel and the windmill were both sources of substantial, if unreliable, mechanical energy, though the number of suitable sites for either type of power was limited. And wind energy trapped by the sail, combined with the development of an efficient rudder, transformed the possibilities of long-distance navigation at sea.

THE SOURCES OF THERMAL ENERGY IN
PRE-INDUSTRIAL SOCIETIES

The relative abundance of *mechanical* energy was of great importance in determining levels of productivity per head in agriculture, overwhelmingly the most important single form of material production. In manufacturing industry also mechanical energy was important, but *thermal* energy was frequently an even more significant bottleneck. Commonly, the prime source of thermal energy was the burning of wood and since in some industries heat was needed in large quantities in order to achieve even modest levels of production, the extent of forest cover could be a major determinant of the location and scale of particular industries. It is no coincidence that Swedish and Russian iron figured so prominently in supplying domestic demand in England in the eighteenth century before an effective substitute for charcoal came into wide use (Thomas 1986; also Ashton 1951: ch. 5; Davis 1962: 213–24). It has been estimated that it was necessary to fell the timber from a total of 40,000 hectares in order to produce 10,000 tons of iron (Benaerts 1933: 454). Very few countries could sustain a large output of iron indefinitely. None could possibly raise iron output to the levels which later became commonplace as long as charcoal was the means of converting ore into metal. To illustrate the extent of the difference between what was feasible in an organically based economy and what was later routine, it is worth noting that, using Benaerts's estimates of fuel needs, and in an era before the advent of coal smelting, to construct the railway network as big as that which Britain possessed by the end of the nineteenth century would have involved removing the timber from some 12 million hectares, or half the surface area of the country.[2]

The thermal energy requirements of iron production were unusually large compared with those of many other industries, but the list of industries for which a supply of thermal energy was vital is long: brick-making, glass-refining, pottery manufacture, the smelting and working of non-ferrous metals, salt-boiling, brewing, dyeing, baking, and many more. Meeting the thermal energy needs of industries such as these in an expanding economy raised the same fundamental problems as were inescapable when trying to secure adequate supplies of mechanical

---

[2] This is a conservative estimate based on the assumption that the railway system consisted of 20,000 miles of single track with rails weighing 90 lbs a yard, which implies a total requirement of 3 million tons of steel rails (for simplicity, iron and steel are treated as requiring similar amounts of heat energy in their manufacture, which adds to the conservative nature of the estimate).

energy. Increasing the output of wood meant setting aside an increasing acreage for that purpose. At some point the food needs of the population were bound to conflict with their wish to command a larger flow of thermal energy, thus creating a situation essentially similar to that associated with increasing fodder supplies for horses and oxen. If human populations were also increasing, such developments inevitably resulted in a more and more severe competition for the use of land.

The problem of meeting the thermal energy needs of advanced agricultural societies led at times to an energetic search for a means of circumventing this restriction. When a tree is cut down and used for fuel, the energy thus released represents the accumulated product of photosynthesis over many decades, even over several centuries. The fact that the gain represented by a cumulative growth process could be realized instantly in this way, that trees are what might be termed a centennial rather than an annual crop, did not, of course, represent an escape route from the general constraints of all organic economies. Only the annual increment of timber growth could be taken if output was to be sustained. In exceptional circumstances, however, an escape was possible, for there are several forms in which plant growth can be cumulated not simply over a century or two but over many millennia, or even over tens of millions of years. The former is true of peat; the latter of coal. Both substances came into increasing use as the more traditional sources of thermal energy became scarce in long-settled areas. In substantial measure the Dutch economy of the Golden Age was a peat-based economy, as the work of De Zeeuw has recently shown, while in England, a land in which probably no more than 15 per cent of the land surface was forested even at the time of the Domesday survey, coal, though little liked, became an increasingly important prop of the industrial economy from the sixteenth century onwards (De Zeeuw 1978; Rackham 1980: 126 and table 96, 127).

The significance of the switch from traditional sources of heat energy is obvious. In favourable circumstances, where the process of accumulating the products of photosynthesis has continued for countless centuries, a society gains access to energy on a scale that is impossible within the confines of an organic economy in which the annual expenditure of energy cannot exceed the ceiling set by the annual cycle of energy capture from insolation. The production horizon of a society which has made the switch is transformed. Some projects which were once literally physically impossible become feasible. To revert to the example quoted earlier, the 3 million tons of steel needed to construct a rail network of the size built in Britain in the nineteenth century can be manufactured without difficulty, since the energy needed to under-write such a project is readily available. Where once steel could be used only to make a suit of armour, after the switch it could be used to make a battle-tank.

In the circumstances of organically based societies a fortunate natural endowment, if allied to restrained population growth, might result in relatively abundant supplies of both mechanical and thermal energy per head of population and hence give rise to a community where living standards were well above those of bare subsistence and which was seldom visited by famine. But, equally, even the most fortunate of such societies could not hope to dispose of energy on a scale to enable output per head to increase other than modestly. In many types of production there were significant advances in productivity per head to be gained from the division of labour in the manner immortalized in Adam Smith's parable about pinmaking (Smith 1961: I, 8–9). But since all material pro-duction involves the expenditure of energy, since there is a close rela-tionship between the input of energy in the production process and the level of output per head, and since the highest attainable levels of energy use per head were very modest by the standards of the last two centuries, it is easy to understand why the classical economists expected growth to end in the 'stationary state'—a state in which the limits to growth had been reached, a state made unavoidable by the limitations inherent in an economy whose sole source of raw materials and energy was the land. In the stationary state, moreover, the lot of the average man was expected to be a miserable one (Wrigley 1987).

Classical economists did not frame the arguments which led them to predict the stationary state in terms of energy availability. They relied instead upon the concept of declining marginal returns to capital and labour.[3] Paralleling the economic arguments for the stationary state, however, there was an underlying physical reality. One of the three factors of production, land, was in fixed supply. This ensured that, at some point, declining returns must take hold either at the intensive or the extensive margins of cultivation, or at both, and since land was the prime source of useful energy, whether in the form of food, fodder, or fuel,[4] the ultimate constraint on growth sprang from what Ricardo

[3] This concept was used explicitly only by Malthus and Ricardo, but Adam Smith used an essentially similar argument.

[4] Land, even when interpreted widely to mean all forms of raw material supply, seldom figures prominently in modern neoclassical economic writing about factors of production and constraints upon growth. Occasionally, a voice of dissent is raised, worried that cru-cially important matters are being ignored. A notable dissentient voice has been Georgescu-Roegen, whose concern was focused on the issue of entropic degradation (1971; 1975).

termed 'a law of nature.'[5] There was a limit to energy output per acre set by a biochemical process whose inefficiency ensured that the bulk of the abundant total inflow of energy from the sun, frustratingly, was not accessible to mankind. As a result, productive capacity was modest in relation to human needs if members of society, other than the elite, were ever to be able to enjoy more than the basic necessities of food, clothing shelter, and fuel.

The expectations of the classical economists, fortunately, proved unduly pessimistic, and in discovering why their expectations were disappointed we can also see how radical was the difference between even the most advanced organic economy and the economies which have characterized the world following the industrial revolution. It is intriguing that Adam Smith referred to the importance of coal only as a factor whose presence, by enabling the average family to meet its fuel needs more cheaply than in areas far from a coalfield, kept the price of labour relatively low and thereby encouraged manufactures to be located in that area (Smith 1961: II, 404). In this a supply of coal was closely similar in its effects to the existence of land of high fertility where corn could be produced cheaply. In a famous passage Smith described how in rich agricultural areas away from water transport corn could be grown cheaply but could not be exported at a profit since it was relatively bulky and heavy and transport costs were therefore high. By enabling workers to live economically, however, cheap corn kept production costs low and, as a result, corn could be 'virtually' exported, in the form of, say, woollen cloth rather than as grain (Smith 1961: I, 430–1).

OVERCOMING THE ENERGY SUPPLY BOTTLENECKS

Smith made no play with the link between available energy and individual productivity. He and the other classical economists were reflecting upon the characteristics of organically based economies and were largely unconscious of the significance of the slow sea change which was taking place in the productive economy of England. Seen from the point of view

[5] In reflecting on the constraints upon growth and, in particular, on the law of diminishing returns associated with the limited supply of agricultural land, Ricardo argued that an increasing proportion of the value of the produce of the land would be taken by labourers even though the absolute quantity available to each labourer would fall. The share of capital in the total return would thereby be reduced and the fortunes of the farmer as capitalist would fall in parallel, a state of affairs which 'will necessarily be rendered permanent by the laws of nature, which have limited the productive powers of the land.' (Ricardo 1951: 126).

of energy usage, defining the 'classic' period of the industrial revolution as that from, say, 1760 to 1830 is both arbitrary and misleading. An increasing dependence upon fossil fuels had been a notable characteristic of the British economy since the later sixteenth century. By 1800 Britain was already producing and consuming 15 millions tons of coal a year, several times the combined coal production of the continent of Europe at the time, and the equivalent in energy terms of the annual produce of about 6 million hectares of woodland (Wrigley 1988: 50–7). Since little of the surface area of Britain was forested and its total area is only about 23 million hectares, much of it, especially in Scotland, of poor quality, it will be obvious that the country's energy economy had already outstripped anything which was feasible within the constraints of a purely organic economy. The history of those English manufacturing industries which depended upon thermal energy illustrates this point. In industry after industry the use of fossil fuel increased at the expense of wood-burning. The transition was simple and swift where, as in salt-boiling, the fire and the object to be heated were separated from one another by a physical barrier such as the base and sides of a cauldron. It was more protracted where a chemical interaction between the fuel and the object to be heated appeared unavoidable, as with the smelting of iron. Where this was the case, it often took some time to overcome the problem. But the advantages of finding a successful solution to such problems were obvious and created a powerful incentive to continue the process of trial and error until a viable solution had been found.

Matters were less straightforward in industries in which the prime need was for mechanical rather than heat energy. During the seventeenth and eighteenth centuries mechanical energy continued to be obtained overwhelmingly from the same sources as had provided it for many centuries, and above all from human and animal muscle. It was the 'burning' of fuel in the form of food or fodder which, translated into useful work by the exercise of muscle power, continued to meet most productive needs, greatly aided, so far as sea transport was concerned, by capturing the energy in the wind by the use of the sail, and further aided in some land-based production processes by the use of water and wind power to drive 'mills'. But muscle power is feeble when compared with the scale of energy use needed to lift a population out of poverty, and other traditional sources of mechanical energy, predominantly wind or water power, were intermittent in their availability and restricted to a limited number of sites.

The problem was especially acute in the coal-mining industry. A single miner in the course of a year's work in seventeenth-century England could produce about 200 tons of coal (Nef 1932: II, 138; Hatcher 1993:

I, 344–6), the equivalent of all the energy produced by photosynthesis over 80 hectares of woodland.[6] Cottrell provides an alternative way of picturing the revolutionary implications of the growth of coal-mining for energy availability, noting that a miner producing 500 pounds of coal a day (a very modest level of output, well below the seventeenth-century English average) would be producing a heat value 500 times greater than the heat value of the food he consumed (Cottrell 1955: 86). Coal was a potential solution to the problem of the deficient energy possibilities of an organic economy, but only a small amount of coal lay close to the surface, and the deeper a mine was dug the more acute became the difficulty in removing the water which seeped into mine workings in enormous quantities. The traditional solution to the removal of surplus water was to harness horses to provide the mechanical energy needed to bring it to the surface. But being dependent on horses for power implied that the maximum depth to which a shaft could be sunk was quite modest. At greater depths the inrush of water could neither be prevented nor counteracted. The imperative need to develop an effective answer to the drainage of coal mines forms the background to the development of a general solution to the problem of mechanical energy supply.

The history of the development of the steam engine has been told many times and needs no rehearsal here. The Newcomen engine, the earliest form in which steam was put to effective use as a source of mechanical energy, was wasteful of fuel and had only limited applications, but during the late eighteenth and nineteenth centuries the steam engine developed rapidly, gaining in power and efficiency so that forces equivalent to the energy provided by many hundreds of horses could be applied in a wider and wider range of contexts. Above all, once the problem of converting heat energy into rotary motion had been solved, machines of all types and sizes could be driven at higher and higher speeds without expending muscular energy, and in addition the great transport bottleneck could be overcome. When one man could tend 20 looms, each acting far more rapidly than a handloom weaver could work, or when a steam hammer could accomplish at a stroke a feat which would have taken a blacksmith a working day, many of the constraints which had always previously been present, and which had served to limit what could be achieved by implementing Adam Smith's parable about the division of labour, fell away. Moreover, goods and people began to travel at what would once have been thought breakneck speeds and at much lower real cost, and yet departure and arrival times could be routinely maintained, since the

---

[6] The heat of combustion of 200 tons of bituminous coal is equivalent to about 400 tons of bone dry wood, and, assuming a yield of 5 tons of wood per hectare per annum, this yields the estimate of approximately 80 hectares (White and Plaskett 1981: 12, 125).

railway and the steamship were far less subject to the vagaries of the weather than the horse-drawn carriage or the sailing vessel.

PRODUCTIVE POWER AND POVERTY

For the first time in human history poverty became problematic. The productive powers to banish poverty existed. Whether or not it was in fact banished depended upon factors such as the institutional framework of the society, its economic structure, and its political constitution, but poverty was no longer an ineluctable necessity. No reform of economic, social, or political structures in an organically based society could have overcome the problem of poverty. Personal productivity was limited severely and inescapably by the paucity of energy in the production process, but, with the marshalling of greater and greater quantities of energy at the elbow of the average worker, the old limitations could be surmounted. Levasseur captured something of the nature of the new regime when, in trying to bring home the scale of the changes during the middle decades of the nineteenth century in France, he made a calculation in which he converted the horsepower available through the use of steam engines into its equivalent in extra human labour. He noted that in 1840 France disposed of the equivalent of 1,185,000 labourers from this source who were both docile and untroubled by exhaustion. By 1885–7, however, this figure had risen to 98,000,000: 'two-and-a-half slaves for each inhabitant of France' (Levasseur 1889: III, 74).

Inasmuch as competition for food, a universal feature of animal life, is competition for energy, it might be said that the search for energy ranks with the urge to reproduce as one of the two main determinants of the behaviour and development of most animal species. But whereas the urge to reproduce is intermittent, the search for food is constant. However, it is also true that hunger can be sated. An animal which has gorged itself will for a time lose all interest in food. A zebra may walk within yards of a lion after a kill in perfect safety. But with men it is different: their material ambitions are not so readily satisfied, and therefore their demand for energy is well nigh unlimited. Occasionally, an individual will renounce all ambition to acquire more goods, considering that fulfilment lies elsewhere, but this attitude has become rare to a degree in the modern world and was perhaps seldom widespread in any society. More usually, the appetite grows by what it feeds upon. The urge to acquire more and more material goods and to enjoy a wider and wider range of services proves insatiable, which in turn implies that the appetite to consume energy is similarly likely to grow without limit. Profound though the changes accompanying the Neolithic food revolution were, they were not such as to allow material acquisitions to rise in parallel with desire. There was still a ceiling to the ability of individuals in the mass to acquire material goods. But with the industrial revolution this constraint was relaxed because societies won access to energy supplies built up over innumerable millennia rather than being dependent upon the annual inflow from the sun. As a result, output could be increased exponentially. The relative share of each distinctive group within society, whether defined by class, occupation, or status, might not change greatly, but as the cake to be divided grew steadily and rapidly larger, the material circumstances of most men and women could improve quickly.

The long-term effects of this radical change remain unclear. Stocks of the main new sources of energy—coal, oil, and gas—will probably become exhausted in a matter of centuries at the most, even at existing rates of consumption, and will disappear much more quickly if the most populous of the Asian countries, and especially China and India, raise their energy consumption per head closer to western levels.

In the long run, therefore, an ability to continue to increase energy consumption will probably depend upon finding new sources of energy which are not subject to steady depletion, such as, for example, a method by which a much higher fraction of the energy reaching the earth's surface each year from the sun can be captured. But short-term problems associated with a change in the world's climatic regime may prove so pressing and serious as to alter the nature or scale of energy use long before conventional energy stocks run low. Meanwhile, however, the last half-dozen generations in the West have lived in circumstances of great privilege compared with their predecessors. The only petition in the Lord's Prayer which deals with the things of this world is a plea that we should each day receive our daily bread. The prayer is still repeated universally in Christian churches in the West, but it must long have ceased to have any serious resonance in the minds of those who repeat it. How serious for any of them is the threat that the day will pass without access to a supply of bread? If bread is not eaten today, it is because it is regarded as an inferior good rather than because it is not affordable. Yet to those who joined in the prayer in an Elizabethan church the threat, though intermittent, was real enough. No matter was of greater concern to Tudor statesmen than the dangers which attended the state if the price of bread rose unduly.

Nor has a greater command of material goods been the only, or even the greatest, benefit flowing from an abundance of energy in this new era. At present about 95 per cent of all new-born children in Britain pass the age of 50, whereas 150 years ago only about two-thirds of each new generation reached the age of 20, and fewer than half reached 50. The reasons for this dramatic change are many and complex, but success in this regard would not have been possible without the great changes associated with the industrial revolution.[7] Similarly, the major changes in average height, weight, and healthiness which have come about over the same period may be presumed to have made a major contribution to human happiness. These, too, would not have been possible in the absence of major economic change. It would be artifical and misleading to tell the story of such changes as if energy were the central causal feature of all that happened. But it was a *sine qua non* of the changes taking place.

There have been many studies which have shown a close and consistent relationship between real income per head and energy consumption. Often, the focus of such studies has been the way in which, with rising living standards, more and more energy is consumed. But one man's consumption of energy is another man's expenditure of energy in producing the goods or other products consumed. In very recent years this relationship has weakened as energy consumption per head has levelled off while living standards have continued to rise. This development was to be expected not only because of the greater efficiency of energy use but also because the proportion of all expenditure directed to the products of tertiary industry has risen steadily, and their production in many cases requires relatively little energy. But where populations are still poor and there is a strong determination to bring about improvement, as in China for example, it may be expected that satisfying their needs will continue to involve substantial and rapid increases in energy use per head. Figure 4.1, drawn from a textbook written in the 1950s, illustrates the nature of the relationship which has prevailed during the bulk of the period since the industrial revolution. The very large number of countries in which energy consumption was less than a quarter of a ton per head per annum is striking. One person in the United States was consuming as much energy as fifty people in the poorer countries. Both the variables displayed were subject to wide margins of measurement error, but the broadly consistent relationship between them is nonetheless striking.

During the last couple of centuries an age-old constraint has disappeared. Where once the annual cycle of vegetable growth set a limit to

[7] The exact percentages reaching different ages will vary both with the overall level of mortality and with the characteristics of each local mortality regime. However, the present situation in Britain is closely approximated by level 24 of model West within the Princeton model-life table series, and the situation 150 years ago is broadly captured by level 10 of model North. The quoted survival percentages are derived from these two life tables. The combined sex expectation of life at birth in the former case is about 75 years, while in the latter it is about 41 years (Coale and Demeny 1966: 25, 229).

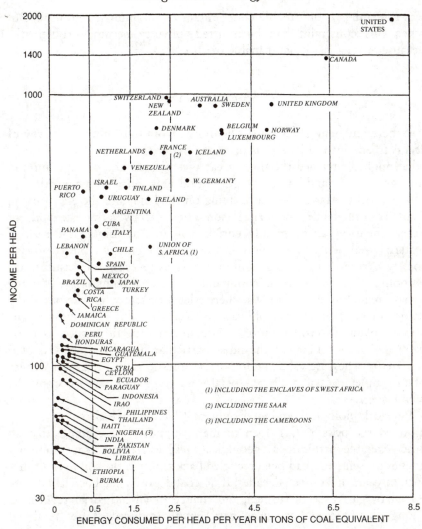

FIG. 4.1 The relationship between income per head and energy consumption per head.

Source: Kindleberger (1958: 24, fig. 2.3). In the original the horizontal axis was labelled, in error, 'pounds' rather than 'tons' of coal equivalent.

every form of activity, the effect of learning to exploit stored energy has been to allow everyone to count on having not only their daily bread but much else besides. Pre-industrial societies were severely limited by their inability to support human effort with other sources of energy. Poverty was a seemingly inescapable concomitant of the human condition. But when this constraint had been lifted, poverty became problematic, because at long last it was capable of cure.

CONCLUSIONS

Are there any general lessons to be drawn from this lightning survey of access to energy and its effects upon the material circumstances of life in what might be termed the three great ages of man: the pre-agricultural, the agricultural, and the post-agricultural eras; or, if you will, the era of living off the land, the era of living on the land, and the era of living apart from the land? The main lesson which I draw is that the study of human history can be greatly enriched if, in determining the relative material well-being of a society in the past, the energy context of each society is regarded as being as illuminating as its economic institutions, its political character, or its command of material technology. Was the society feudal or capitalist? Was there a legal system which favoured the enforcement of contractual obligations? Was the value of including leguminous plants in crop rotations understood? Questions such as these from the most general to the most particular have been chewed over repeatedly. They are valid and important questions. But there is a danger of incompleteness if political, social, and economic issues occupy the whole stage.

Physical, biological, and environmental factors have also always conditioned the possibilities open to man. Suppose, for example that all dead vegetable matter in past geological ages had decayed, as it commonly does at present, and had been recycled back through the soil over a timespan of years or, at most, decades. If no coal deposits had been laid down, no oil or gas reserves formed, the chance of an industrial revolution taking place would have been very greatly reduced, if not rendered impossible. Making an assertion of this kind is apt to arouse scepticism, if not hostility, because it runs counter to the received patterns of conventional discourse on the subject. Yet the case can be pressed with some confidence since the energy requirements associated with the material circumstances of modern life are known with precision and the energy limitations of economies in the era before fossil fuels were widely used are unambiguous.

To avoid being misunderstood it is important to emphasize the logical status of the claim just made. It is not intended as an assertion that the industrial revolution was somehow mysteriously 'caused' by the existence of large coal deposits close to the surface in Britain, or even that their presence explains why the industrial revolution started in England rather than elsewhere. Learning to make effective use of fossil fuels, success in tapping energy supplies so vast that each year energy could be consumed at a rate an order of magnitude greater than that previously attainable, was a necessary, but not a sufficient condition for an industrial revolution to take place.

I should like to conclude by suggesting a tentative agenda for future research about past energy usage. In principle it is possible to use energy production and consumption as a general descriptor of any past society. We are accumstomed to thinking of price as a means of making apples directly comparable to pears, or a Rembrandt etching to an electric light bulb. There are limits to the range of human artefacts and activities which can be measured by price, most obviously in the case of societies which make no use of money. But price nevertheless is a most valuable measuring rod for many purposes. So, equally, is energy, and it can be used to define the scale and nature of the differences between different human groups and periods in a way that can scarcely fail to be illuminating. What is the maximum amount of energy in the form of food which could be secured by a hunter-gatherer community on a sustainable basis in different environments and ecological complexes? How was this maximum altered by, say, the development of the spear and the bow and arrow as devices for multiplying supplies of meat; or by the development of the fishing canoe; or indeed by the spread of the use of fire for cooking? After the advent of agriculture by what factor did access to usable energy increase? As population in medieval England was reaching its later thirteenth-century peak and the proportion of land under cultivation was also approaching a level so high as to include areas, if we are to believe Postan (1966: 556–9), incapable of being farmed continuously without serious soil degradation, how great was the energy capture involved? How did it compare with the comparable capture in the mid-eighteenth century after the radical improvements in agriculture which had taken place in the previous half millennium? As England approached the 'classic' period of the industrial revolution, how did the balance change between traditional sources of energy secured through working the land and new sources of energy obtained by bringing coal to the surface? How great was the contrast between, say, Wiltshire and Lancashire in this regard? How marked was the difference between England and the continent at different dates from, say, 1550 onwards?

This list of questions could be extended almost indefinitely. Approximate answers to most of them could be attempted forthwith by arguing from a general knowledge of the processes involved and the characteristics of the different economies. But each of the questions posed could be answered with greater precision and authority if our current knowledge were extended by further research. With a clearer grasp of such issues, much else would also be clarified. Successful historical investigations commonly involve the exercise of sympathetic imagination. This is taken for granted when, say, studying the treatment of heresy in the past, or when considering the position of women. In such cases, it is essential to enter a different thought world if the functioning of society and the attitudes of men and women are to be understood and trivial moralizing to be avoided. But when describing and analysing the ways in which the material needs of men and women were met in the past, the need for a comparable flexibility of mind is not always so clearly appreciated. The use of economic models which are devoid of historical content can lead to serious error. Arguments resting solely or largely on general categories such as the supply of and demand for labour or capital will fail to encompass much that was crucial to the understanding of the material circumstances of past eras. The physical limitations imposed by environmental circumstances were often severe, and a failure to recognize them and to incorporate them into analysis can easily vitiate attempts to understand the functioning of societies in the past. Energy constraints were among the most pressing and universal of such limitations. In particular, there is a great gulf fixed between us and all those of our forebears who lived on the opposite side of the divide which we call the industrial revolution. If we wish to cross the divide and gain a just impression of the nature of the differences between now and then, no alternative offers a more instructive point of departure than one focused on human energy needs and the means available for satisfying them.

REFERENCES

Ashton, T. S. (1951). *Iron and Steel in the Industrial Revolution* (2nd edn). Manchester: Manchester University Press.

Benaerts, P. (1933). *Les Origines de la grande industrie allemande*. Paris: F. H. Turot.

Boserup, E. (1965). *The Conditions of Agricultural Growth: The Economics of Agrarian Change under Population Pressure*. London: Allen and Unwin.

Coale, A. J. and Demeny, P. (1966). *Regional Model Life Tables and Stable Populations*. Princeton: Princeton University Press.

Cottrell, F. (1955). *Energy and Society. The Relation Between Energy, Social Change, and Economic Development*. New York: McGraw-Hill.

Davis, R. (1962). *The Rise of the English Shipping Industry in the Seventeenth and Eighteenth Centuries*. Newton Abbot: David and Charles.

De Zeeuw, J. W. (1978). 'Peat and the Dutch golden age: the historical meaning of energy attainability'. *A. A. G. Bijdragen*, XXI: 3–31.

Fogel, R. (1994). *Economic Growth, Population Theory, and Physiology: The Bearing of Long-term Processes on the Making of Economic Policy*. NBER working paper, no. 4638. Cambridge, MA: National Bureau of Economic Research.

Georgescu-Roegen, N. (1971). *The Entropy Law and the Economic Process*. Cambridge, MA: Harvard University Press.

Georgescu-Roegen, N. (1975). 'Energy and economic myths'. *Southern Economic Journal*, 41: 347–81.

Hatcher, J. (1993). *The History of the British Coal Industry. I. Before 1700: Towards the Age of Coal*. Oxford: Clarendon Press.

Kindleberger, C. P. (1958). *Economic Development*. New York: McGraw-Hill.

Levasseur, E. (1889). *La Population française*. 3 vols. Paris: Saint-Brieuc.

Nef, J. U. (1932). *The Rise of the British Coal Industry*. 2 vols. London: G. Routledge and Sons.

Pimentel, D. (1984). 'Energy flow in the food system', in D. Pimentel and C. W. Hall (eds), *Food and Energy Resources*. Orlando: Academic Press, 1–24.

Postan, M. M. (1966). 'Medieval agrarian society in its prime: England', in M. M. Postan (ed.), *The Cambridge Economic History of Europe. I. The Agrarian Life of the Middle Ages* (2nd edn). Cambridge: Cambridge University Press, 548–632.

Rackham, O. (1980). *Ancient Woodland: Its History, Vegetation and Uses in England*. London: Edward Arnold.

Ricardo, D. (1951). *On the Principles of Political Economy and Taxation*, in *The Works and Correspondence of David Ricardo*, I, ed. P. Sraffa, with the collaboration of M. H. Dobb. Cambridge: Cambridge University Press.

Smith, A (1961). *An Inquiry into the Nature and Causes of the Wealth of Nations*, ed. E. Cannan (5th edn). 2 vols. London: Methuen.

Thomas, B. (1986). 'Was there an energy crisis in Great Britain in the seventeenth century?' *Explorations in Economic History*, 23: 124–52.

White, L. P. and Plaskett, L. G. (1981). *Biomass as Fuel*. London: Academic Press.

Wrigley, E. A. (1987). 'The classical economists and the industrial revolution', in E. A. Wrigley *People, Cities and Wealth*. Oxford: Basil Blackwell, 21–45.

Wrigley, E. A. (1988). *Continuity, Chance and Change: The Character of the Industrial Revolution in England*. Cambridge: Cambridge University Press.

Wrigley, E. A. (1991). 'Energy availability and agricultural productivity', in B. M. S. Campbell and M. Overton (eds), *Land, Labour and Livestock: Historical Studies in European Agricultural Productivity*. Manchester: Manchester University Press, 323–39.

5

Boundaries and Country Planning: Ancient and Modern

Oliver Rackham

ALL members of Cambridge University know the back wall of Peter-house, where it adjoins the town fen: a wall of ancient stone and brick, much patched and recycled, which runs in a curiously erratic course with many angles and offsets. The college was founded on its present site in 1284, but it was not Peterhouse that established the boundary. The college took over the site of the Friars of the Sack (sacked by the Pope for reasons that do not concern us), but it was not the Friars that established the boundary. They, in turn, had taken over houses in a ribbon development along the main road south of Cambridge, but it was not the house-owners that established the boundary. The house-plots were successors to arable strips laid out between the road and the town fen as part of an exercise in country planning in the Norman or Anglo-Saxon period. The owners of these strips had disturbed the originally regular plan by pushing out their back fences into the fen (*usque ad mariscum*)—farmers, then as now, were not above encroaching on public land (Hall and Lovatt 1989).

This little tale reminds us that landscape history is as much the study of boundaries as of land-use. Boundaries may outlast their original structure and function: set up for one purpose, they continue in use for some different purpose. More than eight centuries on, the zigzags in the wall still faithfully record how some farmers had got away with bolder encroachments than others. They have been preserved by an institution which, although the oldest college in Cambridge, would have been outside the comprehension of those who made the zigzags.

Where boundaries survive in use, they get adapted by successive

Acknowledgements. Much of my work has been done in collaboration with Jennifer Moody (Crete and Texas) and Dick Grove (Mediterranean countries). I acknowledge also the help of Catherine Hall (Cambridge) and Susan Bratton (southeast United States).

generations of users. The degree of adaptation matters. If each generation conserves 90 per cent of the boundaries and alters 10 per cent, after 30 generations only 4 per cent of the original system will survive. If each generation conserves 99 per cent of the boundaries and alters 1 per cent, after 30 generations 74 per cent of the system will still be there. In the latter case any original pattern in the boundaries will still be recognizable, in the former case not. In practice, alterations tend to be made on a large scale at rare intervals. Alterations are often not progressive: those made in one century often have the effect of reversing those made earlier, so that, for example, ancient hedges survive more often than modern ones.

Alternatively, a whole system may be preserved because it was withdrawn from use, the boundaries surviving as banks or rows of trees in woodland, moorland, or especially parkland.

Long-settled countries have accumulations of boundaries, each layer reflecting the ideologies and practicalities of successive ages. In Sardinia there are irregular field-walls, often of huge boulders, associated with Iron Age *nuraghe* towers; medieval strip-cultivation; terraces and hedged fields of unknown date; later splittings of originally wide terraces; long straight field-walls of nineteenth-century privatizations; and boundary walls of railways, often constructed just after the privatization walls and making awkward angles with them.

THE STRUCTURE OF BOUNDARIES

I am concerned with boundaries as structures. Constructing boundaries is not a universal human activity: the Indians and the cowboys of the Wild West and the Australian Aborigines seem not to have had them, although the Aborigines, at least, knew very well where one tribe's territory ended and the neighbours' began.

The idea of territory and the marking of territory is, of course, widespread among beasts, birds, and fishes. But to find parallels for the *construction* of boundaries one has to go far from the human species. Decayed trees provide two examples. Trees have no wound-healing as we know it, but they have an efficient mechanism for damage limitation, for keeping decay separate from disease. When a tree is injured it sets up a barrier, a chemically changed layer within the wood, walling off the part no longer needed to hold up the tree from the part that will remain functional. The shape of the boundary is determined by the size and shape of the wound. Fungi then invade the wounded surface and begin consuming the superfluous wood up to the barrier (Shigo 1983). This is why many old trees have a hollow interior with a hard internal surface, all the rotten wood having disappeared.

If the fungi are of certain kinds, notably *Ustulina* species, each individual fungus will set up its own boundary defining the volume of wood to which it has laid claim. These barriers are often hard, black sheets of fungal material running through the rotten wood, or between rotten and sound wood. When the territories of two individual fungi meet, they set up a double zone-plate with a 'demilitarized zone' between (see figure 5.1). Furniture-makers occasionally treat these as ornamental features.

Territorial and Practical Boundaries

Human administrative and territorial boundaries may or may not be marked on the ground. Although modern Europe had its Iron Curtain and Berlin Wall, it is usual, especially in mountains, to pass from one state

Fig. 5.1 Zone-plates produced by *Ustulina* and other fungi in a sycamore (*Acer pseudoplatanus*) stump. The volume occupied by each individual fungus is defined by a boundary which appears in section as a black line. The line is double where two fungi meet. A small part of the stump remains alive, and is defined by a discoloured zone. This represents a compartment boundary laid down by the living tree, and is adjacent to a black line, representing a zone-plate laid down by the nearest fungus. (*Leigh Woods, Bristol. July 1984*)

into another with no more than a series of inscribed stones—if that—to mark the boundary. The various 'Grim's Ditches' in the chalklands of England are supposed to have marked critical parts of the boundaries between Bronze or Iron Age tribes. However, earthwork boundaries are not straightforward. Offa's Dyke, the great Dark Age linear earthwork, marks approximately (and intermittently) the boundary between England and Wales; yet as far as we know it nowhere corresponds exactly either to the political or the linguistic frontier at any period.

The south-west boundary of East Anglia is marked by four or five linear earthworks—Devil's Ditch, Fleam Dyke, etc.—which run parallel to each other and from 7 to 10 kilometres apart. They cross the chalklands from the fen at one end, where they are prolonged by a Roman canal or other water obstacles, to the boulder-clay at the other, where they mysteriously end. They have been studied for over a century, but no one has established what they were for, why there should have been more than one, or why only this part of the boundary should have needed marking (Malim and others 1996).

More numerous are permanent boundaries between zones assigned for different uses. Since at least the Iron Age, some—but not all—roads have been demarcated by hedges or ditches from adjacent private land. Important boundaries, often defined by ancient and massive hedges, include those between private and common land, or between arable land and meadow (see figure 5.2). In Wales and Cornwall an important boundary, defined by a major wall, separates private land from moorland. In Crete mountain-plains—the flat bottoms of huge karst depressions—are often bounded by walls deliminating cultivated land from the mountain pasture; these walls, however, are no longer kept in repair, it now being the shepherds' responsibility to keep their flocks out of the plain.

Boundaries as Semi-natural Features

A boundary, once established, grows into the landscape: it develops an ecology of its own, sometimes independent of further human intervention. On sloping ground the bottom edge of a field turns into a *lynchet* as soil, creeping down-slope under the influence of the plough, piles up against any cross-slope obstacle such as a hedge, building, or edge of a road.

Hedges can arise in three ways (Rackham 1986a: ch. 9). They may be deliberately planted: the earliest record in England of anyone planting a hedge is in a charter of AD 940. They may, though rarely, represent the boundary of a wood that has been grubbed up. Or they may arise spontaneously, as trees and bushes spring up from wind- and bird-dispersed seeds deposited at the base of fences or on grassy baulks between fields

FIG. 5.2   An ancient hedge. Sinuous in outline, of many different trees, it is composed of massive coppice stools produced by many cycles of plashing. It has recently been plashed or 'laid' again. It marks the ancient boundary between arable and meadow in a part of the country where ancient hedges are few. (*Soham, Cambridgeshire, June 1976*)

(see figure 5.3a, b). The distinction between planted and spontaneous hedges was known to the Romans, for example in the writing of Siculus Flaccus (first century AD) and Palladius Rutilius (?5th century AD).

In England it is usually assumed that most hedges are planted. Ancient hedges usually contain more tree and shrub species than modern. There is a well-known correlation (Hooper's Rule) between species and age: the number of tree-and-shrub species in 30 yards (27 metres) of hedge is approximately equal to the age of hedge in centuries (Pollard and others 1974). This is mostly explained by supposing that hedges, planted with one or two species, gain others with age through natural colonization. However, it can rarely be proved that hedges older than the seventeenth century are of planted origin. Spontaneous hedges, whatever their age, are usually of a mixture of species.

Hooper's Rule is one of the indicators of the age of a hedge. It holds for many thousands of hedges, but the user must beware of exceptions: recent spontaneous hedges, hedges that have been invaded by elm (which displaces other species), new roadside hedges where the hedge on the

FIG. 5.3 (a) Wire fence separating a recently disused railway from the adjacent field, with occasional small bushes at the bases of the posts. (*Hayley Wood, Cambridgeshire, May 1969*)
(b) The same boundary 27 years later. The fence has turned spontaneously into a continuous hedge of many species, which has lately been plashed for the first time. (*November 1996*)

(a)

(b)

FIG. 5.4 Farmland with centuriated fields. In the 150-odd years since it was laid out, many of the boundaries—between fields, between field and road, or along a disused railway—have turned into hedges. Note that the hedges are discontinuous and are more numerous in the vicinity of woods. (*Near Woodstock, Illinois, United States, August 1983*)

other side of the road is ancient, and Victorian imitations of medieval hedges (Rackham 1986a: ch. 9).

In the United States there are hundreds of thousands of miles of hedges or 'fencerows'. Most are spontaneous, arising as trees spring out of fences or dumps of field-stones at the edges of fields.[1] They are usually mixed from the start; they seldom get the management which is typical of most English hedges. In America, as in Anglo-Saxon and medieval England (Rackham 1986a: 185f), hedges are commoner within a mile or so of woodland to act as a seed source; also, they do not necessarily form complete enclosures, but may occur as haphazard bits of hedge (see figure 5.4).

In Australia, in contrast, fences have little tendency to turn into hedges. This is apparently because Australian eucalyptuses and other trees, unlike the blackthorn and hawthorn of England or the hackberry and sumach of North America, have very limited means of seed dispersal. This

---

[1] In Costa Rica fences turn directly into hedges through the fence-stakes taking root; they are often cut from pollard trees selected for having this property.

reminds us that landscape history is only partly the history of people. These are other actors in the play, and the actors are different in different countries.

Boundaries also have secondary uses. Some dry-stone walls are made of stone quarried for the purpose, but many are made of stones picked off the fields. Specially thick 'consumption dykes', for using up stones, are a feature of parts of Scotland and of stony land in Mediterranean countries. Outcrops or immovably large boulders may be disposed of by incorporating them in the line of the wall.

At least since the Middle Ages, hedges have been a major source of fuel, sometimes coppiced on a regular cycle like woods. 'Hedgerowes' in sixteenth-century surveys could occasionally be strips of woodland 100 metres wide.

Perambulations

Before maps became everyday documents, landed estates or political boundaries were defined by verbal descriptions. The annual beating of the bounds is still a ceremonial occasion in some parishes in England: at Little Gransden (Cambridgeshire) they dug a hole and put the Rector's head in it.[2]

The most famous perambulations are those of Anglo-Saxon England, dated from the seventh to the eleventh centuries AD. These mention the streams, hedges, wood edges, downs, free-standing trees, open-fields, 'heathen burials', dragons' hoards, etc. of an already long-settled and cultural landscape. Many can be traced on the ground today; the wealth of detail allows a statistical and geographical analysis of what the countryside looked like (Rackham 1986a). The slightly earlier Welsh perambulations furnish, for example, what is almost certainly the earliest written record in Britain of a wood-lot that still exists. From Crete there are Hellenistic perambulations of the fourth century BC and very detailed Turkish perambulations of the seventeenth century AD, both of which indicate a landscape very like the present (Rackham and Moody 1996). In the United States perambulations are used to this day.

PRACTICAL SHAPES OF BOUNDARIES

Sometimes boundaries are constrained by practicalities. A medieval park was typically a rectangle with rounded corners. It contained deer, strong

---

[2] A recent Rector assures me that this rite is disused.

and agile beasts which needed an expensive fence of cleft-oak stakes (a *park pale*) or a stone wall to keep them in. The shape reflects economy in fencing: the expensive burglar-proof fences round modern prisons are often of the same shape.

Medieval woods, in contrast, have irregular, sinuous, or zigzag outlines. They are surrounded by earthworks which follow every detail of the boundary. Although woodbanks, too, represent a great investment of labour (especially round small woods) they could be constructed piecemeal over the years and did not need to be completed at once. They are our best evidence for the importance of woodland conservation in the Middle Ages. At Hindolveston (Norfolk), the monks of Norwich Cathedral built 6 kilometres of new bank round their two woods in 1297–8 at a cost of £10.10s. They were changing the management of their woods from principally timber to underwood production, which called for more attention to security (Rackham 1980: 157f). One of the woods, with its bank, still exists.

Wood outlines are very stable: many woods have exactly the same shape now as on sixteenth- or seventeenth-century maps. Alterations, if any, result from the definite subtraction of part of the wood to make a field, or the addition of an adjacent field to the area of the wood. Woodbanks were made down the centuries, often recording subdivisions of the ownership of wood-lots (Rackham 1980: fig. 10.1; Rackham 1986b). The later ones tend to be perfunctory. I have seldom seen them in the American colonies, where woodland was plentiful and labour scarce. I have, however, found wood-lot banks on Cumberland Island, Georgia, where there were large numbers of slaves to be found work in slack periods.

Medieval Forests, whether wooded or not, have a third kind of shape:[3] a concave outline, funnelling out into the roads which cross the Forest, often with enclaves of private land within the Forest. (I refer to the shape of the physical Forest, not to the legal boundary as defined in contemporary perambulations.) Most Forests were commons, and this is the characteristic shape of an area of common-land. It is the shape of a piece of land left over after all the private land has been claimed. A forest or common has no bank or pale round it: it is defined by the hedges and ditches of the adjacent farmland, and there was no incentive to shorten the boundary.

---

[3] A Forest, in the sense of Dartmoor Forest or Epping Forest, was a tract of moorland, heath, wood-pasture, etc. on which the king (or some other great magnate) had the right to keep deer. The king was not necessarily the owner of the land: his deer were not the sole users of it, and he could not fence them in.

Left to themselves, people normally create irregularly shaped fields: often very irregular where there are watercourses, rocks, etc. to be incorporated into the boundaries. Even where such natural obstacles are few, boundaries may be very stable. In Lawshall (Suffolk), about 80 per cent of the hedges which are still there are already present on a map of 1611 (Rackham 1985). The most consistent change, before the fashion for destroying boundaries which prevailed between 1955 and 1975, was the narrowing of roads: roadside hedges tend to be eighteenth-century or later, as strips of public land have been filched from the originally wider road.

SHAPES IMPOSED BY PLANNING

Regularities in the landscape normally imply somebody's philosophy or ideology of how land ought to be divided; if on a large scale, they imply the existence of a higher authority capable of imposing that ideology on those who did the work. Ideologists have produced startlingly different ways of dividing land, often successively on the same piece of ground.

The Fens, the great river delta north of Cambridge, are a museum of successive processes of fen drainage and associated ideologies. The seaward belt represents the 'do-it-yourself' pattern of fields set up in the tenth and eleventh centuries by people taking over former salt-marshes; the meandering roads and ditches came from incorporating existing natural creeks. Next inland is a zone of long narrow strips between straight converging ditches, the result of large-scale drainage schemes by the great fenland abbeys in the twelfth and thirteenth centuries. In the south, the last part to be drained, there is a chaos of small-scale rectangular layouts, all at different orientations and dislocated from their neighbours, the work of private capitalists in the seventeenth and eighteenth centuries (Rackham 1986a: ch. 17).

Centuriation

Centuriation is the custom of dividing land, regardless of the terrain, into squares originally of 2,400 Roman feet (710 metres) a side, oriented either north–south and east–west or at 45°. In its later forms, in the United States and Western Australia, the unit is one English mile (1,609 metres), and the orientation is rigidly north–south and east–west.

Centuriation is associated mainly with new colonies. An embryonic example comes from an inscription relating to the Ancient Greek colony of Heraclea in south Italy, founded in 432 BC (Dareste and others 1913:XII, 1). The founder, Dionysus god of wine, had leased his lands and woods to colonists in plots of approximately 80 hectares. The plots were rectangular, but the divisions were not at exactly equal intervals: maybe the surveyors had been worshipping their employer.

Roman professional field-measurers, *agrimensores*, have left treatises on how centuriation was done, and very unusually they tell us why. One such was Hyginus Gromaticus, a writer of unknown date, named after the tool of his trade, the *groma*, a set-square on a staff used for setting out the *cardo* and *decumanus* axes from which all the other divisions were measured off. Two reasons are given. First, the Romans were telling their predecessors: 'You barbarians have lost and we have won, and we are abolishing your land-divisions and substituting our own.' The second reason was theological: the god Terminus liked land to be divided into squares of 2,400 Roman feet, and at every intersection sacrifice to be offered and a hole dug and blood and ashes poured into it. (I cannot say whether this has been confirmed archaeologically.)

Centuriation has been recognized in southern France, Italy, Tunisia, and especially Dalmatia (Bradford 1957): maybe it was the Roman answer to the troubles of Yugoslavia. Anyone who has flown over northern Italy will be familiar with the regular Roman grid of roads, the frame of squares into which a medieval strip-system has later been inserted. If centuriation ever existed in Britain, it survives in so fragmentary a state as to be barely distinguishable from random alignments of scraps of hedge.[4]

A rare, probably late-medieval, example exists on the Lassíthi Plain high in the mountains of east Crete. When the Venetians, lords of Crete, decided to resettle this deserted mountain-plain, they laid it out in 193 rectangles, each an approximate half-square of 5.3 hectares, paying no attention to the natural watercourses. Not having Hyginus with his *groma*, they made the angles 88°, not 90°. The 193 rectangles are still there, though subdivided: by Cretan standards, 5.3 hectares is an impracticably big field (Rackham and Moody 1986: 149ff).

Centuriation was revived in the colonization of the United States. In the Midwest it became the practice to divide land into 'sections', one mile square and separated by a grid of roads. The standard size of farm was a quarter-section, 160 acres, about 25 per cent bigger in area than the Roman unit of centuriation. Americans were just as dogmatic as Romans in carrying straight lines across obstacles: on coming to a bend in a river,

---

[4] It should be possible to test for the existence of centuriation (or any other regular pattern) by predicting where the alignments would cross ancient woodland and then seeing what is there within the wood.

they would build two bridges rather than go round. The result is the mind-boggling grid of roads and boundaries that repeats itself mile after mile after mile, from north Texas to North Dakota and on into Saskatchewan. Its thousandfold monotony is interrupted by dislocations at state boundaries, where accumulated errors of measurement and the discrepancies produced by the curvature of the earth were released before moving on into the next state.

Straight One-Way Plans

Not all ideologists and bureaucrats think in two dimensions. There are one-way types of plan, in which regular alignments in one direction are subdivided by more-or-less random cross-walls in the other.

A simple example is from the hinterland of the Ancient Greek colony of Metapontum in southern Italy. Two sets of parallel straight ditches, 210–240 metres apart, cover the landscape, paying little regard to the terrain; they are joined or intersected by innumerable contemporary and later field boundaries, and fragmented by the development of erosion gullies (Schmiedt and Chevallier 1959). The huge scale (48 and 64 square kilometres) makes it almost certain that the layout belongs to the founding of the colony in *c.* 700 BC.

On the plain of Khaniá in Crete, fields are set out between straight axes which diverge slightly out of the city and are subdivided by cross-hedges at irregular intervals. The system, to judge by the antiquities on the surface, is of late Roman or early Byzantine date. It seems that some catastrophe, such as a mudflow emerging from the Thérisso Gorge, had buried all the earlier archaeology and effaced the previous land-divisions (Moody and Rackham 1996: 146). The recolonization of the plain was planned by an organization man who had forgotten about centuriation and had new, rather sophisticated ideas of geometry.

For a modern one-way system I turn to Pómbia in the Mesará, south Crete. Up to 1965 the land was organized into fields of irregular shape, averaging 0.157 hectares per field. These were of various types: tiny squares (perhaps of Roman origin), rectangles, the apparent remains of a system of strip-fields (see later), and the multitude of shapes produced by centuries of people buying, selling, and subdividing land, but few triangles or polygons (see figure 5.5a). Professional agronomists are irritated by small fields, thinking them 'inefficient' and imagining that time spent travelling between plots is wasted. The farmers may not agree, but tend to assume that academics and politicians must be right. All over southern Europe there has been a fashion among administrators for reorganizing field systems and replacing traditional fields with neat rectangles. At Pómbia there was, additionally, a practical reason: it was proposed to provide irrigation by means of concrete channels, which could not easily be taken to odd-shaped plots (Grove and Rackham 2000: ch. 5).

The reorganization was duly carried out; an elaborate attempt was made to reallocate land and olive trees according to quality, though probably not to everyone's satisfaction. The result is a triumph of geometry, with parallel roads exactly 200 metres apart; everyone's field is a rectangle 100 metres long, and varying in width according to his entitlement (see figure 5.5b). Whether or not it contains olive trees depends on the previous, unrelated ownerships. The fields average 0.357 hectares each. This is a monument, not only to ideology, but to a brief phase in irrigation technology. By 1983 the clumsy concrete ditches had been superseded by plastic pipes, which make it easy to convey water to any plot however awkwardly shaped.

Reaves and Not-Quite-Straight One-Way Plans

One-way plans are not uncommon in Britain. These are of a more sophisticated kind, in which the axes are parallel but not quite straight: each axis displays wobbles which are faithfully repeated by its neighbours. The most thoroughly investigated are the Dartmoor *reaves*, which survive as low earthen banks, sometimes faced or cored with stone. They exist in disuse (and thus accessible to survey and excavation) over about one-third of the high moorland of Dartmoor in southwest England; around their lower edges they have often been adapted and incorporated into later fields. They are associated with houses, barrows, and stone circles; they represent the boundaries of what were then pasture and arable fields in the Bronze Age, 1700–1600 BC (Fleming 1988).

One-way plans of similar complex geometry to reaves occur widely, and are not contemporary. The Céidhe Fields in County Mayo (Ireland), of Neolithic date, were excavated beneath a peat-bog. Others cover many square kilometres of south Norfolk, north-east Suffolk, and mid- and south Essex. These survive (or did until recently) in use as the hedged boundaries of modern fields, and therefore have undergone centuries of piecemeal alteration; their regularity becomes more perfect if one undoes some of these alterations by studying early maps (Williamson 1987). They can be shown to be earlier than Roman roads, which either conform to the pattern or cut across it, like a railway or motorway. They are generally supposed to be Iron Age, but an earlier origin cannot be excluded.

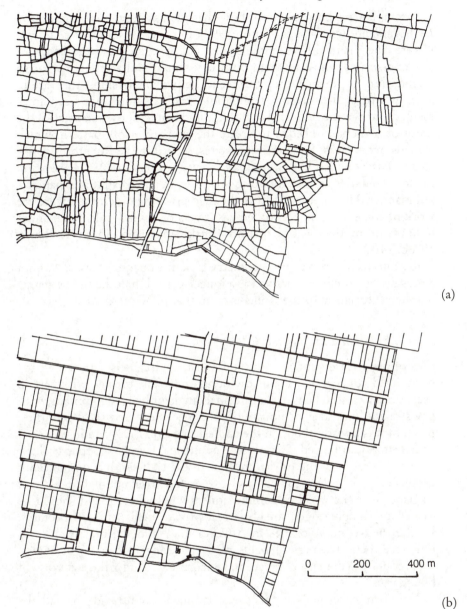

(a)

(b)

FIG. 5.5 Part of Pómbia, Crete: (a) after German air photograph of 1944;
(b) after reorganization.

Attempts have been made to show that such systems were laid out by medieval landowners (e.g. Hinton 1997), but there is an obvious test. If it were true, planned field systems would be as extensive as the estates of the landowners who laid them out: they would end at estate or parish boundaries. In practice, they transcend known ownerships: they are in areas where landownership throughout historic times has been fragmented and chaotic. Domesday Book, for example, shows no trace of the unity of ownership needed to create the south Norfolk pattern, which extends over at least fifty separate estates, or that in the Rochford Peninsula in Essex, which had more than twenty owners in 1086. Parish and estate boundaries are fitted into the patterns in a makeshift and haphazard manner. The inference is that the field grids are older: they were the work of someone who controlled vast tracts of countryside in a manner unheard-of in the historic period (Rackham 1986a: 156ff; Rackham 1986b: 14ff).

Reasons for the reave-type geometry are quite opaque to us. It was not a passing fashion: it was active for a longer period than the time separating the centuriation of the Romans from that of Western Australia.

Strip-cultivation and Planned Countryside

One of the great distinctions in the English landscape is between what I have called Ancient and Planned Countryside. The former, with certain exceptions as in the Fens, is an informal tangle of hedges and roads, with few straight lines. It is demonstrably the piecemeal growth of centuries: much of it is already there on the earliest maps (*c.* 1600) and in medieval verbal surveys. Planned Countryside is a formal layout, set up, parish by parish, as a result of the Enclosure Acts of the eighteenth and nineteenth centuries, which reorganized land-ownership over about one-fifth of England. It is the work of commissioners who believed land should be owned in straight-edged, quadrilateral private fields of 5–20 hectares. Unlike their contemporaries in America, they allowed practicalities to influence them. Corners of fields were not obliged to be right angles; watercourses were straightened and incorporated into the network of boundaries.

This distinction goes with others. Planned Countryside has all the ancient farmsteads grouped in villages, not scattered in hamlets or alone in the fields as in Ancient Countryside; its hedges are flimsily built of hawthorn only; its ancient woods tend to be few and large. The distinction between the two types of landscape corresponds to no known ethnic, tribal, or administrative boundary. It is well over a thousand years old, being already there in the Anglo-Saxon charters.

As is well known, Planned Countryside is the successor either to common pasture or to arable land in the form of strip-cultivation. Before the Enclosure Acts, the lands of each village had typically been divided into two or three great fields, each divided into furlongs which, in turn, were subdivided into multitudes of strips. The strips were of about half an acre in extent, roughly 220 × 11 yards (200 × 10 metres), of a curving shape, characteristically with a 'reversed-S' double curve. Each farmer had a number of strips scattered more or less randomly over the parish. Open-field would go on to the boundary of the parish and would zigzag into the open-fields of the next parish (Rackham 1986a: ch. 8).

Where the land has remained in pasture since enclosure, the strips are often fossilized in the form of ridge-and-furrow, the ridges exactly corresponding to the strips as shown on pre-Enclosure maps. They grow into the landscape, with different types of grassland on the ridges and in the furrows.

This distinction is not peculiar to England. In France there is the traditional difference between hedged *bocage* and open-field *champagne*, conspicuous to this day in (for example) west versus east Normandy. Similar distinctions occur in Portugal, the Alps, Sardinia, and Italy. Crete has its village landscapes and hamlet landscapes: Pómbia is a large village, but has traces of earlier hamlets. As a rough rule, hamlet and enclosed terrain is more common in mountains; villages and open-field in plains.

It used to be thought that open-field and strip-cultivation were aboriginal, or at least introduced by the Anglo-Saxon invaders who, 1,500 years ago, were supposed to have begun to create the cultural landscape of England. All the farmland in England had once been open-field: enclosure had happened in Ancient Countryside much as in Planned, but less formally and at an earlier date. This method of subdividing land, however 'inefficient' it might seem to modern eyes, had its roots in the deep instincts of human behaviour. People split up their land among children and grandchildren; or small farmers contributed oxen to a common plough-team and shared out the proceeds; or peasants ploughed up common pasture and divided it in proportion to the labour invested or the grazing foregone.

In reality, however, this cannot be. People had presumably been doing all these things for 5,000 years from the Neolithic onwards, without creating strip-cultivation. Open-field is not aboriginal: it is first heard of around AD 700. It is not universal, but characteristic of parts of Europe in the last 1,300 years. The earliest evidence for it is in the Anglo-Saxon charters of southern England. It spread gradually over several centuries to cover much of central and north-west Europe: it still covers large tracts of France and Germany. It ranged west into Wales, east to Russia, and south into the Mediterranean. Its incidence was curiously sporadic. It was common in Leicestershire, almost unknown in south Essex; it covered the boulder-clay of west Cambridgeshire but not of east Cambridgeshire; in much of Suffolk it never got beyond an embryonic stage; it still covers much of Sardinia but is apparently unknown in Corsica.

Open-field bears the marks of an agricultural and social revolution no less definite than the later revolution which abolished it. It went with a kind of collectivization of farming, gathering the population into villages and introducing communal working practices.[5] Strip-farming has had a bad press: its disadvantages were recounted by those who had an interest in abolishing it, but we are not told of its virtues. Virtues there must have been, for as late as the seventeenth century it was introduced, briefly, into the American colonies. Perhaps it had to do with making intensive use of land in the face of growing population and lack of room for expansion. Stalin or Ceaucescu, maybe, could have explained it better than I.

Strip-cultivation usually involved reorganizing land which had already been farmed for centuries. The idea that land ought to be divided into strips of a particular shape, as near as practicable to 200 × 10 metres, is as much the mark of an ideology as the 710-metre squares of the Romans or the mile squares of America. Open-field systems, or at least groups of furlongs, seem to have been laid out as a whole, not to have grown up piecemeal. Presumably, most such schemes were set up by lords with the power to impose their theories on their inferiors, although Cambridge city somehow acquired a very complex open-field system without having a recognizable lord of the manor.

Strips made some concessions to practicality, being varied to fit slopes, drainages, and watercourses. Sometimes the strips were fitted into an earlier, regular field-system, as with the Roman centuriation of the Po plain, or the rectangular, probably Iron Age, fields of Cambridge city. The site of Peterhouse had been farmland for at least a thousand years: the strips were fitted between a pre-existing road at one end and the pre-existing fen at the other.

In some countries every trace of a hedge was eradicated. In England, nearly every open-field system had at least a few hedges, often haphazard bits of hedge between the strips not forming enclosures; occasionally they survive among the later enclosure hedges. How many of these were survivals of pre-open-field hedges and how many had grown up on

---

[5] It must also have involved devising means for recording and identifying the thousands of strips. Manorial court records are not clogged with disputes about people accidentally harvesting their neighbours' crops.

baulks, I cannot say. There were also hedges at the limits of the open-field, where it abutted on common land, meadow, the next parish, or the edge of the village.

PLANNING AND SEMI-PLANNING:
AN EXAMPLE FROM TEXAS

The middle of Texas has a rectangular two-way layout differing from the familiar centuriation. The axes are at approximately 30° west and 60° east of north, but there are smaller areas at 45°; a junction between two orientations causes a curious dislocation in the middle of Waco city. Each axis seldom continues for more than a mile or two: one searches in vain for the long, monotonous mile axes of a normal American plan. If this is regular centuriation it has changed more in 150 years than Dalmatia has in 2,000.

Texas, part of Spanish Mexico, proved difficult for Europeans and was long left uncolonized. Settlement, when it happened, spread out partly from the inland Spanish (or rather Canary Island) colony of San Antonio, founded in the early eighteenth century, and partly from United States colonists spreading westward into east Texas from 1800 onwards. The Spanish authorities, and later those of independent Mexico, tried to regularize the latter colonization by means of formal land grants to middlemen or companies. Land grants had got well ahead of actual settlement when Texas went to war with Mexico and became independent at the Battle of San Jacinto in 1836. The Republic of Texas continued to follow Latin American principles of land distribution until it was taken over by the United States in 1846.

The modern history of Texas is reflected in its country boundaries (see figure 5.6), which correspond to the patterns of land division prevailing in different phases of colonisation. The block of counties in the middle and south, with predominantly 30° and 60° orientation, corresponds to Spanish land grants and their successors. In the east are irregular boundaries, often following natural features, corresponding to the phase of informal United States settlement. After 1846, and particularly after the United States Civil War ended in 1866, the organization men triumphed: south, west, and north Texas belong to the grid of rectangles extending all the way into Canada. Only in the wild western deserts beyond the Río Pecos is there a different system of random polygons.

The 30° and 60° orientation was established by the Spanish and continued by the Mexican land office; it may have been determined by the

FIG. 5.6　Counties of Texas.

fact that the main Rio Brazos de Dios (the River Brazos) runs mainly 30°
east of south. The original grants were on a generous scale. This is the
perambulation of a grant of one *labor* of land made by the government
of the State of Coahuila & Texas in 1825 to Robert Leftwick, of 'la
Comp[añi]a de Nashville' [Nashville, Texas, now deserted]:

Comesando en il rincon de aeriba del sitio No. 6 y sigue el ria . . . sigunido las
vuoltos . . . y paso . . . desemboicoura del arroyo clamidi en Ingles Davigtons
Creek . . . a unae estaue eiue arbol Clamado en Ingles Sycamore 6 puilgs en
demitros N 8°E 8 vs tambein un nogal N 25°E en 4 vs De alli S 60°E 9958 vs en
3600 vs si encontro un alio Davingtons Creek y entre al montre y paso al rincon
y clavo una esteua un arbol caudio en Ingles Live Oak 10 pulg de diametro N
10°E en 20 vs alli S 30°E 2500 vs a una pala de pidros arriba de en baerario alto
De alli N 60°E 9728 vs a donde connero en 317 vs paso el suon NE del Sitio No
6 y a alli eon la leinia NE coleindente con el Sitio No 6 al lugar donde Comico.

Y comprehende vaite y catro labors de terire. (Meridian County Clerk's Office, County Surveyor's Record, vol. B: 560)

The unit of measurement is the Spanish *vara*, 0.847 metres, of which 1,900 are supposed to go to the English mile. I translate the doggerel Spanish thus:

Beginning at the rear corner of Plot No. 6; following the river [Brazos] . . . following the bends [of which measurements and directions are given] . . . passes the mouth of the canyon called in English Davingtons Creek . . . to a stake; a tree called in English sycamore [*Platanus occidentalis*] 6 inches in diameter N 8°W at 8 varas, also a walnut [probably pecan, *Carya illinoenis*] N 25°W at 4 varas. From there S 60°W [for] 9958 varas; at 3600 varas pass another Davingtons Creek and enter the forest; pass to the corner and drive a stake; a tree called in English Live Oak [*Quercus fusiformis*] 10 inches in diameter N 10°W at 20 varas. From there S 30°E 2,500 varas to a pile of stones behind a high post [?]. From there N 60°E [for] 9728 varas; in which note at 317 varas the NW corner of Plot No. 6; from there along a NE line, coinciding with Plot No. 6, to the place where it began. This includes twenty-four *labors* [about 20 sq.km, 8 sq.miles] of land.

Grants by the State of Texas were usually of one square mile of land, but defined and oriented in the Spanish manner. For example, Jesse G. Thomas received '640 Acres of land situated on Hog Creek', forming a square 1,900 × 1,900 *varas*:

Beginning at the North boundary line of a Survey made for John Letcher and S60W 1700 v[ara]s from Letcher's N.E. corner for the S.E. corner of this survey, from which a Post Oak [*Quercus stellata*] bears N49E 17 vs and a Live Oak S60W 11 vs—Running thence S60 W 520 vs to Hog Creek—1900 vs to the S.W corner—thence N30W 1900 vs to the N.W corner, from which a Post Oak marked A, bears S15E 4 vs & another B, N35W 5 vs—Thence N60E, 1900 vs to the N.E. corner, from which an ash [*Fraxinus texensis*] bears S3W 17 vs and a Cedar [*Juniperus ashei*] bears S66E 30 vs—Thence S30E 1900 vs to the beginning—surveyed July 25, 1845. *G.B. Erath*, Dep. Surveyor. (Meridian County Clerk's Office, County Surveyor's Record, vol. B: 80)

Grants were also made of half a square mile; sometimes a rectangle of 1,900 × 850 *varas*, but more usually a square of 1900/√2 *varas* a side. The original grantees chose their land and had it staked out by surveyors such as the great George B. Erath (after whom Erath County is named). Little attempt was made to coordinate the grants or to see that they joined up. This left many odd L- and T-shaped bits of land, often in rocky, cedar-choked canyons, to be taken up (if at all) by later grantees. Some land was granted twice, by the Mexican and Texan governments; this made work for lawyers for the rest of the century (some claims are said still to be pending).

Such, then, is why the middle Texas landscape is made up of short straight lines, mostly at 30° and 60°, but seldom prolonged for more than a few miles. Roads are seldom mentioned in the surveys, and seem to have arisen haphazardly at a later date.

Survey lines often deviate from the canonical direction by a degree or two. The compass is not a precision instrument, and surveyors did well to drag measuring chains across rattlesnake-infested canyons, down cliffs, and through cat-briar, poison ivy, and cedar-brakes. But there was perhaps another factor. By the 1840s there was a third claimant to the land, the Comanche Indians, who were taking an interest in the doings of surveyors. Men like Erath, with valuable scalps on their heads, had every reason for not lingering over their work.

From the survey particulars one can work out the appearance of what had been an American Indian cultural landscape: to ascertain the extent and character of prairie (with no trees), savanna (with scattered trees), and forest. A century and a half on, much is still recognizable. The boundaries have grown into the landscape. Those of the Jesse G. Thomas grant are massive mixed hedges, which if they were in England would be thought to be medieval. Woodland has greatly increased through the infilling of savanna, but the ex-savanna woods can be distinguished from original woodland. The prairies are mostly still open; most have been through a phase of cultivation, and some are still cultivated. There are innumerable deserted farmsteads. Remains of settlers' fences are to be found embedded in hedges, the stakes often charred from the last prairie fire: the prairies are much less grassy and the landscape has become less combustible. There are still post-oaks, live-oaks, ashes, and cedars—although seldom the actual trees of 1845—close to the corners where the surveys mention them.

REFERENCES

Bradford, J. S. P. (1957). *Ancient Landscapes: Studies in Field Archaeology*. London: Bell.

Dareste, R. and others (1913). *Receuil des inscriptions juridiques grecques*. Paris: Leroux.

Fleming, A. (1988). *The Dartmoor Reaves*. London: Batsford.

Hall, C. and Lovatt, R. (1989). 'The site and foundation of Peterhouse'. *Proceedings of the Cambridge Antiquarian Society*, 78: 5–46.

Grove, A. T. and Rackham, O. *The Nature of Mediterranean Europe*. New Haven: Yale University Press. (provisional title: expected 2000)

Hinton, D. A. (1997). 'The "Scole-Dickleburgh field system" examined'. *Landscape History*, 19: 5–12.

Malim, T. and others (1996). 'New evidence on the Cambridgeshire dykes and Worsted Street Roman road'. *Proceedings of the Cambridge Antiquarian Society*, 85: 27–121.

Pollard, E., Hooper, M. D., and Moore, N. W. (1974). *Hedges*. London: Collins.

Rackham, O. (1980). *Ancient Woodland: Its History, Vegetation and Uses in England*. London: Edward Arnold.

Rackham, O. (1985). 'Ancient woodland and hedges in England'. in S. R. J. Woodell (ed.), *The English Landscape: Past, Present, and Future*. Oxford: Oxford University Press, 68–105.

Rackham, O. (1986a). *The History of the Countryside*. London: Dent.

Rackham, O. (1986b). *Ancient Woodland of England: The Woods of South-East Essex*. Rochford District Council.

Rackham, O. and Moody, J. A. (1996). *The Making of the Cretan Landscape*. Manchester: Manchester University Press.

Schmiedt, G. and Chevallier, R. (1959). *Caulonia e Metaponto. Applicazioni della fotografia aerea in ricerce di topografia antica nella Magna Graecia*. Firenze: Istituto Geografico Militare.

Shigo, A. L. (1983). *Tree Defects: A Photo Guide*. Broomall, PA: United States Department of Agriculture, Northeastern Forest Experimental Station.

Williamson, T. (1987). 'Early co-axial field systems on the East Anglian boulder clays'. *Proceedings of the Prehistoric Society*, 53: 419–31.

6

Environments and Identities: Landscape as Cultural Projection in the English Provincial Past

Charles Phythian-Adams

INTRODUCTION

THE haunting opening passage of *Christ Stopped at Eboli* by Carlo Levi contains some observations that derived from his experience when exiled by the Fascists to an isolated part of southern Italy:

> closed in one room, in a world apart, I am glad to travel in my memory to that other world, hedged in by custom and sorrow, cut off from History and the State, eternally patient, to that land without comfort or solace, where the peasant lives out his motionless civilization on barren ground in remote poverty, and in the presence of death. (Levi 1982: 11)

Such a statement points up a difference between, on the one hand, the personal sentiments of a sympathetic observer who has lived for some time in the company of those whose immediate world he seeks to conjure up, and, on the other, the inevitable objectifications by historians of how the natural world or the landscape was formerly explained, perceived, or evoked, very largely by educated outsiders. Amongst historians, one thinks immediately here of Keith Thomas's path-breaking survey of developing opinions to do with numerous environmental matters over many centuries in his *Man and the Natural World* (1983); or of Simon Schama, and his boldly conceived *Landscape and Memory* (1995), which pursues the different metaphorical traditions attached to a range of landscapes by intellectuals, literati, and artists from a cross-section of different European and American cultures. With such broad avenues so brilliantly illuminated, perhaps an historian of the English

I am particularly grateful to Mrs Pauline Whitmore for typing this essay and to Mr Kenneth Smith for drawing the maps.

provinces may therefore be forgiven for stepping off the trunk routes to follow rather more dimly lit byways, if not as a contemporary observer, at least as one who seeks to understand how specific landscapes were represented as the cultural constructs of the actual regional or local societies inhabiting them.

To attempt this we shall need to narrow the focus in both space and time. In the first place, it may be useful to try to reconstruct how contrasted localized settings—restricted environments—might have been apprehended in cultural terms by the folks who dwelt in such landscapes and left their marks upon them. In the second place, it may be relevant to take heed of Levi's distinction between, on the one hand, the traditional pairing of 'history' with the state and, on the other, what he calls the 'motionless civilisation' of the peasant in the localities (Levi 1982: 11–12, 78–9, 133–5, 137–8, 238). How relevant to these last contexts is the idea of 'history' with change as its leading sequential feature? After all, like his, the worlds into which I want to peer were inhabited by *customary* societies. For them, as a member of one of them at the turn of this century remarked in connection with the skills of the wheelwright, it was tradition that was dominant: 'Reasoned science for us did not exist . . . What we had to do was to live up to the local wisdom of our kind; to follow the customs, and work to the measurements, which had been tested and corrected long before our time in every village shop all across the country' (Sturt 1963: 19).

We have to accept that in a very real sense before mass urbanization most country folk were themselves integral parts of their own environment. The list of practical ways in which people were tied to intensely regionalized geographical contexts is both obvious and tediously long. It is thus only necessary to recall such matters as the influence of local soils on farming and diet, of local materials on vernacular building types or handicraft skills, or of distinctive tracts of relatively homogeneous countrysides or *pays*—like fenland, moor or wold—on a whole range of associated characteristics such as average parish size, the incidence of manorialization, or settlement forms.

To these, the current small change of academic approaches to English local pasts, may be briefly added a mention of the impact of differing seasonal rhythms on that most sensitive indicator of shared local identity, the communal calendar, which differed in detail from place to place. Common to all places, however, used to be the ceaseless repetitive cycle of ritualized seasons and days, such as Christmas, May Day, or Midsummer, when 'culture' itself—in the shape of each settlement—was temporarily transformed into 'nature' for the duration of each ritual, by the lavish decoration of streets and housefronts, and sometimes interiors, by masses of foliage brought in from the countryside (Phythian-Adams 1983: 88–9). The visual *volte face* involved was almost certainly far greater than historians may infer from their documents (Laver 1947: 8–9). On some such occasions too, in different regions, there even survived down to more modern times ancient traditions involving changing forms of ritual animal disguise (Cawte 1978: 230–49). Stag- or fox-hunting are but similar survivals of this immediate ritual relationship between man and nature.

I wish then to begin from the premise that in contrast to the historian seeking to objectify past realities at a distance, the experience of customary societies was not only immediate but, to an unknown extent, deeply subjective. In that respect, we can hardly disagree with the judgement of W. G. Hoskins (1955: 46) that the Old English settlers, for example, probably 'had no eye for scenery, any more than other hard-working farmers of later centuries'. Is it therefore possible to reconstruct some of the alternative ways in which specific local or regional societies as it were 'appropriated' to themselves their particular surroundings by projecting salient cultural characteristics onto their environment and so merging their own identities with it? Conversely, can we recreate the manner in which the social memory was itself perpetuated through this shared mental mapping of local or regional landscapes (Fentress and Wickham 1992: 17–18)?

The evidence available with which even to begin to answer these large questions is inevitably fragile, but, given the fulfilment of certain preconditions, at least an attempt may be made. The necessary circumstances required for such reconstructions would seem to include the known presence of a self-identifying society or social grouping; information on a widely shared outdoor working culture; the perdurance of key names or associations in the landscape; evidence for a repetitive oral culture; and indications of known opportunities for the regular re-activation of the social memory. What will be in question here, therefore, will not be an enquiry into how environments may have *determined* facets of culture. The object of this investigation will be to trace the mechanisms whereby select cultural assumptions were fitted into physical contexts, whilst still remaining true to what was relevant to such purposes in the landscape itself.

On this collective basis, then, I would like to discuss three different examples of ways in which landscapes may have been 'appropriated' in cultural terms by the societies inhabiting them. The first, the earliest, and inevitably the least well-evidenced, is what I would dub the 'epic landscape', which I shall discuss fairly briefly in the context of early Dark Age Cumbria. The second might be described as the 'ethnic environment' which can be extensively examined in relation to the Lincolnshire of the twelfth and thirteenth centuries and traced through even to the seventeenth and beyond in order to inspect the longevity of it as such a construct. The last examples should illustrate what I shall call 'the topography of superstition' and will be derived from the late nineteenth- and early twentieth-century West Country. In taking the long view, I shall also seek eventually to narrow in from broad regional contexts to very much more specific locales, where we can inspect actual patterns of cultural projection in much more detail. Throughout, I shall be concerned to identify ways in which each mental map may have been triggered from time to time in the minds of contemporaries.

EPIC LANDSCAPE: NORTHERN CUMBRIA

My first example, which I can only advance somewhat tentatively, concerns the Celtic society that dominated the Solway basin before it was finally brought under Anglian rule in the seventh century, and, in particular, the area of what later became the county of Cumberland together with the northern element of Westmorland centred on Appleby. As continued to be the case for centuries thereafter, this Highland-Zone region must have practised a pastoral economy that involved the seasonal movement of livestock to pastures at some distance from the settlements, which were thus fully inhabited only from autumn to spring, but where lay such arable as there was to be cultivated and the adjacent pastures which needed resting (Fox 1996: 8–9). The proportion of the population involved in this summertime transhumance to what later became known as shielings is unknown, but at this period—as would indeed be the case on the late medieval Border, where the surname groups customarily shielded together—it is probable that kinship groups moved together, perhaps leaving behind only a small core of males to work the meadowlands and the arable (Robson 1989: 41–3; Ramm *et al.* 1970: 4).

There is every likelihood too that, as elsewhere, the landscape was already subdivided into broadly identifiable territories, each centred in the lowlands on some royal or lordly hall to which services and renders were owed. In other parts of England evidence survives at least to suggest that when incoming Angles finally ran up against firmly established British populations, they may have labelled the inhabitants by simply attaching an Old English term meaning 'settlers' (*saetna*) to the pre-existing Celtic topographical name for their territory: such as the Chilterns or the Peak (District) (Phythian-Adams 1993b: 21–2).

In Cumbria, where marked clusters of Celtic names for particular places coincide with specific physical features still known by those few Brittonic names for major *topographical* conformations or whole countrysides which had escaped renaming by Angle or Scandinavian, we may thus wonder whether the topographical names in each case similarly denoted earlier British territories. Three in particular stand out: the *moel* area in the vicinity of Great Mell Fell (meaning 'a bare hill'); the locality known as *barroc* (or 'crest') in the area of Inglewood Forest south-east of Carlisle, from which Barrock Fell takes its name; and the intriguing distribution of names in *iâl*—meaning 'a fertile upland region'—which straddles the later line of the Cumberland/Northumberland boundary up on the Pennine ridge (Phythian-Adams 1996: 79–82).

Now, the most common British place-name type in the region to mark some form of habitation is *caer*. In Cumbria, unlike Cornwall, there is no reason to doubt that an early *caer* was or had been a defensible place and as such may have been a significant place. The most important in the region, after all, was Carlisle—*Caer Luel* as it was called from the ninth century at the latest. Most of the remaining eight places bearing this name also look as though they had been Roman or native defensive sites. In these cases, however, location militates against their having been regarded as permanent sub-regional central places. On the contrary, such sites are to be found in precisely the situations chosen as shielings: on the uplands, in wooded valleys, or near the seashore. These places are spaced across the region such that the three British 'districts' already suggested have but one apiece; and when allowance is made for the development of later lordly territories in some sort of relation to earlier British arrangements, such divisions of the region, outside the heavily Scandinavianized areas, also contain only one *caer* each, usually on or towards a physical margin or significant boundary. The implication seems to be, consequently, that each *caer* served a particular territory in the context of its seasonal transhumance patterns (Phythian-Adams 1996: 83–5).

In performing some such function, therefore, the *caers* may further have been connected with the earlier history of what most historians would probably accept as having been archaic customs peculiar to still-Celtic territories, even though they are evidenced only in later times. The first was the ancient render of cattle, the *noutgeld*, a payment that seems to have been expected in such regions on 1 May, the Celtic feast of Beltane, the very same date as, or shortly after, that at which the movement of people and stock to the summer pastures also customarily began in the north (Camden 1637: 806; Ramm *et al.* 1970: 4, n.6.). In subsequent centuries this render was made by those who not only held their lands specifically by free tenure but who also, because of this, were expected to ride in defence of the king wherever he might move within the boundaries of his kingdom. There is a strong inference, therefore, that *caers* were simultaneously the summer stations and the fortified hosting places of local leaders. Here their wealth in cattle might be displayed (and, if necessary, coralled for protection) and here perhaps mustered those who were qualified to fight in the war bands. We need hardly doubt that summertime was the campaign season. Males of servile tenure, by contrast, may have been left behind at the farmsteads (as in other transhumant societies) to deal with the hay harvest and so on.

What is so interesting in this context is that out of all the surviving British place-names in the region, only eight probably incorporate the personal name of a Celt, and of these as many as five are linked with *caers*. One other *caer* has an Old English personal name attached to it; three more, in areas of low British survival, look as though they ceased to sustain their traditional functions, as in these cases, instead of personal names, there are descriptive elements which refer either to sheep or to cobbles. Given both the rarity of personal naming and the antiquity and obvious status of the *caers*, it may reasonably be proposed that we are not here dealing with the peasantry. It is much more likely that the people in question were people of reputation whose exploits were deemed to merit their commemoration in the landscape and, we need hardly doubt in the case of this particular society, people who were celebrated by the bards.[1] The Briton who gave his name, Luguvalos, both to a district and then to the *caer* of that district, Carlisle, will hardly have been a nonentity. Certainly it looks as though the fame of some endured sufficiently long to earn entries in the ninth-century *Annales Cambriae* (Morris 1980: 85–6, 45). It is usually accepted by scholars, for example, that the reference therein to the battle of Arthuret in 573 'between the sons of Eliffer and Gwenddolau son of Ceido; in which battle Gwenddolau fell' is to be linked to the place-name Carwinley (the *caer* of Gwenddolau) close by to, and possibly originally coincident with, the erstwhile Roman fort at Netherby in what later became the parish of Arthuret. In the case of the annal for 595, where is recorded 'The death of King Dunod son of Pabo', there may be an echo in the name Cardunneth (possibly *Caer Dunod*) high up in the *iâl* district of the Pennines (and further perhaps at Powdonnet Well in Morland parish). The name Pabo, moreover, has been suggestively associated with an Anglian place-name element cognate with *caer* at Papcastle (originally *Papceaster*) in West Cumberland. *Ceaster* was the Old English for a Roman fortified site, and the Roman fort at Papcastle represented the nodal point for the communication system between the coastal strip and the routes eastward

---

[1] Place-name interpretation is constantly changing. Provided names in *caer* are still taken to be linked with British *personal* names (albeit perhaps revised), the general points made here about probable connections with persons of reputation should still stand, even though such reputation may now be lost to us.

through the lake district (Miller 1975; Phythian-Adams 1996: 86, 127–8).

It is not unlikely, then, that the names of such princely individuals were attached to all *caers* in this region originally to denote the overlordship of the territories concerned towards their edges. In so doing, what was probably further evoked in many cases were the locally known, closing episodes in the proud independent history of an entire Celtic society before it was merged within the sovereignty of Northumbria. For present purposes, the precise date at which these personal names were given to features on the landscape (though it can hardly have been very long after the events concerned) matters less than that they surely expressed a lasting sense of British, as opposed to English, identity, which was echoed in other ways too: in the survival of the Brittonic language, in the incidence of church dedications to British saints or in the refashioning of the lives of such indigenous saints over the five and more centuries after 600, and in the face of domination and colonization by other peoples whether Angle, Norse, or Gael (Phythian-Adams 1996: 167–71). So long as transhumance was practised even by a minority of Celtic-speaking people, evocations of the past could be triggered annually around the shieling fires and the social memory renewed. To that extent it may be claimed that the landscape of early *Cumbra land* may have been overlaid by a mental map of a lost heroic age but in ways that still related to environmental realities.

LOCAL, PROVINCIAL AND ETHNIC IDENTITIES: LINCOLNSHIRE AND THE NORTH SEA LITTORAL

Twelfth-century Lincolnshire, towards the close of the last genuinely multi-racial era in British history, furnishes a useful ethnic contrast to the earlier epic cultural projections of the north-west. Heavily settled by Danes from the later ninth century, comprising part of the tenth-century Scandinavian confederation of the Five Boroughs, which included Lincoln and Stamford, and providing a springboard for the events of 1013, 1014, and 1016, which led to the accession of the Danish King Cnut, Lincolnshire continued to house an ethnically distinct immigrant population for 300 years after the period of Viking settlement. Cicely Clark (1992: 555) put the scale of this in perspective when commenting on studies derived from nominal lists that are far from comprising total head-counts, but which show relative incidences of Scandinavian personal-name patterns in the twelfth century, 'average levels of Scandinavian influence . . . from district to district being graded 15–20 per cent in Bedfordshire and in Suffolk, through 35–40 per cent in the east Midlands and in Norfolk, to 60 per cent and more in Yorkshire and in north Lincolnshire'.

It is on north-east Lincolnshire that we must concentrate, and with special attention to its aspect. Here, the Lincolnshire marshlands are cut off from the rest of the county to the west by the great swell of the wolds rising up almost from sea level, the coastal settlements thus being obliged to look either across the Humber or seawards. In this area we have just enough information to derive a long view on the interrelationship between different spatial levels of identity: local, provincial, and 'national'. It will be best to take each of these in turn.

To begin with, we are lucky to have preserved for us one of the earliest local origin myths to stem from what is clearly a localized oral tradition. In the tale of Haveloc the Dane, which is first encountered in a written source largely compiled in Lincolnshire, Geffrei Gaimar's *L'Estoire des Engleis* (of probably 1136/7) (Short 1994: 337–8), the founding of Grimsby is implied on two different occasions, and it is mentioned three times explicitly in a later, fuller, and free-standing version of the same tale dating from *c.* 1190–1220 (Bell 1925: 25). The myth tells how a Dane called Grim, having brought from Denmark by sea with his own family the orphaned young son of the Danish king to what is a *British* kingdom of Lindsey, then settles at the spot which will become Grimsby in a marshland area that was not popular with other settlers. His great ship is sawn in two and refashioned into a house; Grim himself fishes from a boat to gather a rich harvest from the sea (including turbot, salmon, mullet, whale, porpoise, and mackerel), exchanges his catch for bread, saves his money, and sets up as a salter (Bell 1960: 12–14). In all of this he thus personifies the typical activities of those inhabiting this long coastline down to and around the Wash at this time (Bennett and Bennett 1993: 28–9, 56–7). By the next stage in the development of the myth—as found in the already mentioned later version known as *Le Lai d'Haveloc*—yet more emphasis is being placed on Grimsby as a hitherto uninhabited haven in which Grim's 'house' was then the first, and where soon he was joined by so many country folk that the place developed into a market town with the name of Grimsby (Bell 1925: 181, 207). Immediately across the Humber estuary, similar origins were to be ascribed to the now inundated medieval town of Ravenserod off Spurn Head, where, perhaps in the 1230s, 'a certain ship' was said to have been 'cast aground at a place where there were no houses built, and a certain man took the ship and made a cabin out of it to live in and dwelt there, selling food and drink to merchants whom he received there, and so others came there to dwell' (Beresford 1957: 136). In every respect, therefore, Grim is to be regarded as the ideal version of the typical Danish colonizer of such a coastline, one who sets up in the wasteland edge of a foreign country without prior personal advantages or prejudice to others (indeed his ship had been mauled by pirates), and whose industry as a successful trader even helps to create prosperity for the indigenous inhabitants. At Grimsby he remains until the end of his days; having destroyed his great ship he had committed himself to Lindsey for life. He may thus stand for, and so legitimize, all those others locally who had colonized this region and in so doing had lent their personal names to settlements with place-names ending in -*by* (Fellows Jensen 1978: 10–12, 15–17, 151, 251).

The Danish Grim is the protector of Haveloc, the heir to the dead king of Denmark, whom he rears under an assumed British name with his own family. On reaching a physically powerful maturity, moreover, Haveloc is eventually hired as a scullion in the British under-king's kitchens at Lincoln. Still incognito, there he is mis-married in terms of overt social status to none other than the orphaned daughter of another Dane, also an under-king, this time of Norfolk. Since the deaths of her father and her mother. who was the sister of the British under-king of Lindsey, the daughter had been the ward of the latter who marries her off below her station in order to get his own hands on Norfolk. Despite all, Haveloc, of course, eventually becomes King of Denmark. Having defeated the wicked King of Lindsey, he then becomes king of both Lindsey and Norfolk (Bell 1925).

In Gaimar's subsequent teasing out of the implications of this tale, which he places, after a short but significant prologue and link-passage, at the very beginning of his *History of the English* (itself but a sequel to a now lost history of the Britons), it becomes clear that Haveloc is regarded as but one of an earlier sequence of Danish kings in England, including the aforesaid King of Norfolk, that stretches back to the days of a mythical King Dane (Bell 1960: lvii–lviii, 66, 137). The Haveloc myth itself, moreover, is set chronologically by Gaimar not in the days of the Vikings, but in the reign of King Arthur's nephew, Constantine, over-king of Britain, under whom, therefore, Lindsey and Norfolk are held. In other words, and Gaimar is explicit on the matter, the Danes had had a legitimate place in Britain not only prior to the Vikings but even since before the arrival of the first Saxons, Danish hatred of whom is emphasized in Gaimar's introductory sequence (Bell 1960: 1–2).

A dozen miles along the road from Grimsby to Lincoln lies Caistor. Situated on an edge of the *west*-facing flank of the Lincolnshire wolds this erstwhile Roman station (from which its Old English name of *ceaster* derives) occupies a commanding position from which to oversee hostile approaches from the Humber into the physically enclosed interior of Lincolnshire. In the late eleventh century, moreover, Caistor was a more important place than upstart Grimsby, a settlement of but modest standing, albeit that references in Domesday to customs and a ferry there suggest the first stirrings of commercial activity (Foster and Longley 1992: ff.343, 342v.; 338v.). Caistor, by contrast, was of long-established importance in its district. It was a royal vill (and for a time previously had boasted a mint which indicates some form of urban status); it was the 'capital' of the North Riding of Lindsey (in which Grimsby too lay); and it seems to have possessed a 'minster' church (Smart 1987: 262; Bennett and Bennett 1993: 38–9; Stocker 1993: 117).

In 1190 Caistor is represented for the first time in the surviving documentary record as *Thwancastre*, or later, vulgarly, 'Thwangcaster', from the Old English word for a 'thong', although this name is likely to have been in circulation orally well before it was noted in writing (Cameron 1991: 87–8). Whether the legend about this place as recited in the pages of Geoffrey of Monmouth's *History of the Kings of Britain*, which was completed only a year or so before Gaimar's work, has influenced this extended version of the place-name, or whether an existing vernacular name stimulated the construction of the legend, cannot now be determined. Nevertheless, if, as surely we must, we accept J. S. P. Tatlock's identification of Caistor with the *Thanceastre* of Geoffrey of Monmouth, the legend in question will have been circulating in Lincolnshire at precisely the same time as were the mythical associations of Grim and Haveloc with Grimsby (Tatlock 1950: 24).

This legend tells how Hengist, a leader of the first Saxon warriors to reach Britain in the fifth century, is rewarded for his military help against enemies north of the Humber by his patron, the British King Vortigern, with lands in Lindsey but not, as he sees it, with either the residence or the title that would be appropriate for one of his royal descent. Both of these demands, however, Vortigern refuses to concede, on the grounds that Hengist and his followers are both pagans and foreigners, and that the princes of Britain would not consent. Hengist instead, therefore, successfully begs licence of Vortigern simply to build a *promontorium*—a word which can imply a fortress—on the land already granted and of such limited extent that its area could be defined by no more than what could be encircled by a single thong. This, of course, Hengist cunningly effects by creating so long a continuous thong, cut artfully from the hide of one bull, that it is enough to surround a much larger area than Vortigern had intended (Thorpe 1966: 157–8; Tatlock 1950: 23, 384–5). It was thus the supposed remains of this stronghold (in fact the polygonal Roman defences of the place—as Geoffrey's Latin version of the name,

Castrum corrigie, clearly indicates) which locals later thought had been demolished to build the church on the same spot (Jackson 1870: 61–2). It may even have been its shape which led to the idea that the place had been pegged out (Leahy 1993: 29).

Hengist's original land-fall and eventual major holding, however, was Kent. This was said to have been allotted to him only as a result of a banquet he gave for the British king at Thancaster, a grant that represented the price paid by a sexually aroused Vortigern for the hand of Hengist's newly introduced and alluring daughter. Through this second ruse, Hengist thereby became the father-in-law of the king of Britain (Thorpe 1966: 159–60). In Lawman's version of Geoffrey of Monmouth (*c.* 1199–1225), moreover, it was only a night's ride away from Thancaster that Vortimer, son of Vortigern by a previous marriage and military champion of the Britons, was later poisoned by his new Saxon step-mother, who then fled there (Weiss and Allen 1997: 135–6). (It is perhaps worth recalling here that in the pre-Conquest pages of the *British History* ascribed to Nennius, Vortimer was said to have been buried at Lincoln (Morris 1980: 72, cap. 44).) Throughout, therefore, Thancaster is depicted as an illegitimately contrived but nevertheless very early Saxon foothold in the British territory of Lindsey.

In all of this the myths surrounding Grimsby and Caistor, the two dominant settlements of northern Lincolnshire in the twelfth century, complement each other. Both appeal to wider rival allegiances. The origins of Grimsby are acceptable and Danish; those of Caistor unacceptable and Saxon. The true contrast, however, is not between two nearby places but between the protagonists concerned on a wider 'historical' canvas and hence over a yet more extensive mental map. For the purposes of this broader picture, the comparison must be between Hengist and Haveloc rather than with Grim, who is but a vehicle whereby the wider implications of the matter may be brought about. The basic opposition, which is overtly expressed in Gaimar's *History*, is that between the Saxon claim to parts or all of England by both Hengist and the subsequent royal line of Wessex, on the one hand, and the just rights of the Danish King Dane and his eventual successor Haveloc, who recovers the Danish inheritance, on the other. It is Hengist and Haveloc who are severally seen or claimed to be connected to British Lindsey in the post-Arthurian period. As near contemporaries, it was therefore they who were the direct mythic rivals in the regional context and, beyond the pages of Gaimar, are likely to have been thought of as such in the collective memories of the two different ethnic traditions during the twelfth century. How close was that mutual complementarity becomes clear if we summarize and compare the salient characteristics of each of

TABLE 6.1 *Mythical 'founding' heroes compared*

	Hengist	Haveloc
Continuing continental connections	Saxony	Denmark
English seaboard link	Kent (Lindsey)	'Norfolk' (Lindsey)
Status	Royal family	Royal family
Physique	Huge; powerful fighter	Huge; powerful fighter
Condition	Exiled; returns to England with foreign force	Exiled/fled; returns to England with foreign force
Story-type	Trickster	Bears supernatural marks
Plot	Exploits own daughter to marry British king and to poison the king's son	Marries royal daughter who is niece of British king, and defeats the king
First footholds in Lindsey on virgin land	Builds from scratch a fortress which develops into a town (Thancaster)	Nurtured in a newly contrived boat 'house' which develops into a town (Grimsby)
Long-term function:	Originates Saxon claims	Resumes and transmits Danish claims

the two hero types (see table 6.1). The reason for this is transparent. In the Haveloc myth the Saxons have been brushed aside, and the Danes have simply been substituted for their continental neighbours, the Angles, who had previously occupied eastern England. To judge from what Gaimar adds elsewhere in his *History*, at one and the same time therefore, the Vikings could now be seen as simply claiming their rightful inheritance of Britain (Bell 1960: 66, l.2084), and their successors locally, a large alien minority, could thus be repackaged as the legitimate descendants of the earliest English whose *History* Gaimar was then writing.[2]

We must turn now, however, to the wider cognitive map that the Haveloc myth conjures up. First, it is in Lindsey proper that the myth locates the sites of action: Grimsby itself, where Haveloc first arrives from Denmark; the lost 'Charlfleet', further down the coast and perhaps the predecessor of Saltfleet Haven (Bell 1925: 27 and n.1), where he

---

[2] It is worth remarking that a recent trend in archaeological interpretation has been to emphasize a Danish presence or influence in both Lindsey and East Anglia early in the Anglo-Saxon settlement period. (Hines 1984; Leahy 1993: 37; Newton 1992: 65–74; Hines 1992: 315–29; Hedeager 1992: 279–300).

lands on his return as King of Denmark; and Tetford, up on the southern end of the wolds, where he finally defeats the British king in battle. Above all, there is Lincoln, where the king has his court. Second, there is a wider Lindsey because the kingdom is said to extend from the Humber as far as Rutland and Stamford and, by implication (since Rutland and the county of Lincolnshire together so seem to comprise the territory in question), to include also the fenland district known as Holland, which borders on Norfolk. Third, further to the south lies the 'kingdom'of Norfolk which its erstwhile Danish king is said to have extended through the conquest of what, because of the form of its name, is evidently to be understood as the British 'Cair Coel' 'with all the country', which presumably implies the addition of territory of the East Saxons that now lies in Essex (Bell 1925: 183–4, 219). This Danish realm, which could then be said to stretch 'from Colchester as far as Holland', therefore included Suffolk, and it is at the 'city of Thetford', which straddles the Norfolk/Suffolk border, that the Danish king dies (though he is buried symbolically at British Colchester (Bell 1960: 3)).

Taking this region as a whole, therefore, in it are included both the former Anglian territory of a wider Lindsey and also—although significantly not by name—all of East Anglia. Yet at the period of the narration, when we are usually led to understand that some sense of England as a nation was rapidly gathering ground, there is not one mention of the English. The physical setting of the myth, however, embraces the entire eastern littoral of England from the Humber to the northern reaches of the Thames estuary at the least. Every single place mentioned—except Tetford—could be reached by water. Grimsby, as we have seen, develops into a fishing haven. In real life, down to 1200, Charlfleet seems to have functioned as a disembarkation point for fleets from Denmark, and one fleet of 480 ships is woven into the myth (Bell 1925: 215–16). Above all, this is a world that looks east across the North Sea to its Danish roots. More than a quarter of the earliest version of the myth is devoted to action in Denmark itself, in two distinct episodes involving three separate sea voyages, and by the end of the tale Danish sovereignty is established not only over greater Norfolk but also over greater Lindsey; all this, of course, in exactly the areas south of Humber and east of Leicestershire in which place-names revealed the greatest presence of late Scandinavian settlement.

In the twelfth-century versions of the myth, therefore, whatever the proponents of an emergent English national identity may tell us, the eastern seaboard is still being represented as a cultural outlier of the Scandinavian world. As their own geographical situation demanded, descendants of the Danes belonged sentimentally as much to the maritime community of the North Sea as they did to something called England. There is a telling episode to underline this. In the *Lai*, when Haveloc is about to leave home, Grim speaks of how the former is not meant for a life there with the poor fishers of Grimsby, and goes on to enjoin his 'son' Haveloc: 'Va t'en, bel fiz, en Engleterre'—go into *England* (Bell 1925: 182, l.175).

A Middle English *re*working of this myth, presumably originating in its present form somewhat earlier than later in the period 1174–1303, is given a Latin title which smacks rather of a saint's life: *Vita Havelok* (who is now also described as sometime king of England and Denmark) (Skeat 1915: xxiii–xxiv, 1). This new version marks certain suggestive shifts in the nature of the myth. Here, the provincial level is entirely replaced by a setting that is now the realm of England as a whole, from Dover to Roxburgh on the Tweed, with Winchester—the capital of Wessex—as the seat of a king with an Old English name (Skeat 1915: 6). The *Vita* places no less emphasis than its predecessor on Havelok's connection with, and doings in, Denmark of which he again becomes king, but the Danes are no longer surrogate Angles; they are now unambiguously Danish. When Havelok returns to England to defeat the evil regent (as opposed to a British subking), he now fights specifically *against* the English, and, having won the crown of England, he wears it before *both* English *and* Dane. This time, therefore, England as a whole is more directly portrayed as part of a Scandinavian dominion spanning the North Sea, over which Danes rule supreme. Havelok entrusts the governance of Denmark to his Danish justiciar, whilst remaining himself in England (Skeat 1915: 90–1, 100). The conclusion seems inescapable. No longer does Havelok displace Hengist as an alternative to the 'Saxon' originator of the English nation. The second version of the myth is resurrecting an *imperium* and a polity that, in a highly generalized way, retrospectively reflects the union of Denmark and England in the earlier eleventh century under Cnut who, incidentally, was buried at Winchester. Since Cnut's empire included Norway, moreover, a yet wider Scandinavian connection may then have been understood. Grimsby's evident links to Norway in the twelfth century have led one authority to describe post-Conquest Lincolnshire as 'a kind of remoter suburb of Norway' (Gillett 1970: 8). In the thirteenth century, therefore, the myth is still appealing to those with Scandinavian roots, but in a somewhat more ambitious way. It must therefore be more than coincidence that, from the later part of that century through to the second half of the fourteenth, perhaps as many as fifty Middle English versions of Havelok are known to have emanated from around the Norfolk end of the Wash in the vicinity of that other North Sea port, King's Lynn (McIntosh 1989: 230).[3]

At the same time as the scope of the story widens, however, we may watch its fictional locale also narrow. Lindsey is now mentioned only to locate Grimsby, and it is Grimsby that takes on a much greater importance. Through Grim, the town is seen as a source for the supply of fish to Lincoln (where much of the action still takes place) as well as acting as the starting point for Havelok's life in England and the stopping-off point on his return to Denmark. Grimsby replaces both Charlfleet (the probable predecessor of Saltfleet Haven) as the disembarkation point for Havelok's invasion fleet, and Tetford on the wolds as the site of his victory over the evil regent of England. In this version, moreover, Havelok swears to found a monastery at Grimsby and even goes so far as to marry off one of Grim's daughters there to a new character, the Earl of Chester (Skeat 1915: 85, 97–8). Since the real Norman Earls of Chester had had a near contemporary claim to a tower in the castle of Lincoln, to the constableship of Lincoln and Lincolnshire, and even to an hereditary sheriffdom for the county, this represented an extraordinary attempt at absorbing them, as it were, into the Danish descent of Lindsey (Hill 1965: 93–6, 177–81). The lengths to which the town itself would go in self-promotion, indeed, are to be measured eventually by royal authentication of the myth through the central approval in the late thirteenth century for the grant of a town seal on which Grim is shown with Havelok and his queen, Goldeburgh, on either side of him, the former below a crown and the latter with sceptre and diadem (Skeat 1915: frontispiece).

In the fresh urban emphasis of the second version, the stronger and more detailed focus is on Lincoln, where, by 1338, it was even reported independently that within the castle could be seen a large stone thrown by Havelok in one of his feats of strength, as well as the chapel where he had been married (Skeat 1915: xvi). Lincoln, moreover, is supplied by Grim with fish from Grimsby, even though there is no hint of such a connection in the records of that borough (Rigby 1993: 61). The whole sense of the myth, however, is to bind these two urban centres together— at a time that Grimsby itself had in fact been overtaken economically and as a source of supply for the city by Boston at the mouth of the navigable River Witham to the south (Poole 1955: 96).

---

[3] It seems most likely that both versions of the myth were widely circulated, and probably orally in the first instance, however much they may have been tidied up for literary presentation. Gaimar certainly seems to be exploiting for his 'historical' purposes what he takes to be a local tradition that looks as though it may reach back even to before the days of the Five Boroughs.

What should be noted, then, is the penultimate stage of the myth. By the late sixteenth and the seventeenth centuries, 'Grime' himself seems to have been reduced to the status of either an English merchant or a Humber fisherman. 'Grime' now simply fosters the foundling (discovered floating in a boat) who is only identified much later as a son of the king of Denmark. Havelok does still act as a scullion in the king's kitchen, and then marries a daughter of the English king, but it is not clear that he is then crowned king of England. In one version, the political link across the North Sea, and the related questions of ethnic and provincial identity, are thereby blurred. Instead, Grimsby itself seems at last to have become the sole focus of the myth which has now become thoroughly Anglo-centric. Being rewarded by Havelok, Grime is newly said to have 'builded a fayre Towne' himself, to which Havelok grants advantageous trading privileges in Denmark. By the seventeenth century, the town even boasts its own Havelok stone. An effigy, now mistaken to be that of 'Grime their founder', but in reality that of Sir Thomas Hastlerton, which had been relocated in the parish church from the dissolved nunnery of Saint Leonard's, indicates that Grimsby had even conspired to invest Grime with knightly status in the eyes of the public (Cole 1911: 6).

By the nineteenth century, Grim was being said in one new tradition to have thrown down stones from Grimsby church tower in an attempt to block the attack of a hostile fleet, one of which became 'Havelok's stone', an incident that was clearly derived incorrectly from the original adventures of Havelok himself in Denmark (Briggs 1970–1: B, II, 223). Some miles to the south, moreover, Little Grimsby was being related to someone now called 'Little Grim' in a legend concerning two magic stones brought over by him and his 'best man' from Denmark (Rudkin 1936: 69–70).

An origin myth that had once embraced the realm of England in an Anglo-Scandinavian universe had thus contracted to the point where it had meaning not even for the North Sea littoral, but only for a small port on one of its remoter edges. What had gradually been lost was, first, an ethnic perception of early provincial sovereignty and, second, a sense, albeit mythical, of a decisive provincial contribution to the sovereignty of the realm as a whole. In each case a provincial dimension was rooted in a racial identity that was associated with, and made synonymous with, highly particularized environmental settings. With the slow evaporation of both ethnic and territorial identity and influence, however, a popular geographical vision seems to have shrunk. The protracted accompanying process of localization in its turn is probably to be associated with the multiplication of fixed physical referrants, such as named stones and the like. Indeed, had the explanations of the stones survived but not the versions of myths, we would never have guessed at their implications for the wider associations they must once have triggered.

TOPOGRAPHIES OF SUPERSTITION:
THE WEST COUNTRY

In the cases both of the epic landscape and of the ethnic environment already described there is an appreciable distinction between some overall sense of territory or sphere of identity and, within such a frame, the diversity of environmental conditions. In reaching outwards, the cognitive map embraces such physical variations until defined limits are realized. This then seems to be a quite opposite process to that whereby broad separate categories of such natural feature as mountain, river, or forest may be evoked or construed metaphorically by and for a national intelligentsia. What seems to have been of more concern in the cultural appropriations of landscape by the earlier regionalized societies presently under discussion was the horizon of their vision. And what emerges unambiguously in that connection is the relevance of river-drainage basins or whole seas as cultural arenas. In the north-west, when the necessary allowance has been made for the subsequent disruption, by Angle and Norse alike, of Celtic place-name patterns in the south-western coastal strip of Cumberland, the formal territory and the informal cultural region of the British period may be seen to have coincided with the inner Solway basin. In Lincolnshire the area is subtly subdivided because the inner clay vale landscape of the county was separated from the sea by the wolds. In both Lincolnshire and Cumberland, however, under Scandinavian influence, formal territoriality was overlapped along coastal edges by informal, external cultural associations with the seaward sides of unambiguous internal watersheds and hence with the Irish Sea and the North Sea respectively (Phythian-Adams 1996: 170).

As the sense of semi-independent provincial identity dwindled and as minority ethnic identities were transmuted into broader regional senses of belonging, it becomes necessary to ask whether there were alternative ways of mentally mapping the different environments in which distinct societies were resident. What other preoccupations were there, over and above the world of work, which transcended local particularities? One answer, which will only be given when my colleague, Dr Graham Jones, has completed his study of medieval saints' cults parish by parish across the whole of England, will certainly lie in the regionality of popular religious beliefs. To come down to more recent times, and to judge from the burden of the erstwhile oral testimony to have reached us, however, another and not unrelated answer might concern those mutual anxieties to do with uncertainties concerning such matters as personal health, survival, and fortune on the one hand, and the vagaries of climate and livestock disease on the other. In post-Reformation times, in particular, such problems did not necessarily seem responsive to the invocations of formal religion. In other words, the continuing popular concerns for the powers and manifestations of the supernatural, and preoccupations with the superstitions surrounding these, certainly qualify for inclusion in any discussion of the ways in which culture impinged upon the natural world.

Three points should be made at the outset. First we have at our disposal for these purposes a fairly rich storehouse of folktales or 'narrations' that were recorded before the older ways of life were finally extinguished in this century (Philip 1992: xiii–xxxvii). Second, these reveal not only regional but also local differences of emphasis. Most even specify the place and landscape features where events are said to have occurred. Third, it has to be appreciated that such tales often made a far deeper impression on contemporary audiences than they do today. We have the contemporary witness of W. H. Barrett (1963: ix–x), who was memorizing such stories from his youth in the Fens, that 'they often became gruesome, yet the more spine-chilling they became the more the listeners enjoyed them. Being riddled with superstition they would huddle together when the session was over, having a feeling that the closer together they were the less was the dread of the unknown.' For all these reasons, this rare form of evidence is worth taking seriously.

There is only space to consider two such landscapes, one—and briefly—in Somerset; the other in Cornwall. The first of these two illustrations of what I would call 'the topography of superstition' is based on sixteen folktales mainly collected earlier this century in a restricted area of Somerset that reaches from the Quantocks to the River Parrett, and is bordered by the sea coast to the north (see figure 6.1).[4] On the map all

---

[4] Somerset tales were collected by Ruth Tongue, on whose transmission of the material in its original form some doubts have been expressed (Philip 1992: xxx). The present exercise, indeed, began as a way of testing for inconsistencies in her collection of stories by adopting a measure that was broadly independent of story structures and content: her employment of landscape features set against the locations of her informants. I conclude that while many of her tales may have been tidied up linguistically for publication, their internal logic is consistent (and when set against tales from elsewhere, unremarkable), and that, in the absence of inadvertent contradictions, their genuine associations with local settings look very probable. One may also doubt whether the formidable Katharine Briggs, with whom Ruth Tongue worked closely, would have let serious distortions of such materials slip through her net.

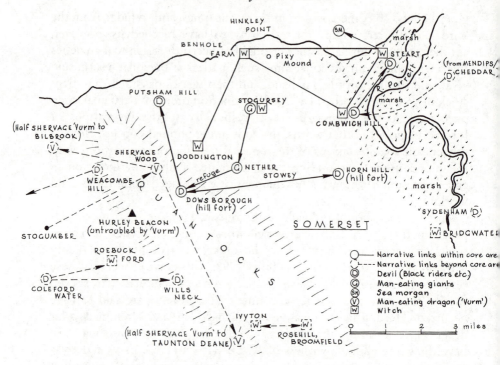

FIG. 6.1   The topography of superstition: localized narrative links in folktales from a district of Somerset.

the places and landmarks mentioned in connection with a range of supernatural beings and occurrences have been included across an area which
embraces what was undeveloped land running down to the coastline;
marshlands; and the wooded combes of the Quantocks, as well as the
foothills at their eastern skirts. It will be seen immediately that there is
an inner core area in which places are mutually interlinked by narrative
incidents within quite a narrow compass, and a scatter of narrative incidents outside and separate from the core. It will be best to deal with the
latter first.

What emerges to the west, and hardly surprisingly, is the effective

The tales used here are most conveniently found, by volume, in Briggs 1970–1: 'A Good
Black Dog' (BI: 13–14); 'The Black Rider' (BI: 51); 'How the Devil Made Cheddar Gorge'
(BI: 103); 'The Hunted Soul' (BI: 103–4); 'Madam Widecombe's Coach' (BI: 114); 'The
Unholy Pig' (and the Yeth hounds) (BI: 149); 'The Great Vurm of Shervage Wood' (BI:
162); 'The Broken Ped' (BI: 185); 'The Pixy Threshers' (BI: 343); 'The Sea Morgan and
the Conger Eels' (BI: 351); 'The Giants of Stowey' (BI: 615–16); 'The Bridgewater Rabbit'
(BII: 626); 'The Dung Putt' (BII: 640); 'The Elder-tree Witch' (BII: 644–6); 'Harriet, the
Witch of Keenthorne' (BII: 668–9).

barrier represented by the Quantocks. Diabolical manifestations connected with Weacombe Hill or between Roebuck Ford and Wills Neck, are restricted to the western flank. Even the bizarre event in Shervage Wood involves a 'stranger from Stogumber' to the west, who goes up to cut wood, ignorant of the peril he is risking, and who sits on a log to eat his bread and cheese only to discover that the log 'begins to squirmy about under'n'. He had sat in fact on 'the gurt vurm of Shervage Wood'. When the stranger cuts this man-eating dragon in two with his axe, one half of it sets off the ten miles to Bilbrook to the west, and the other half to the Vale of Taunton Deane eight miles to the south, and therefore not down into the core area. To the south and south-east, neither the witch at Broomfield, nor the witch at Bridgwater, nor the sensational appearance of a malevolent black monkey astride a pig at Sydenham, just to the east of the latter, appear to interconnect with the core area.

What we seem to have, therefore, is a spatially self-defining oral community occupying some dozen parishes for whom local features across this landscape relate logically to each other within an area of no more than 40 square miles. Even including the sea morgan who tempts coastal fishers of conger eels to their fate in the quicksands off Steart, all types of habitat are interlinked. Most marked is the way the devil defines the outer limits of this community, as he rides either on horseback or on a boar or, most threateningly of all in stag country, as a horned rider with the horned 'yeth hounds' between the two hill forts at Horn Hill, Cannington, and at Dowsborough Hill. It is the devil whose last shovelful of spoil from the excavation of the Cheddar Gorge is dropped accidentally west of Parrett to create Combwich or 'Cummage Hill', which in turn links him in space to two witches: Madam Withycombe (the hill is called Withycombe Hill) and, in the marshland, the Black Witch of Steart (whose demise, incidentally, leads to the fortunate release of one Granny Thatcher from being overlooked). Both witches have separate tales devoted to them, and both are suspects in the case of the elder-tree witch, who seeks to milk the cows on an 'unket' piece of land probably near Benhole farm by the coast, but who turns out to be a witch, this time from Doddington. At Stogursey not only is there another witch, but there are also man-eating giants under the castle mound, who raid the rival giants of Nether Stowey castle, which they flatten. Again and again, in fact, we see a frame of reference that comprises sets of easily recalled links between, for example, similar types of earthwork—castles or forts—that can be shared only by an audience that is familiar with this particular countryside.

This, then, is surely the nub. When what is in question is familiarity with a locale rather than with a former territory or external cultural sphere of influence, it will be the spatially constricted knowledge of the *connotations* attached to local landmarks that will lend not only some sense of identity to those residents who share that knowledge, but also indeed even some sense of residential possession precisely because of this. Not only does this fit very well with the sort of localized kinship neighbourhood that some of us have been seeking to reconstruct elsewhere (an exercise, however, that has still to be attempted in this district) (Phythian-Adams 1993a), it also helps to explain why the supernatural emphasis may change so markedly from one such neighbourhood to another, and hence from one district to another, despite the underlying similarity of the supernatural vocabulary. A cultural neighbourhood of the kind mapped simultaneously interlocks characteristics from the *different* natural environments within it, whether sea—marshland, coastal or upland—and connects in a generalized way to its regional cultural horizons. As we have seen, some of these tales are specifically linked to locations that are unnecessary to the stories being told. The places so mentioned, however, are all situated towards the lowland edges of the wider natural arena—effectively, the wider Somerset region which drains into the Bristol Channel: to Cheddar and the Mendips to the north-east; to Kingston St Mary and the Vale of Taunton Deane to the south; and to Bilbrook in the last low-lying stretch of the coastal zone where the Brendon Hills run into Exmoor and so block off Somerset from Devon to the west.

The difficulties involved in tracing and understanding the ways in which environments are coloured by the cultural assumptions of their inhabitants are most likely to be overcome by looking, finally, at a yet more narrowly defined landscape still, in an even more densely evidenced area, the northern claw of the westernmost extreme of Cornwall (see figure 6.2).

A century ago Zennor belonged to a group of three remote and impoverished neighbouring townships: Madron parish, which included the chapelry of Morvah; Zennor parish; and Towednack, which, like the little town of St Ives, lay in the parish of Lelant. Zennor itself is a large parish of more than 4,000 acres some five miles west of St Ives, containing scattered farms and tiny hamlets with but one small nucleated centre, Zennor Church Town, and a close neighbour, the hamlet of Trewey (or Treva). The harsh landscape is littered with granite boulders, many of which have been used in the construction of a lace-like pattern of ancient field enclosures, or for buildings on the coastal strip where farming has predominated, and up on the moor and elsewhere for different prehistoric purposes. In the nineteenth century the inhabitants got their living from agriculture, tin-mining, quarrying, and from the sea: fishing, smuggling,

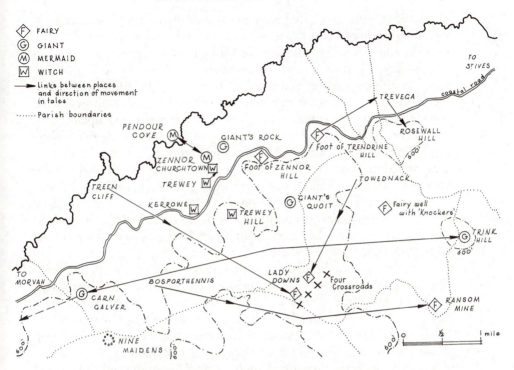

FIG. 6.2 The topography of superstition: landmarks and the supernatural in the west Cornish parishes of Zennor and Towednack.

and exploiting wrecks on the treacherous Atlantic coastline. Towednack, its easterly neighbour which reaches towards the skirts of the Lelant Hills, was rather more concerned with tin-mining.

Taken together, the supernatural associations that may be pinned to this landscape help both to define a cultural space and to categorize its component elements in a number of ways.[5] In the first instance, tales and superstitions mark out a territory by precisely emphasizing boundaries and edges. The giant of Carn Galver (the peak broadly marking the boundary between Morvah and Zennor), for example, was said to have

[5] The Zennor tales quoted are usefully gathered together, by volume, in Briggs 1970–1: 'Betty Stogs and the Fairies' (BI: 178–9); 'Cherry of Zennor' (BI: 199–202), but the full version is in Philip 1992: 320–6; 'The Fairy Miners' (BI: 236–7); 'The Fairy Tools' (BI: 242–3); 'The Fairy Widower' (BI: 244–7); 'Nursing a Fairy' (BI: 330–2); 'Skillywidden' (BI: 355–6), but the full version is conveniently given in Philip (1992: 313–16); 'The Giant of Carn Calva' (BI: 610–11), with the full version in Philip (1992: 281–83); 'The Witch of Treva' (BII: 746–7).

protected the whole of what were known locally as 'the high countries', including Chun or Chun castle (a prehistoric hill settlement), off the map, near the south-western boundary of Morvah, and, in the opposite direction, to have faced the enemies of the district as far away as Trink (a hill fort) close to the eastern boundary of Towednack. In doing so, most of the high land separating the entire northern coastal strip from the Penzance area to the south was delimited. It was across this upland division, between the impoverished 'high countries' and the more prosperous valleys or 'low countries' to the south, that girls from the Zennor area hoped to find places in service. Neither of the two girls who attempted this crossing in two tales managed to get beyond the four crossroads on the Lady Downs on the watershed zone. One of them came from Towednack, the boundary of which is marked by one of these crossroads; and the other came from Treen Cliff on the extreme coastal edge of Zennor, to where she had to return.

Within the area delimited, moreover, it is clear that a mental distinction was made between what was below terrestrial level and what was at it. Below the plane of social activity was another world into which humanity might occasionally trespass at its peril, or which might emerge briefly onto the terrestrial plane before returning below. Half a dozen stories involving this immediate vicinity tell of fairies, and in terms that clearly indicate their usual underground situation: either as heard by male miners as 'knockers' working on the lodes down mines or wells; or as visited in their usually lush fairy world by girls who are inveigled into nursing a male fairy child. To judge from the locations of such stories, and more particularly the points where fairies are thought to have surfaced, this fairy world was regarded as being situated within the moorland zone down to the point where the landscape flattened out at the level on which most human settlement was located. In these situations, of course, it thereby reflected to a considerable extent the area of the tin-mines.[6] The other world below the surface also comprised a perilous sphere of male working activity, the sea. There, the Zennor mermaid, an ageless beauty (whose chair is kept in the church), was said to have tempted a male chorister from the church which she had attended for years, to become her mate in the deeps of Pendour Cove, where, ever since, the two have been heard singing together (Courtney 1989: 70). Sea and church were linked not only by the mermaid but also by St Azenor or Senara (to whom Zennor seemingly owed its name and the church its dedication), who had prudently avoided drowning

---

[6] I am extremely grateful to Dr Margaret Pelling for drawing my attention to a precise parallel from the sixteenth-century demonology of mines in Switzerland in Webster 1982.

on her legendary voyage from Ireland by being nailed down in a barrel (Padel 1988: 181; Symons 1992: 164–5; Farmer 1987: 65 *sub* 'Budoc').

Located on the surface, at all contours, by contrast, were both the 'human' relics of the past, whether mythological or traditional, and associations with the supernatural in the present. Quasi-human myths were commemorated by the Nine Maidens, a stone circle said to represent nine petrified dancers; or by the erstwhile signs of giants at play like the logan stone on Carn Galver, the Giant's Quoit and the Giant's Rock (Hunt 1896: 49–52); tradition was represented by the church and its link with the otherwise unknown Celtic St Azenor. At the other extreme, temporally speaking, were those members of society who *currently* had access to the supernatural: on the one hand, the local incumbent (who exorcised the corpse of a witch in one of the tales) and, on the other, the embodiments of evil: not only the witch herself, who is unambiguously situated within the normal social world, but also the animals into which witches might be transformed like hares or cats. All of these were perceived as operating at terrestrial level.

Within the overall spatial context, there was a very clear central topographical antithesis between, on the one hand, the evil associations of Trewey Hill, and the nearby hamlets of Trewey and Kerrowe, and, on the other hand, the church and its yard at the very foot of the same hill; both supernatural zones being kept distinct in local lore from the moorland zone. Trewey Hill was reputed to have been the meeting place for the witches of West Cornwall and on it, the Witches' Rock, when touched nine times at midnight, was said to prevent a person being 'overlooked' (Courtney 1989: 41). At Kerrowe it was told how a hunt had chased a hare which they had wounded into a cottage where, of course, they then discovered a bleeding old woman instead—a well-known symptom of witchcraft (Symons 1992: 138). A tension between the two extremes of the supernatural was expressed in ways too numerous to be dismissed as coincidence. Zennor church represented a consecrated place of assembly; whereas the witches' assembly place opposite on Trewey Hill may well have been a pagan site. Church rituals tended to be male-dominated not only because of the parson and churchwardens, but also because coffin-bearers were invariably male. Witches, by contrast, were female and, like the witch of Trewey, practised shape-changing into animals. Candles were customarily lit on the church tower on Christmas Eve through to 1866, and then again in 1883 (Courtney 1989: 7). On Midsummer Eve there were bonfires on Trewey Hill.

This supernatural opposition is climactically and precisely located in the tale of 'The Witch of Treva' (or Trewey), where her coffin is borne underhand, according to Zennor custom, by six aged men from the hamlet towards the church. Halfway from Trewey, a hare leaps over the coffin, so frightening the bearers into dropping it. New bearers take up the task, only to be deterred themselves by a cat, which suddenly appears sitting on the coffin. A third lot of bearers is now persuaded to carry the coffin very quickly towards the sacred space of the churchyard, with the parson ceaselessly reciting the Lord's Prayer before them, until, symbolically, they reach a liminal line: the church stile. There, to quote the nineteenth-century summary of the story, 'they rested the corpse, the parson paused to commence the ordinary burial service, and there stood the hare, which, as soon as the clergyman began "I am the resurrection and the life", uttered a diabolical howl, changed into a black unshapen creature, and disappeared' (Briggs 1970–1, Part B II: 746–7).

This spatial organization of the topography of superstition is therefore distinctive and, within its own terms of reference, logical. In particular, the location of witch associations within a tightly defined area, in close relation to the settlement core of Zennor parish, yet apart from the zones associated with fairies, partly recalls the wider Somerset pattern. There, witchcraft was associated with communities, whereas manifestations of the devil in various guises, and the location of the man-eating dragon in particular, related more to uninhabited countrysides. With that, however, any slight resemblence ends. The supernatural emphases in each district, despite their not dissimilar situations, are quite different. In the one, the devil figures prominently, both giants and dragons consume people, and supernatural pigs are a puzzling repeated motif. In the other, the giants are playful and the most emphasis is placed on an alternative fairy world which manifestly complements the working context of the Cornish tin-miner. There is nothing inevitable about the relationship between culture and the environment, unless it is that cultural meanings in the past will be as diverse as the locations to which they are attached.

CONCLUSION

But if there is nothing inevitable in the relationship, there do seem to be some underlying consistencies in its realization. At a first, immediate level, there are landscapes of need and supply, specific environments in which the interaction of humankind and nature may be directly ritualized. Above that, is the second, wider level under consideration here, at which different *pays* are subsumed together into some more embracing cultural notion, that allows of a shared sense of belonging amongst those inhabiting them. Unlike the metaphorical evocations of 'empty' wilderness by polite culture in terms of pastoralism or romanticism, for example, the concern in more subjectively apprehended regional contexts is specifically to embrace the *occupied* landscape and to seek to give it and its inhabitants associational meanings. Crucial to this way of looking, therefore, is the fact that named settlements intervene, as it were, between the individual and the landscape, and thereby the environment itself is reorganized in interlinked terms to create a kind of cultural rather than environmental map. It is noticeable then that the links in question connect culture to the environment through predominant occupational activities or seasonal rhythms that are characteristic of the local working relationships between settlements and nature. It is these relationships, therefore, that also interconnect the two levels. At the second level, moreover, what allows of some degree of inclusiveness is, above all, a shared aspect, in which people in localized societies may look collectively inwards and/or outwards towards the sea from a physically defined arena delimited inland by a horizon, which is usually a pronounced watershed.[7] At this level, too, as formal associations with archaic territories are displaced by informal strands of attachment, identification with regional figureheads, whether real or surrogate for some ethnic group, will be superseded by less single-minded mental assumptions, which nevertheless, may more nearly reflect much more localized environments.

Closely linked to provincial appropriations of the landscape, however, is an ahistorical sense of time, which, if not quite amounting to that 'motionless civilization' of which Carlo Levi speaks, tends to be extraordinarily enduring, whether in terms of names in the landscape or with respect to oral traditions. Here the past seems to be either fixed or even co-existent with the present—certainly not perceptibly changing—in the sense that fairies and mermaids, for example, seem to inhabit a form of parallel time that is without end. Such change as there is involves the almost imperceptible displacement of broader cultural understandings and the shrinkage of associations until, in so many cases, they come to refer to but a stone or isolated landmark. Possibly that is why we today are so concerned to fill the resulting emptiness of our own landscapes with projections from the fictions of such disparate authors as Thomas Hardy or Catherine Cookson. Novels like these themselves once owed something to a contemporary sense of regional genius which they thus condensed. Every generation, perhaps, needs landscapes to tell stories rather than histories.

[7] Special valley examples of self-contained landscapes with cultural identities at both provincial and national levels are discussed in Phythian-Adams (forthcoming).

REFERENCES

Barrett, W. H. (1963). *Tales from the Fens*, ed. E. Porter. London: Routledge and Kegan Paul.

Bell, A. (ed.) (1925). *Le Lai d'Haveloc and Gaimar's Haveloc Episode*. Manchester: University of Manchester Press.

Bell, A. (ed.) (1960). *L'Estoire des Engleis by Geffrei Gaimar*. Anglo-Norman Texts XIV–XVI. Oxford: Blackwell.

Bennett, S. and Bennett, N. (eds) (1993). *An Historical Atlas of Lincolnshire*. Hull: University of Hull Press.

Beresford, M. W. (1957). *History on the Ground: Six Studies in Maps and Landscapes*. London: Lutterworth.

Briggs, K. M. (ed.) (1970–1). *A Dictionary of British Folk-tales in the English Language Incorporating the F. J. Norton Collection*, Part A, I and II (1970); Part B, I and II (1971). London: Routledge and Kegan Paul.

Camden, W. (1637). *Britain or a Chorographicall Description of the Most Flourishing Kingdomes, England, Scotland and Ireland*, translated by Philemon Holland. London: Andrew Crooke.

Cameron, K. (1991). *The Place-names of Lincolnshire, ii, Lincolnshire, Lindsey, North Riding and the Wapentake of Yarborough*. English Place-Name Society, LXIV/LXV.

Carver, M. O. H. (ed.) (1992). *The Age of Sutton Hoo: The Seventh Century in North-Western Europe*. Woodbridge: The Boydell Press.

Cawte, E. C. (1978). *Ritual Animal Disguise: A Historical and Geographical Study of Animal Disguise in the British Isles*. Folklore Society Mistletoe Series. Cambridge: Brewer.

Clark, C. (1992). 'Onomastics', in N. Blake (ed.), *The Cambridge History of the English Language*, II, *1066–1476*. Cambridge: Cambridge University Press.

Cole, R. E. G. (ed.) (1911). *Lincolnshire Notes Made by Gervase Holles A.D. 1634 to A.D. 1642*. Publications of the Lincoln Record Society, I.

Courtney, M. A. (1989). *Folklore and Legends of Cornwall* (originally *Cornish Feasts and Customs*: 1890). Exeter: Wheaton Publishers.

Farmer, D. H. (1987). *The Oxford Dictionary of Saints*. Oxford: Oxford University Press.

Fellows Jensen, G. (1978). *Scandinavian Settlement Names in the East Midlands*. Navnestudier Udgivet af Institut for Navneforskning, 16. Copenhagen: Academisk Forlag.

Fentress, J. and Wickham, C. (1992). *Social Memory*. Oxford: Blackwell.

Foster, C. W. and Longley, T. (1992). 'Lincolnshire'. Translation revised by D. R. Roffe in *The Lincolnshire Domesday*. The County Edition of Domesday Book. London: Alecto Historical Editions.

Fox, H. S. A. (1996). 'Introduction: Transhumance and Seasonal Settlement', in H. S. A. Fox (ed.), *Seasonal Settlement*. Vaughan Papers in Adult Education, 1–23.

Gillett, E. (1970). *A History of Grimsby*. London: Oxford University Press for the University of Hull.

Hedeager, L. (1992). 'Kingdoms, ethnicity and material culture: Denmark in a European perspective', in M. O. H. Carver (ed.), *The Age of Sutton Hoo*. Woodbridge: The Boydell Press, 279–300.

Hill, F. (1965). *Medieval Lincoln*. Cambridge: Cambridge University Press.

Hines, J. (1984). *The Scandinavian Character of Anglian England in the pre-Viking Period*. Oxford: British Archaeological Reports, 124.

Hines, J. (1992). 'The Scandinavian Character of Anglian England: An Update', in M. O. H. Carver (ed.), *The Age of Sutton Hoo*. Woodbridge: The Boydell Press, 315–29.

Hoskins, W. G. (1955). *The Making of the English Landscape*. London: Hodder and Stoughton.

Hunt, R. (1896). *Popular Romances of the West of England, or, The Drolls, Traditions and Superstitions of Old Cornwall*. London: Chatto and Windus.

Jackson, C. (ed.) (1870). *The Diary of Abraham de la Pryme: The Yorkshire Antiquary*. Surtees Society for the year 1869, LIV.

Laver, J. (1947). *Isabella's Triumph (May 31st, 1615): Denis Van Alsloot*. London: Faber and Faber.

Leahy, K. (1993). 'The Anglo-Saxon Settlement of Lindsey', in A. Vince (ed.), *Pre-Viking Lindsey*. Lincoln: City of Lincoln Archaeology Unit, 29–44.

Levi, C. (1982). *Christ Stopped at Eboli*. Harmondsworth: Penguin.

McIntosh, A. (1989). 'The Language of the Extant Versions of *Havelok the Dane*', in Laing, M. (ed.), *Middle English Dialectology: Essays on Source Principles and Problems*. Aberdeen: Aberdeen University Press, 224–36.

Miller, M. (1975). 'The Commanders at Arthuret'. *Transactions of the Cumberland and Westmorland Antiquarian and Archaeological Society*, New Series, LXXXV: 96–118.

Morris, J. (ed.) (1980). *Nennius: British History and the Welsh Annals*. History from the Sources. London and Chichester: Phillimore.

Newton, S. (1992). 'Beowulf and the East Anglian Royal Pedigree', in M. O. H. Carver (ed.), *The Age of Sutton Hoo*. Woodbridge: The Boydell Press, 65–75.

Padel, O. J. (1988). *A Popular Dictionary of Cornish Place-Names*. Penzance: Alison Hodge.

Philip, N. (1992). *The Penguin Book of British Folktales*. Harmondsworth: Penguin Books.

Phythian-Adams, C. V. (1983). 'Milk and Soot: The Changing Vocabulary of a Popular Ritual in Stuart and Hanoverian London', in D. Fraser and A. Sutcliffe (eds), *The Pursuit of Urban History*. London: Arnold, 83–104.

Phythian-Adams, C. V. (ed.) (1993a). *Societies, Cultures and Kinship, 1580–1850: Cultural Provinces and English Local History*. Leicester: Leicester University Press.

Phythian-Adams, C. V. (1993b). 'Genesi e Primo Sviluppo del Territorio locale in Inghilterra'. *Proposte e Ricerche: Economia e Società nella Storia dell'Italia Centrale*, 30: 19–34.

Phythian-Adams, C. V. (1996). *Land of the Cumbrians: A Study in British Provincial Origins A.D. 400–1120*. Aldershot: Scolar.

Phythian-Adams, C. V. (forthcoming). 'Frontier valleys', in J. Thirsk (ed.), *The Oxford Illustrated History of the English Rural Landscape*. Oxford: Oxford University Press.

Poole, A. L. (1955). *From Domesday Book to Magna Carta 1087–1216*. (2nd edn). Oxford: Oxford University Press.

Ramm, H. G., McDowall, R. W., and Mercer, E. (1970). *Shielings and Bastles*. Royal Commission on Historical Monuments (England). London: HMSO.

Rigby, S. (1993). *Medieval Grimsby: Growth and Decline*. Monographs in Regional and Local History, 3. Hull: University of Hull Press.

Robson, R. (1989). *The English Highland Clans: Tudor Responses to a Medieval Problem*. Edinburgh: Donald.

Rudkin, E. H. (1936). *Lincolnshire Folklore*. Burgh le Marsh, Lincolnshire: Richard Pacey.

Schama, S. (1995). *Landscape and Memory*. London: Harper Collins.

Short, I. (1995). 'Gaimar's Epilogue and Geoffrey of Monmouth's *Liber Vetustissimus*'. *Speculum*, 69: 323–43.

Skeat, W. W. (1915). *The Lay of Havelok the Dane: Re-edited from the MS. Laud Misc. 108 in the Bodleian Library, Oxford* (2nd edn, revised by K. Sisam). Oxford: Oxford University Press.

Smart, V. (1987). 'Moneyers of the Late Anglo-Saxon Coinage: The Danish Dynasty 1017–42'. *Anglo-Saxon England*, 16: 233–308.

Stocker, D. (1993). 'The early church in Lincolnshire: A study of the sites and their significance', in A. Vince (ed.), *Pre-Viking Lindsey*. Lincoln: City of Lincoln Archaeology Unit, 101–22.

Sturt, G. (1963). *The Wheelwright's Shop*. Cambridge: Cambridge University Press.

Symons, A. (1992). *Tremedda Days: A View of Zennor, 1900–1944*. Padstow: Tabb House.

Tatlock, J. S. P. (1950). *The Legendary History of Britain: Geoffrey of Monmouth's Historia Regum Britanniae and its Early Vernacular Versions*. Berkeley and Los Angeles: University of California Press.

Thomas, K. (1983). *Man and the Natural World: Changing Attitudes in England 1500–1800*. London: Allen Lane.

Thorpe, L. (ed.) (1966). *Geoffrey of Monmouth: The History of the Kings of Britain*. Harmondsworth: Penguin Books.

Vince, A. (ed.) (1993). *Pre-Viking Lindsey*. Lincoln: City of Lincoln Archaeology Unit.

Webster, C. (1982). 'Paracelsus and demons: science as a synthesis of popular belief', in *Scienza Credenza Occulte Livelli di Cultura*. Florence: Leo S. Olschki.

Weiss, J. and Allen, R. (eds) (1997). *Wace and Lawman: The Life of King Arthur*. London: Everyman.

7

The Renaturing of African Animals:
Film and Literature in the 1950s and 1960s

William Beinart

OUR world is saturated with images from photography, film, and television which are intricately bound up with our patterns of knowledge. This essay has its deeper origins in entrancing Sunday evenings watching wildlife on television with my young children, many years ago. My interest took academic shape in 1990, when I began teaching a course on the environmental history of Africa to undergraduates at the University of Bristol, just a few hundred metres from the BBC's Natural History Unit. British students, sadly, probably knew more about African animals than about African people. After some months in which they learnt about peasants and settlers, tsetse and drought, a couple of sessions at the end of the course on the history of natural history film and literature proved to be popular and familiar terrain for them. I will suggest that this history has something to tell us about changing Western approaches to African animals.

Sufficient has been written about Western attitudes to animals for historians to know that great caution should be exercised in pinpointing trends. For example, Keith Thomas (1983) suggested that the period around 1800 might be considered something of a watershed in England, when more modern sympathies had begun to displace older patterns of domination, aggression, and mistreatment. There was undoubtedly an increased interest in pets and in animal protection. Yet the first half of the nineteenth century probably saw more intensive use of working animals in this country. Fox-hunting flourished as did extraordinarily predatory hunting of wild animals overseas, not least in Africa.

Similarly, few would disagree that publicly expressed attitudes to animals in the last half-century have become more protective and benign; yet factory farming, James Serpell notes, has simultaneously reached its apogee: 'We nurture and care for [pets] like our own kith and kin, and display outrage and disgust when they are subjected to ill-treatment', but we condemn useful animals like pigs to a sacrifical life as if they were 'worthless objects devoid of feelings and sensations' (1996: 19). The domestication and use of animals in particular produce complex tensions and contradictory impulses in human approaches which allow for the nurture of other mammal species, and also for dispensing with, and often consuming them. Jostling sets of moral values are not least evident with regard to wild animals: fascination and respect run parallel to fear and carelessness about their habitat. At any particular time, there has been a wide range of practices, as well as strikingly different views about particular groups of animal, whether classified as wild, vermin, domestic, or pet (Lewinsohn 1954).

Despite these cautions I want to explore the idea that during the 1950s and 1960s significant changes can be discerned in the way that African wildlife was presented to Western audiences. A small number of highly committed, even obsessive people, who worked at the interface with African animals, especially in Kenya, played a central role in this process: I will discuss, amongst others, the Denises, Adamsons, and Harthoorns. The success of their project, however, suggests that their audiences, relatively few of whom had direct contact with Africa, were highly receptive. It was a relationship mediated by new developments in such diverse spheres as veterinary medicine, ecology and ethology, film, television, air transport, and popular publishing. These changes were not without their impact on African countries.

AUTHORS AND FILMMAKERS—A COLLECTIVE BIOGRAPHY

African animals have long held a grip on a small corner of the British imagination. In the nineteenth century hunting and its literary aftermath fascinated large numbers of Western people (Ritvo 1987; MacKenzie 1988). This type of engagement persisted well into the twentieth century in the elite East African safari hunt, and is still alive on the increasing number of game farms in Southern Africa—as well as in Wilbur Smith novels. Victorian African hunting and adventure sagas had often included illustrations of animals. When cameras became available, hunters liked to be photographed with their kills displayed before them, sometimes with a foot firmly on the neck of the animal in a pose of domination. Even those who wished to photograph live animals sometimes found that they had to make do with immobile dead subjects (Guggisberg 1977: 13). Although camera technology was sufficiently developed by the 1880s to take photographs at one-thousandth of a second, and stop birds in flight, getting heavy equipment on location in Africa was far more difficult.

Around the turn of the twentieth century, predatory hunting started to give way, very unevenly, to increasing concern about game preservation in the British empire. Game reserves were gradually established in which hunting was strictly controlled. Conservationist approaches were mirrored in photographic books and lantern slides which displayed live animals. Pioneer photographers such as Carl Schillings and A. R. Dugmore waited patiently in hides to shoot—in the metaphor of the time—graphic wildlife pictures which included predators hunting (Guggisberg 1977).

The possiblties for filming wild animals in Africa were quickly realized in the early twentieth century, soon after the technology became available. Some of the early film was preoccupied with capture and spectacle. *Paul J. Rainey's African Hunt*, released in 1912, grossed $500,000 and clearly struck a chord in Western expectations about Africa (Imperato and Imperato 1992: 97). Cherry Kearton, perhaps the most innovative and important early British filmmaker, accompanied Theodore Roosevelt's much-publicized hunting safari to East Africa in 1909 (Kearton 1935; Guggisberg 1977). In 1911 he filmed an expedition to Kenya by an American military officer, Colonel C. J. Jones, who was a leading figure in the movement to preserve the American buffalo (Scull 1911). Alarmed that African animals might meet the same fate, Jones took skilled cowboys with him to demonstrate that it was possible to capture animals by lassoo. On a subsequent trip Kearton staged a spectacular reconstruction of a Maasai lion hunt. His pith helmet, lack of anthropological sensibility, and chats with penguins now seem redolent of the imperial ethos and an uneasy anthropomorphism.

Martin Johnson, the key inter-war American filmer of African animals, started out presenting slide- and talk-shows of his trip with Jack London to the South Sea islands, including sequences on 'Cannibals' and 'Dances of the Head Hunters' (Imperato and Imperato 1992). His first film in 1917, called *Jungle Adventures*, dwelt on the thrills, spills, and wildness of the tropics. In many successful feature films on Africa, released in the 1920s and 1930s, he and his wife Osa never dispensed with an element of showmanship. They induced elephants, rhinos, and lions to charge at Osa, the vulnerable white woman, who, with assistants, was ready to shoot if the animals came too close.

But it would be be misleading to argue either that this early work was entirely one-dimensional or, as I will illustrate, that such approaches disappeared from natural history film by mid-century. Kearton came to

Africa after he had established himself as the most systematic photographer of British birds. He had used a wide range of strategies to approach his subjects in their nests, lowering himself on ropes to photograph cliff birds or lying in a hollow model cow near hedgerows; he transferred many of his careful photographic techniques to film. He was a committed conservationist, and by the 1930s he felt that the art of natural history film was taking a step backwards. Kearton believed that his 'true to life' techniques, 'the real natural history film of which I had been a pioneer, ignominiously died' in the face of rampant commercialism, overexposed audiences, and changing tastes (Kearton 1935: 275–7).

Similarly, the Johnsons, after meeting with Carl Akeley, a major figure at the American Museum of Natural History, became absorbed in a project to compile an accurate record of animals whose survival was by no means certain (Haraway 1989; Bodry-Sanders 1991; Imperato and Imperato 1992). They spent long periods in Kenya during the 1920s, especially in the dry north at Mount Marsabit. It was an isolated spot, where the wildlife was less nervous than in areas more frequented by hunters; a small lake, which they called Lake Paradise, attracted many thirsty animals which they could capture on film from their hides. Much of their film taken in the 1920s concentrated on animals in their habitat. Akeley, who had developed a lighter, more manoeuvrable camera, visited them in Kenya; so did George Eastman, head of Kodak, who recognized the potential of their work. Both Kearton and the Johnsons wrote many illustrated books, so that film and publishing reinforced each other from the start (Guggisberg 1977; also see Imperato and Imperato 1992 for a bibliography).

The Johnsons, in particular, transformed wildlife film and Armand Denis (b.1897) entered the field just as their work was receiving its peak exposure. His career also displays the tension between a rather commercial, exploitative approach to animals and careful conservationism, which became more marked from the late 1940s. Denis opened his autobiography, *On Safari*, with a typical manifesto: 'I have had two great passions in my life—travel and animals' (1963:15). Similar sentiments were expressed by others in the field. Belgian-born and Oxford-trained, he worked as a research chemist in the USA in the 1920s and collected unusual animals. With money he made from inventing a method of volume-control for radios, he financed a filming trip to Bali. When the film stock was damaged, he made contact with Kodak and worked for them. His Bali film, *Goona Goona*, satisfied a fascination for the exotic and was a hit in Paris and New York, where Goona Goona milkshakes went on sale in Times Square.

Zoos and circuses were popular in the 1930s, and the task of stocking them with a variety of large wild animals became the basis for a particularly fertile narrative of masculine prowess, capture, and control. RKO, one of the biggest US film studios, released *Bring 'em Back Alive* in 1932, starring Frank Buck, who had already achieved some renown in this sphere. Denis was employed to help on its successor, *Wild Cargo* (1934). The films focused on the drama of capture as well as ersatz battles between animals. An old tiger, which was to have fought with Frank Buck in a pit, drowned in a torrential downpour; Buck resolved the problem by being filmed wrestling hand to hand with the corpse (Denis 1963: 62). *King Kong*, released in 1933, achieved its dramatic tension by inverting these same themes of capture. Control was lost over the wild ape-like monster, which threatened both the symbols of purity, a white woman, and of modernity, a skyscraper (Haraway 1989: 162).

Denis reacted strongly against his experience of popular animal cinematography and in the mid-1930s made a film independently about big game in the Albert Park, Belgian Congo. He remained involved with some of the more dubious aspects of the African wildlife enterprise, such as the search for the four-tusked elephant of the Ituri forest with the grandiose New York Explorers Society. In 1940, when the war interfered with filming, he started a chimpanzee farm in Florida, partly for research on the origins of cancer, partly as a tourist attraction. He was only one of many who helped to fuel a market for exotic animals which was proving highly destructive. Wild animals were still there to be sold, possessed, researched on, caged, and displayed. In 1950, he was employed on the MGM remake of *King Solomon's Mines* on location in East Africa, a story which glorified the great white hunter.

But he also developed a lyrical, celebratory natural history film, which reached fruition in *Savage Splendour*, released in 1949. It is, from our vantage point, a sometimes uneasy fusion of people and animals in the 'wild'. And it did feature animal capture, notably of a rhino and giraffe by lassoo, a technique which Denis (1963: 263), like Colonel Jones, felt would prove that large animals could be captured for zoos or moved to safe reserves without loss of life. But considerable footage was 'true to nature' and by constructing an underwater tank Denis managed to secure perhaps the first film of hippos in 'their monumental underwater ballet' at Mzima springs in Kenya (1963: 246). The aim of the film was to record and educate, to view the wild rather than to capture it. It was RKO's most profitable feature film of the year and its reception suggested strongly that tastes were shifting.

In 1950 Denis married Michaela, then a fashion designer 'moving among the smart set in New York', who also claimed she had 'devoured animal books' and developed an 'African fixation' as a child in London

(Denis 1955: 11, 22). As in the case of the Johnsons, the Denises became a glamorous, media-friendly team. One of Michaela's first jobs was to stand in for Deborah Kerr when animal shots were required for *King Solomon's Mines*. During a visit to Britain in 1953, to promote a further African film, *Below the Sahara*, Armand Denis was invited to show footage and talk on BBC television. 'The public response was quite extraordinary. In all my years of film making I had never known anything like it. A week or two later . . . we did another half-hour programme . . . It seemed that we had become famous' (1963: 280).

The Denises did not find success in a vacuum. A mass market for animal films and books—as well as illustrated magazines such as *National Geographic*—was well established and the early 1950s seem to have been a particularly fertile period for a newly sympathetic approach. Hans Hass (1973) was making prize-winning underwater films in the 1940s and early 1950s. Konrad Lorenz, 'the man who talks with animals', published his popularization of advances in ethology, *King Solomon's Ring*, in 1952. The Disney Corporation produced the first of their 'True Life Adventure' series, *The Living Desert*, in 1953. Jacques Cousteau's best-selling *The Silent World* appeared in the same year and the film version soon afterwards (Cousteau, 1953; Munson, 1989). Gerald Durrell's *Overloaded Ark* (1953), about a collecting trip to Cameroon, was the first of his spate of books. Bernhard Grzimek, zoo director and champion of African wildlife, catered to a similar readership soon afterwards (1956; 1960).

Animals had featured on British television's *Zoo Hour* in the 1940s, when George Cansdale, superintendent of London Zoo, brought some of his charges to the Alexandra Palace studios (Attenborough 1980: 7). This was a didactic exercise to demonstrate anatomy, behaviour, and party tricks, a tradition continued by Johnny Morris, based at Bristol Zoo, in *Animal Magic* in the 1960s. Even if Cansdale's animals were captive, their unpredictability, whether urinating or escaping, could make good television. David Attenborough, a young television producer with a zoology degree, made a series of three programmes with Julian Huxley to illustrate animal colourings and shapes.

The Denis's BBC contract did, however, represent something new: a commitment to location filming of animals in their habitat in a regular half hour slot. They made Nairobi a permanent base, built their dream house there, and assembled a filming team. Armand produced his own films, Michaela wrote books, and their long-running series helped to define television natural history and attract attention to Kenya's parks. The 'breath-taking animal sequences which thrill millions', Michaela recorded (1955: 65), were only 'the highspots of weeks and even months of routine work, of constant disappointment, and backbreaking journeys'. Kenya was becoming a significant submetropole of natural history filmmaking, drawing on the infrastructure of colonial rule (despite Mau Mau) and on networks of specialists, including the Leakeys, white game-rangers, and African intermediaries (Denis 1955; 1967). Denis began to make explicitly conservationist films, for example illustrating how the crude wire traps set by poachers cut into the legs of elephants, and explained his switch to television partly in terms of its potential for such messages; feature-film distributors were still hesitant on this front.

In turn, their programme, and the growing television audience, provided a platform for Peter Scott's *Look* series and Attenborough's *Zoo Quest*, both broadcast in 1954 (Parsons 1982; Attenborough 1980). The first *Zoo Quest*, in some senses a step backwards, filmed an animal capture expedition to Sierra Leone, but it also aimed at a more scientific approach and transmitted concern for small exotic animals as well as large. George Michael, a Lebanese-South African jazz musician, who ran a gun shop in Pretoria and organized hunting safaris for an elite tourist market, made a feature-length film called *African Fury* in 1952 (Michael, 1958; 1959). On a trip to the United States to sell his film, he conceived of a family television programme *The Michaels in Africa*. Its success, his wife believed (1958: 98), came from its sincerity of purpose: 'we don't use actors, and we never fake shots to make them look better than they might otherwise appear.' There was no television outlet for them in South Africa, but their material was screened in Britain, the USA, and Europe.

The involvement of George and Joy Adamson in the linked production of books and films, as authors and subjects, illustrates some further key developments. Born in India in 1906, George Adamson found work in 1938 as a game warden in Kenya after a chequered career of hunting and trading (Adamson 1968; 1986). Based in Isiolo, north of Mount Kenya, where the fertile highlands end, he fell in love with the arid north and then with Joy in 1942. She was an Austrian botanical illustrator, already on her second marriage, talented and impetuous. Her relationship with Adamson, whom she married in 1944, was always deeply troubled, although it created important opportunities for both of them.

As part of his duties, Adamson shot a lioness in 1956 which was believed to have attacked a Boran homestead; he found himself with three motherless cubs of about ten days old which he brought home. It was by no means unusual for Africans or Europeans to keep wild animals. The Keartons had a pet chimpanzee, the Johnsons a gibbon, the Denises kept a menagerie in Nairobi, and so did the Michaels in Pretoria, including a leopard, a springbok, and a lion in the garden. Joy had already kept unusual pets, and in earlier years, when she was drawing plants on Mount Kenya, she had stayed with Raymond Hook, who trained cheetahs for hunting and racing—a practice which had been common in India (House 1995: 55; Divyabhanusinh 1995). In Zambia, soon afterwards, Norman Carr (1962), warden of the new Kafue National Park, found himself with three motherless lions cubs, of which he adopted two. (The third went on to participate in the film *Cleopatra*.)

'At once', Adamson (1968: 219) recalled, 'Joy took absolute possession of the cubs':

How little did Joy or I imagine that the story of the smallest of the three cubs, and the cubs she herself would have one day, would be translated into thirty-three languages, sell several million copies, be made into a film and, as we hope and believe, make a lasting impact on the way in which human beings regard wild animals.

Two cubs were sent to zoos in Europe, but they kept Elsa, who went everywhere with them. At two years old, the lioness started hunting local stock and they decided, after some conflict with the authorities, to put her back into the wild—a long and difficult process.

Joy Adamson wrote about the experience in a short book, *Born Free*, which appeared in 1960, with its extraordinary photographs. Collins, who published the text with maximum publicity, had been looking to expand in this area and became an important outlet for popular wildlife books. In the next couple of years, the Adamsons maintained some contact with Elsa, who gave birth to three cubs, and Joy wrote two further books, *Living Free* and *Forever Free* (1961; 1962). A children's book was produced, David Attenborough made a film, and Joy travelled the world on a speaking tour, promoting her publications and raising money for a trust fund she had established for animal conservation. *Born Free* sold one million copies in England and five million copies overall; it is still one the easiest books to find in the nature section of second-hand bookshops.

In 1964, George Adamson participated in a film based on their experiences, produced by Carl Foreman who had made *Guns of Navarone* and *Dr Zhivago*. Both the film crew and the lead actors, Virginia McKenna and Bill Travers, were determined that they should capture the spirit of *Born Free* as closely as possible. George again domesticated and lived with lions on a daily basis, in an even more intense way than before: film produced a reality which was as extraordinary as the earlier events it was portraying. Partly because of the publicity around the books, the film had an enormous impact when it was released. The experience of making it deeply influenced Travers and McKenna, also a husband-and-wife team. She wrote that Adamson's 'attitude towards lions, and indeed all living creatures, was our chief influence during those very difficult months of filming, and will always be a guiding light to us on questions of animal treatment, animal-human co-existence in the world' (McKenna 1970: 36). Already animal lovers, the 'incredible experience of working with the lions' persuaded them to devote their energies to conservation.

Adamson managed to secure some of the lions involved in the film, and repeated the process of restoring them to the wild in Meru reserve. Travers filmed this as a documentary called *The Lions are Free* (1967). It included a scene at Whipsnade Zoo in England, where two of the film lions had been taken, showing them bounding up to greet McKenna, but trapped by a fence (McKenna 1970: 42). The film was shown three times in 1967 on prime-time US television to estimated audiences of 35 million, and netted large profits. Travers and McKenna later made films in Scotland of Gavin Maxwell's *Ring of Bright Water*, and in Tsavo National Park with the Sheldricks. The drama of Elsa's life and its aftermath played to a large Western audience.

When the Adamsons required veterinary attention for their lions in the 1960s, they turned to Drs Toni and Sue Harthoorn. Sue Hart trained at the Royal Veterinary College in London, married a South African in 1950, and lived on a farm in the Eastern Transvaal, where she started a veterinary practice. In 1957, she met James Stevenson-Hamilton, legendary retired first warden of the nearby Kruger National Park, a year before his death. Hart (1995: ix, 77) maintained strong contact with Stevenson-Hamilton's wife Hilda (who kept zebra on her farm) and later suggested that the couple had greatly influenced her to focus on wild animals. She wrote animal stories and 'spread the gospel of conservation' in her *Dr Sue* series on South African radio, later transposed to BBC Playschool (Hart 1973).

Toni Harthoorn, a friend of hers from veterinary college working in Kenya, was a pioneer in the use of drugs to immobilize animals (Harthoorn 1970). In 1958 he experimented with these techniques to transplant antelopes. In 1959, he participated in Operation Noah, rescuing animals threatened by the flooding of the Zambezi valley during the construction of the Kariba dam (Lagus 1959). He was called in because the team, while successful with many smaller animals, could not move black rhino without immobilization (Hart 1995: 83). He worked with both Denis and Adamson, and the Natal Parks Board requested his help in moving white rhino, a successful operation which resulted in transfers of this rare species to the Kruger National Park, Zimbabwe and Kenya (Player, 1972). During his visits to South Africa, he met Sue Hart again; they married and moved to Kenya.

Immobilization techniques had tremendous potential in the veterinary context, in scientific work on live animals, such as weighing, measuring, tagging, and radio tracing, as well as in conservation. The new drugs anaesthetized animals quickly and evenly, so that they did not damage themselves, and there was an effective antidote. They also had implications for the management of animals for film, and the techniques themselves became the subject of television broadcasts. Film soon also found the Harthoorns. Ivan Tors, an American director who made the successful *Flipper the Dolphin* series, came to Kenya to shoot *Cowboy in Africa*, at much the same time as Foreman was filming *Born Free*. Sue Hart acted as vet, animal manager, and minder of the African child actor, Charles Malinda (Hart 1969: 139 ff.) The film explored the idea of ranching wild animals, already being developed in southern Africa, as a temporary means of saving them. Its villain tried to set the animals free, but the animals, understanding their best interests, returned. Many species had to be captured to make the film, and immobilization was essential. Despite the rather dubious message, great trouble was taken to train the animals. 'Nothing was faked', Hart protested, except when the rhino captured for the film battered off its horn, and had to star with a rubber replacement.

Using the Harthoorns as models, Tors developed the *Daktari* series ('doctor' in Swahili), shown widely in the USA and Europe in the late 1960s and early 1970s. *Daktari* became big business, with spin-offs like the *Daktari Annual*. Its hero Marsh Tracy expounded many of the values which people like the Adamsons and Harthoorns were trying to publicize, although this did include advice on how to capture animals (for benign causes, of course). In a nice inversion of reality, in one story called 'Fame comes to Clarence' (the louche lion), Tracy is approached by an oily American film director with 'pig-like eyes', who solicits his help, only to be told that Daktari was 'not interested in our animals as film stars, only as patients' (Morrisey 1967: 5). The *Daktari* films did not, however, call directly on African networks, as they were shot in 'Wameru', southern California. Sue Hart called her autobiographical book *Life with Daktari*.

While they did not achieve anything like the personal profile of the Adamsons, the Harthoorn's house in Nairobi was a meeting point for people associated with wildlife and film. Sue Hart was involved with the animal orphanage in Nairobi National Park. Perhaps her most interesting initiative was a TV series called *Animal Ark*, made for Kenyan, not metropolitan audiences and acted by Kenyan children with African producers. Morris Mwenda, television controller after independence, was keen to develop a children's programme which did not directly transmit British material and values. Hart (1969: 168) saw it as an opportunity to continue her South African work and spread the conservationist message: 'I concluded—and confirmed—my suspicions that the African child knows far less about wild African animals than the European.' Knowledge about animals, Hart argued, would quickly lead to love and care for them.

FILM, LITERATURE, AND WILDLIFE

My sources have largely been autobiographies and animal books, many well illustrated, as well as biographical accounts and films. Our subjects were eager to express their ideas, promote their causes, and advertise their motives, although their books were sometimes quickly written and are frustratingly short on historical detail. Let me try to draw some general themes from their accounts without losing sight of their individual emphases.

Some of those discussed, such as Toni Harthoorn, were primarily scientists, some were park wardens or self-trained writers and researchers, and others, such as Armand Denis, were professional filmmakers who had to be alert to the mass market they served. But they were all animal lovers and their work was increasingly sensitive to ecological thinking which saw people as part of nature, to conservationist ideas which advocated protected areas for wildlife, and to filming techniques which presented animals in their habitats. As privileged interlocutors with wild animals, they were all also experimenting with and publicizing what they felt to be a new set of relationships with and images of animals. They were not necessarily the first to do so, but they had access to the combined force of literature, photography, film, and television.

The Denises, Adamsons and Harthoorns transmitted a strong affection, even love, for animals. Occasionally this is expressed with intentional humour. Armand Denis, discussing his turtle collection in the 1920s, recalled that 'my love was an all or nothing affair' (1963: 31). But throughout his life, Denis surrounded himself with unusual animals and tried to relate to them on an individual basis. When he and Michaela settled in Nairobi, they developed a 'long and agreeable friendship with Voodoo the vulture', which they had found injured. Voodoo was free, but followed them when they were out walking and filming, swooping down to perch nearby or on Denis's head. He was 'remarkably gentle . . . He would never peck or misbehave' (Denis 1963: 284). Their house in Nairobi was home to many pets and half-wild animals. On one occasion they briefly adopted a baby elephant; on another, they tried to tame an aardvark. Denis (1963: 317) ended his book: 'I am still happiest when I am with animals, particularly if I can tame them or live close to them in the wild.'

Joy Adamson, George thought, was also happiest when she was on safari or deeply involved with animals. She kept the rock hyrax Pati as a pet for many years; it helped to domesticate the lion cubs in 1956. After Elsa, Joy's energy went into Pippa, the cheetah (Adamson 1969). *Born Free* was not only a minutely observed record of a lion growing up in captivity; what made it unique were the frequent descriptions of emotional interaction between Elsa and the Adamsons. We read about 'gentle caresses', 'smacks' (by the lion), playfulness, and humour. Elsa's expressions were interpreted by the Adamsons and, in turn, she was seen to understand theirs. Elsa could apparently experience emotional conflict, like a child in relation to parents, even over 'the meaning of "No" . . . when tempted by an antelope' (Adamson 1960: 32). There was a good deal about trust. When the lioness formed a relationship with a wild lion, 'she returned to George's tent for a few moments, put her paw affectionately around him and moaned softly, as if to say to him "You know that I love you, but I have a friend outside to whom I simply *must* go"' (Adamson 1960: 129). The pictures expressed it all: as one caption had it—'Elsa affectionate as ever' (Adamson 1960: 97).

The classic images of George Adamson are those of his walks with Elsa and, later, with the film lions Boy and Girl, his back to them while they followed like large dogs. Talking about the filming of *Born Free*, George noted: 'Most of the people of the unit were extremely nice and friendly but their way of life was not mine. There were too many dramas and "goings on" for my peace of mind. I felt safer with the lions' (1968: 255). As part of training the lioness Mara, he moved his tent into her enclosure:

For the next three months she slept regularly in it, usually stretched out on the floor alongside my bed and sometimes on it. Although many of the nights were far from reposeful, particularly when Mara decided to share the bed, she never gave me any cause for anxiety regarding my personal safety. (1968: 258)

In the preparatory work with another lioness, who had to do a bedroom scene with Bill Travers, Adamson spent 'nights with her in the room . . . Before dawn I would be woken up by feeling a rough tongue rasping my face and her heavy body pinning me to the bed' (1968: 261).

Hart wrote: 'one only had to be with George and his lions, [to] sense and see their unique relationship . . . a sort of man-to-man understanding which . . . broke the barriers of previous animal–man communication' (1969: 56). When she arrived to attend to the film lion Ugas's eye, she recounted how George summoned him: ' "Oogas", he called, pitching his voice in such as way that it sounded like the call of a lion . . . over and over again until the lion appeared, walked straight over to him, leaned on him and purred loudly. It was the most amazing sight I had ever seen' (1969: 52). Describing Joy Adamson and a baby leopard, she noted the 'incredible play of emotions' (1969: 87).

Sue Hart herself expressed profound attachment to animals, including a baby elephant: 'not very long after my first meeting I grew to love that little elephant as I had never loved an animal before in spite of the fact that it was not my own' (1969: 193). In a discussion of Stinkie, a baby rhino reared in the animal orphanage, Hart approvingly quoted Yuilleen Kearney's argument that 'a baby animal can sense whether you really love it . . . When it knows that, then it grows confident. It *knows* because it can scent your love' (1969: 189). A caption to a photo of Hart with a chimp has: 'Moment of love: Hugo and the author' (Hart 1995: 23). She described how the animals in *Cowboy in Africa*, which the film villain had set free, returned:

with gentle guidance they allowed themselves to be herded into the corrals where they knew that food, water and sanctuary awaited them. It was like something out of the Bible; gone were fear and apprehension, the barriers between man and beast. The scene contained a dream-like, almost fairy-tale quality that made one want to rub one's eyes in disbelief. (1969: 152)

Household affections were not only reciprocally transmitted between humans and animals, but seen to be operating between different species. One of the most striking images expressing this is Hart's picture of Helen the baby elephant, Stinkie the rhino, and Maureen, a child, resting together, a tricycle in the background (Hart 1969: facing 192).

If the drama of earlier animal literature and film had been the hunt, the charge, the capture, this phase depended on interaction and the play of emotion between people and animals, a theme which has remained important to the present in films such as *Free Willy*. Natural history documentaries tended to depart, if hesitantly, from these strategies in the late 1960s. There were already well-established 'true to nature' alternatives: for example those espoused by the BBC Natural History Unit (established 1957), especially in filming British birds (Parsons 1971; 1982). The Unit had difficulties with the Denis's series soon after they took it over in 1958. Despite its popularity, the presenters were seen to be too intrusive. In later years, people were more often extracted from the narrative and, where presenters remained involved, they focused more on the animals themselves; filmmakers sought to avoid anthropomorphization and imputing human emotions to animals.

But, again, we should not see too sharp a break in the type of film screened on television. The BBC Natural History Unit was hardly consistent in initiating *Animal Magic* in 1962; Johnny Morris, filmed with animals in Bristol Zoo, was even more present than the Denises, although his style was different. Moreover, people like the Denises and Adamsons also saw themselves as representing nature more accurately. Like the zoologists of this post-war era, they were deeply aware of the importance of understanding animal behaviour in the context of notionally undisturbed natural habitats. Their strategies for handling animals depended to a significant degree not just on kindness, but on study and experience of instinctive animal responses—especially how to avoid aggression. (In their view, aggressiveness had been exaggerated as a trait of large mammals, even if part of the attraction of their films was a sense of immanent danger and wonder at the filmmakers' bravery.) Moreover, it may be possible to argue that the depiction of intense human–animal interactions, by grasping Western imaginations, helped to open the way for a more animal-centric vision. Dispassionate strategies, it may be added, could also dissemble, in that wild animals were now inevitably affected by encroachments of human society, not least during filming. In openly depicting this, the early presenters were in some ways ahead of their time (House 1995: 244).

Emotional involvement with wild animals, so explicitly expressed in print and film in the 1950s and 1960s, blurred the boundaries of the wild and domestic. All of our subjects reared injured or motherless animals, which became part of their households for a time. They were, in some senses, making pets of wild animals, including the largest and most dangerous, although these animals were more than pets in that they often demanded more attention. Collapsing the barriers between people and animals was seen as important for human society as well. When the Denises visited the southern Maasai game reserve to film lion sequences for *Below the Sahara*, they found that the warden kept 'two half-grown lion cubs, and seven dogs' as pets. Michaela (1955: 59–60) wrote that 'out of the bush they created a Garden of Eden where they lived in complete concord with wild animal life', achieving 'what more than half the world is looking for and will never find: a new Golden Age'. In her more intense moments, Joy Adamson saw herself as an innovator in the progress of civilization. These authors expressed not so much a yearning, in the manner of their contemporary, van der Post, to celebrate ancient human archetypes epitomized by the San who were seen to live close to nature, but, rather, an alternative vision of modernity in those decades of technological and scientific hubris. Although they have not perhaps been claimed, they did surely influence some strands of popular modern environmentalism, especially its animal-centric anglophone forms.

A significant feature of these relationships was not just an appreciation for other species, but for individuals amongst them. The Adamsons' lion experiments came under considerable criticism. Local African people feared for their stock. Wildlife officials argued that animals reintroduced to the wild, but habituated to people, might be unpredictable and dangerous in game reserves, and, second, that lions were by no means a threatened species. George Adamson justified his work after *Born Free* partly on the grounds that the animals deserved their freedom, but partly because these were not just any lions, they were individuals.

Both individuality and partial domestication were signified by the naming of all these animals—an element in their absorption into human households, or interactive contexts, where they could become the object of warmth and care (Thomas 1983: 113–15). They were generally given the names of animals, rather than people: lions were called Gog and Magog, Boy and Girl; elephants became Whiskey and Soda; Stinkie, initially Tinker Bell, was named after its smell; even Voodoo the vulture 'would answer to his name and come waddling over' (Denis 1963: 283). There also are examples of the use of European and African names, usually reserved for people. Naming wild animals helped to project them to the public, to incorporate them partially into human civil society, and hence to accord them rights, at least of survival—a long-debated issue. I suspect that the emphasis on families and domestication struck a chord with audiences during the 1950s, a conservative post-war decade, when stability was valued. Not only human but animal families were projected as desirable states to the public. *Born Free* ends, as does Carl Foreman's photobook of its making, with 'the family—Elsa, her mate and the cubs relax on their rock' (Foreman 1966: endpage). (He was dissuaded from an alternative scenario in which Virginia McKenna was to cuddle Elsa's three cubs.) For Western audiences, these were also a more comfortable vision of Africa than images of Mau Mau in Kenya, Nkrumah in Ghana, or apartheid and the ANC in South Africa.

Film, and especially television, was a medium which lent itself to the project of familiarising Western audiences with wildlife. Film captured movement, dramatic encounter, and violence and had enormous advantages in transmitting energy and excitement, even in the black and white pictures to which television was limited at the time. Animal film had often concentrated on dramatic moments of running, fighting, and killing. These remained important motifs but television, together with new techniques, helped enlarge the scope by capturing such activities as mating and giving birth. It is true that African animals were perhaps no longer exotic to the film-watching public nor intrinsically photogenic: for much of the time they graze or rest. But through cutting and juxta-position of scenes filmed at different times, even the most prosaic activ-ities could be spliced into an absorbing narrative. Action could be achieved partly by compressing time on film. And on television, images of wild animals were brought, literally, into people's front rooms to produce what Haraway (1989: 42) called the 'absurdly intimate filmic reality we now take for granted'. No moment of animal life was immune. Through film and television, Western audiences could see a vastly enlarged scope of animal behaviour which few had encountered in the flesh.

The language of film, as it had developed for Western audiences, also contained a powerful strain of sentimentality. Feature producers such as Carl Foreman clearly saw how natural history and drama could be married to make animals cosy. Perhaps this combination of new know-ledge and sentimentality helped to transfer the protective impulses which British people, though not them alone, felt towards pets. Denis could argue: 'there are grave drawbacks to television and I would be the last to underestimate them, but the mass wave of sympathy and understanding it has produced for wildlife during the last ten years must certainly be counted among its positive benefits' (1963: 316). Even when film styles changed, this intimacy was retained and enlarged through colour, slow motion, underwater cameras, cameras placed to represent the vantage point of the animal, and time-lapse photography. As the number of many rare species dwindles, we know them, visually, better than ever before, 'an index of our power over nature, as well as our distance from it' (Wilson 1992: 122).

I have used the idea of renaturing not because these filmmakers and authors were changing the behaviour of whole species, but to emphasize that they were consciously projecting wild animals in a new way and that human understanding of nature is clothed in a cultural cloak. In the main, they were not simply attempting to domesticate wild animals. All of them believed that the best place for wild animals was in the wild, even if human care was sometimes necessary and even if, ironically, the wild now had to be protected. They were against hunting and only in favour of capture in specific circumstances, although their special role at the inter-face between humans and animals, and their professional need to handle animals, might justify the occasional transgression.

Just as the nature of wild animals was being reinterpreted, so, too, by the 1950s and 1960s, returning animals to the wild did not necessarily imply losing them completely. Few places had in the past escaped the human imprint and the areas designated as game reserves and national parks, some of which had been recently and regularly occupied by African people, were increasingly being managed by specialists. Some species could be encouraged, others discouraged, depending on their perceived balance. Animals were being moved between areas; predators were allowed in some reserves but not in others. Waterholes were provided to facilitate viewing as well as animal survival in the smaller areas now reserved for them; except in the largest reserves, animals could no longer migrate. Debates developed about whether to cull and burn or whether to let nature take its course. In a few cases, the future of species depended on human management. Light aircraft, immobilizing darts, radio tracking, roads, landrovers, and microbuses shouldered their way into these preserves making them and their animals more accessible to scientists and tourists alike. Patrick Marnham (1987: 24–5) has decried such strategies as 'elephant farming', even though they were clearly less managerial than the commercial game farms being developed in Southern Africa; his was the voice of backward-looking romanticism. Nevertheless, the very fascination with imagined wilderness—fed by some of the visual representations discussed—helped to create the conditions for this simultaneous protection and intrusion.

I suggested at the outset that these popular representations were not without their ramifications for Africa. The images of African animals projected at this time were essentially for Western people, a moment largely, if not exclusively, in European and American culture. They were part of a late imperial phase which asserted the need to conquer and control nature in distant parts of the world, from the ocean depths to the top of Everest, even if those at the interface with nature also admitted to doubts—and assumed responsibilities—in connection with that conquest. Thus although elements of the conservationist project were deeply subversive of an earlier imperial ethos, they were not directly a challenge to the pre-eminence of western ideas.

Such approaches also drew on well-established colonial ideas that Africans tended to be careless of nature while whites, if sometimes initially penitent butchers, nevertheless had taken upon themselves the mantel of protection and care. Although the concept of trusteeship was being abandoned in respect of African people at this time, as they surged towards independence, a creed of responsibility was ever more strongly emphasised in relation to African animals. It is striking that natural history literature and film at this period—and even to the present—often tends to write out or diminish the presence of African people who had lived so long with wild animals.

It is important not to oversimplify this point for three reasons. First, especially up to the 1940s, many filmmakers focused on both African people and animals as part of natural Africa. This approach could still include uncomfortable images of nearly naked people, especially women, which had long titillated Western audiences. But more sensitive portrayals, reflecting a new cultural relativism, projected an element of symbiosis between Africans and the natural world they inhabited. One of Kearton's last major filming efforts tried to weave a narrative around such a construction of the relations between African people and animals. Denis shot dramatic sequences of a gorilla hunt by forest people, an activity which he saw as justified: 'To the protein-starved forest dwellers hunting is a necessity not a luxury as it is with the white man. The risks are more equal, and I tell myself that it will go on whether I witness it or not' (1963: 196). Joy Adamson's successful animal books created the opportunity for publication of an artistic project on which she had worked before: a careful record of Kenya's 'tribal' people in typical dress (House 1995: 175, 292). There was also a strong tradition of anthropological film, reflecting shifts in that discipline, which continues to the present.

Second, African people were in fact essential auxiliaries and intermediaries in every phase of these ventures. The literature produced, to a greater extent than the photographs and film, does often name and discuss those involved. It is true that they usually appear as the porters and servants, literally and figuratively, of an essentially European project. For example, even though the Johnsons became close to the Africans who worked with them, their films pandered to their audiences' sense of racial superiority (Imperato and Imperato 1992: 101). The Michaels depended on an African employee, called only Penga, to feed their pet lion. Although it was Penga who developed a day-to-day relationship with the lion, at least until he was mauled, he is depicted in Marjorie Michael's book (1958: 73–8) as rather hapless and irresponsible (see also Michael, G. 1959: 52). Amidst a written reverie on Africa, Michaela Denis includes a typically colonial discussion of the weaknesses of her servant, Kirmani (1967: 24). Yet there is no doubt that Africans are part of the record.

And, third, especially but not only after independence in the early 1960s, some of the authors are more generous in their recognition of African involvement. George Adamson worked for sustained periods with African communities and assistants whom he reports as deeply involved in his projects; the pictorial record gives an inkling of this, notably striking photographs of a Turkana assistant, Makedde, with Elsa. *Born Free* included both African and Indian actors and some attempt was made to win the support of the new Kenyan government. Sue Hart in particular tried to incorporate African people in filming and viewing wildlife. She goes out of her way to appreciate African skills: for example Malutu, 'appointed to keep the rhino [Stinkie] company' was described as 'a young African who had a way with animals' (1969: 189). After she returned to South Africa in 1972, she pursued conservation projects in African educational institutions.

Despite these qualifications, this phase of natural history film and literature was ultimately a drama played out between African animals and white men and women. Together with many other historical processes, it fed into changing Western attitudes as well as the exclusive reservation of parts of Africa for wildlife, scientists, and tourists. But it is important not to leave the analysis here. Debates and conflicts on these issues have become increasingly central to wildlife management and, more recently, also the subject of fascinating environmental films which go beyond the earlier natural history genres to incorporate political discussion of the costs and benefits of conservation. Local African knowledge and skills, always an element in conservation projects, are now being more explicitly researched and celebrated. African societies have themselves undergone far-reaching transformation and it cannot be assumed that they would have found it possible to continue to live with animals. The parks and their animals are an important heritage which thus far some African governments, at least, have been reluctant to renounce.

REFERENCES

Adamson, G. (1968). *Bwana Game: The Life Story of George Adamson*. London: Collins and Harvill Press.

Adamson, G. (1986). *My Pride and Joy: An Autobiography*. London: Collins Harvill.

Adamson, J. (1960). *Born Free: A Lioness of Two Worlds*. London: Collins.

Adamson, J. (1961). *Living Free: The Story of Elsa and Her Cubs*. London: Collins.

Adamson, J. (1962). *Forever Free*. London: Collins.

Adamson, J. (1969). *The Spotted Sphinx*. London: Collins and Harvill Press.

Attenborough, D. (1980). *The Zoo Quest Expeditions: Travels in Guyana, Indonesia and Paraguay*. London: Penguin Books.

Bodry-Sanders, P. (1991). *Carl Akeley: Africa's Collector; Africa's Saviour*. New York: Paragon House.

Carr, N. (1962). *Return to the Wild: A Story of Two Lions*. London: Collins.

Cousteau, J. Y. (1953). *The Silent World*. London: Hamish Hamilton.

Denis, A. (1963). *On Safari: The Story of My Life*. London: Collins.

Denis, M. (1955). *Leopard in my Lap*. London: W.H. Allen.

Denis, M. (1967). *Ride a Rhino*. London: Sphere Books (first published, 1959).

Divyabhanusinh (1995). *The End of a Trail: The Cheetah in India*. New Delhi: Banyan Books.

Durrell, G. M. (1953). *The Overloaded Ark*. London: Faber and Faber.

Foreman, C. (1966). *A Cast of Lions: The Story of the Making of the Film Born Free*. London: Collins, Fontana Books.

Grzimek, B. (1956). *No Room for Wild Animals*. London: Thames and Hudson.

Grzimek, B. (1960). *Serengeti Shall Not Die*. London: Hamish Hamilton.

Guggisberg, C. A. W. (1977). *Early Wildlife Photographers*. Newton Abbot: David and Charles.

Haraway, D. (1989). *Primate Visions: Gender, Race, and Nature in the World of Modern Science*. New York: Routledge.

Hart, S. (1969). *Life with Daktari: Two Vets in East Africa*. London: The Companion Book Club.

Hart, S. (1973). *In the Wild*. Johannesburg: Africana Book Society.

Hart, S. (1995). *Dr Sue: A Vet in Africa*. Johannesburg: Ravan Press.

Harthoorn, A. M. (1970). *The Flying Syringe: Ten Years of Immobilising Wild Animals in Africa*. London: Godfrey Bles.

Hass, H. (1973). *Challenging the Deep: Thirty Years of Undersea Adventure*. New York: William Morrow and Company.

House, A. (1995). *The Great Safari: The Lives of George and Joy Adamson*. London: Harper Collins.

Imperato, P. J. and E. M. (1992). *They Married Adventure: The Wandering Lives of Martin and Osa Johnson*. New Brunswick, NJ: Rutgers University Press.

Kearton, C. (1935). *Adventures with Animals and Men*. London: Longman, Green and Co.

Lagus, C. (1959). *Operation Noah*. London: Fauna Preservation Society, William Kimber.

Lewinsohn, R. (1954). *Animals, Men and Myths*. New York: Harper and Brothers.

Lorenz, K. Z. (1952). *King Solomon's Ring: New Light on Animal Ways*. London: Methuen (paperback, London: Pan Books, 1957).

Marnham, P. (1987). *Fantastic Invasion: Dispatches from Africa*. Harmondsworth: Penguin Books.

MacKenzie, J. M. (1988). *The Empire of Nature: Hunting, Conservation and British Imperialism*. Manchester: Manchester University Press.

McKenna, V. (1970). *Some of My Friends have Tails*. London: Collins and Harvill Press.

Michael, G. (1959). *The Michaels in Africa*. London: Frederick Muller.

Michael, M. (1958). *I Married a Hunter*. London: Popular Books.

Morrisey, J. L. *et al.* (1967). *Daktari Annual*. Manchester: World Distributors.

Munson, R. (1989). *Cousteau: the Captain and his World*. New York: William Morrow.

Parsons, C. (1971). *Making Wildlife Movies: An Introduction*. Newton Abbot: David and Charles.

Parsons, C. (1982). *True to Nature*. Cambridge: Patrick Stephens.

Player, I. (1972). *The White Rhino Saga*. London: Collins.

Ritvo, H. (1987). *The Animal Estate: the English and Other Creatures in the Victorian Age*. London: Penguin Books.

Scull, G. H. (1911). *Lassoing Wild Animals in Africa*. New York: Frederick A. Stokes.

Serpell, J. (1996). *In the Company of Animals: A Study of Human–Animal Relationships*. Cambridge: Cambridge University Press.

Thomas, K. (1983). *Man and the Natural World: Changing Attitudes in England 1500–1800*. London: Allen Lane.

Wilson, A. (1992). *The Culture of Nature: North American Landscape from Disney to the Exxon Valdez*. Oxford: Blackwell.

8

From Hunting to Mining: The History of Human Environmental Relations in Eastern Arnhem Land

Howard Morphy

INTRODUCTION

HUMAN beings have been in Australia for at least forty thousand years. The popularly accepted view is that, except for the last two hundred years, the history of Australia has been one of continuity and stability. The Australia that Europeans first encountered, it is thought, was a continent of hunters and gatherers that had long been cut off from the rest of the world: a continent with a stable population in balance with the resources of its environment. Its population was conservative: an unchanging people in an unchanging land. And then a little more than two hundred years ago came the catastrophe of the European invasion, in which Australia rejoined the rest of the world—a world at the end of the age of enlightenment and on the edge of the industrial revolution (see Butlin 1993: 185). The invasion was thought to have created an unbridgeable gulf between a prehistoric past that comprised forty thousand years of undifferentiated stability and a historic past connected to a present that is characterized by change. In Crosby's (1986: 18) words: 'when Captain Cook and the Australians of Botany Bay looked at each other in the eighteenth century they did so from opposite sides of the Neolithic Revolution'.

Aborigines became the archetype of people without a history, their present used to represent other people's pasts, their way of life the location of myths. Aborigines were our Stone Age past: 'So far, no fossil remains of man have been discovered in Australasia; but there is no need to seek there for fossil forms. Ancient and primitive man still survive— more primitive than any fossil form of man yet to be found in Europe'

(Spencer 1921). Aborigines became and to an extent have remained the location of our myths. They are portrayed as being in contact with the earth, spiritual people, existing in harmonious balance with the forces of nature. In the popular imagination the 'Dreamtime' becomes a fundamental symbol of the difference between Aborigines and the rest of the world, often a positive sign but nonetheless one that reinforces a sense of otherness.

This view is a myth, consisting of a set of sub-myths. The most pernicious of these have been the myth of nomadism, and the conceptualization of the nomad. Nomadism has had both positive and negative connotations to Europeans. On the one hand, the nomad is rootless, wandering, detached from place. On the other hand, in the romantic view most recently promulgated by Chatwyn (1987), nomads are free, in touch with nature, and close to the roots of the human psyche. The former view made Aborigines virtually invisible to the early colonists, not because they were unseen but because they were held to be of no account. As hunter-gatherers they were closer to animals than to humans: failing to use the resources of the land, they had no rights to the present and nothing to say about the future. They failed to make their mark on the landscape.

The real story is far more complex and much more interesting. Once we remove the myths we are able to see that the history of Aboriginal people has much more in common with the history of the rest of the world. The gap between the Aboriginal past of Australia and the colonial present, far from being unbridgeable, has been bridged many times by Aboriginal people themselves. While the invaders did not find it necessary to understand the Aborigines, the Aborigines have spent two hundred years trying to understand and influence the invaders. In the recent political history of Australia both land rights legislation and the Mabo judgement have been important steps in establishing continuity with the past. These legal events have not simply been imposed from above, although superficially it looks that way. They have happened as the culmination of a process of interactions in which Aboriginal people have finally persuaded the state of the need to recognize their rights. The gap, thus, is not unbridgeable. The European invasion was, nevertheless, an important moment, and a determining one. The moment before the invasion becomes, in the light of the invasion, a moment of immense conceptual significance and a space from which to rethink subsequent developments. From an Aboriginal perspective it is the colonizing Europeans who are the nomads, who leave too great a mark on the landscape before moving on.

THE ABORIGINAL MODE OF ADAPTATION

Rather than surveying Australia as a whole, I will focus on a small segment—on Arnhem Land in Northern Australia and the Yolngu Aboriginal people of the area. I am not taking Arnhem Land because its history is typical; there is no typical history of Australia. While common continent-wide themes can be identified, they have to be understood in the context of regional variation. As a continent Australia exhibits an enormous diversity of environments, from desert to monsoon rainforest, and over the period of human occupation its climate, vegetation, and shape have changed dramatically. The ways of life of the Aboriginal population—their social organization, material culture, and religious practice—have differed greatly in space and time. Population densities and economic activities varied with climatic change, extreme aridity even resulting in the abandonment of certain regions for a time. Arnhem Land can be used as an exemplar of this process of change and diversity.

I will begin, however, not with events but with a model of what Eastern Arnhem Land society was like at the moment of colonization, focusing in particular on the relationship between Aborigines and land. Because this differs significantly from what we know of hunter-gatherer societies elsewhere, I will refer to it as the Aboriginal mode of adaptation. My analysis draws heavily on the work of Nicholas Peterson (1972, 1975, 1986), who has produced the most clearly thought-out ecological model of Arnhem Land Aboriginal society. The model applies in a modified way to many other parts of Australia, but it is necessary to include the caveat 'where equivalent data exists'. Although Australian Aborigines are often used as the paradigm case of the balanced relationship between people and environment in hunting and gathering societies, there are almost no detailed studies of the subsistence pattern of hunter-gatherer societies in Australia or elsewhere.

It is fair to say that, until recently, understanding of the hunter-gatherer mode of adaptation was at best simplistic. We still know far more about the foraging life of animals than we do about human hunter-gatherers. Far more money goes into researching primate foraging activities. This is partly because it is much harder to gather the evidence about human hunting and gathering. The Heisenberg effect is too great, the chances of the researcher dying of malnutrition too high, and there are just too few contemporary hunter-gatherers left to study.

In the nineteenth century the modelling of hunter-gatherer societies was little concerned with how they gained their living. Hunter-gatherers were presumed to represent the earliest form of human society. On to them were projected all the myths of origin that were necessary to account for the development of 'civilized' human society and the human psyche. The model that came to prevail was the patrilineal horde, a development of the primal horde that congregated around a patriarchal super ego. As sociological language gained in sophistication, the patrilineal horde became the patrilineal clan, seen as the original form of society (Durkheim 1971). The details of the model were never filled in but it was assumed that groups of hunters and gatherers comprised men who were linked together by patrilineal descent, their children who belonged to their clan, and their wives who were members of another clan. No one ever recorded such a group on the ground or modelled how it would operate and change over time. In the 1950s and 1960s this model came to be replaced by another. The new model was ecologically based (Lee and DeVore 1968) but nearly as unfounded in empirical data. It was assumed that hunting and gathering involved utilizing the existing products of the environment rather than changing the environment to produce sources of food, and that, therefore, the constraints on hunter-gatherer life would be similar to those operating on other animal populations. There would have to be a balance between population and resources. The size of the population would be self-limiting and vary according to the carrying capacity of the land. Because in most environments seasonal factors meant that resources were differentially dispersed according to the time of the year, group size would have to vary accordingly. The catch-phrase for hunter-gatherer society became 'flexible band organization'. This model had the advantage over the patrilineal clan model in that it was not contradicted by the evidence and that it apparently took account of the ecological and demographic realities of hunter-gatherer societies. But it posited no mechanism for group organization: flexibility would somehow be achieved by some rule of nature. One of the key problems facing the hunter-gatherer researcher is 'how is this flexibility achieved?'. For Australian hunter-gatherers, at least, we have gone a long way towards answering that question in recent years.

In order to understand the relationship between hunters and gatherers and the land in Arnhem Land it is necessary to understand the relationship between two kinds of group. As we have seen, one has conventionally been termed the band, the other the clan. Bands are groups of people who live and travel together foraging off the land and distributing the products of their labour among the members. A band is associated with a particular area of land that is referred to as its range. Although the ranges of different bands may overlap a little at the edges, they are in effect life-spaces—areas of land that are able to support a given number of people over the long term. Ranges will differ in their resources according to whether they are inland or coastal, and the size of the range will likewise vary according to the carrying capacity of the land. On the whole, coastal Arnhem Land had a much higher population density than the inland: there were more bands per square kilometre of coast than per square kilometre of inland. Some ranges were also seasonally exploitable: hence, any band that occupied such a range would have to disperse at other times of the year, amalgamating with other groups on other ranges.

Clans are descent groups which have rights in certain property or resources. In Arnhem Land clans are corporate groups with respect to land and sacred property, and they have a major influence on the pattern of marriages between groups. Just as the whole of Arnhem Land is included in the ranges of one band or another, so too is the entire land divided up on the basis of clanship. Enormous cultural energy is invested in establishing and maintaing social and spiritual relationships with land. Each clan owns defined areas of land, as well as the songs, paintings, sacred objects, dances, and power names associated with it (see Williams 1986 and Morphy 1991 for detailed discussion). Language is identified in relation to clanship; each clan is said to speak a different dialect and each has its own vocabulary of names for people, plants, dogs, boats, and so on. People are believed to have conception spirits associated with the land, and on death their spirits return to the land. The pattern of relationship to the land is believed to have been set in the past by the ancestral beings who created the land, and clan lands are part of a sacred endowment.

It is tempting to characterize the difference between bands and clans as that between groups that exist on the ground and groups that exist in the head. The band is a 'real' group of people involved in the nitty-gritty task of survival, whereas the clan is a group that never meets together as a unit and which has rights in esoteric property. Even its rights in land seem fairly ethereal—they rarely involve anything as vulgar as exclusive entitlement to the resources of the land and seem more concerned with esoteric knowledge. However, viewed from another perspective, it is the clan that becomes the more concrete and the band that becomes the more abstract entity. The band varies in size according to season and is comprised of different individuals over time. During the wet season, when resources are restricted, the band is at its maximum size. Large numbers of people congregate together in one place, usually the site of a seasonally abundant resource. With the onset of the dry season people's options widen and members of the band disperse into smaller groups, often a few individuals or an extended family. While there is usually a degree of overlap over a number of years, the detailed composition of the band changes over time. Thus the band is a group which breaks up into smaller groups according the exigencies of the seasons and the environment and whose composition varies over time. The clan, on the other hand, although it seldom meets as a group, has an agreed membership, a structure of authority based on seniority and gender, and acknowledged rights in sacra and land.

Peterson's important contribution (1972, 1986) was to show that there is a close interrelationship between the clan and the band. He discovered by conducting a survey that the average size of the two groups was identical, at around fifty members. Clans varied more in size than bands, ranging from one to more than a hundred members. However, the median size for a clan was around fifty and there was evidence that the larger clans were in the process of splitting into smaller clans which would take over the resources and affiliations of clans that were nearing extinction. In the case of bands, the exigencies of hunter-gatherer life and the desiderata of social and religious life meant that the actual size of the group of people living together varied from a single family to several hundred people, but again the average size was a group of around forty to fifty individuals. Taking another perspective, Peterson was able to show that there were a similar number of clan territories and band ranges. However, far from overlapping, clan territories and band ranges appeared to be quite independent of each other.

Nonetheless, Peterson was able to demonstrate a close relationship between clan organization and the hunter-gatherer band adaptation. The functional relationship between clan and band is quite a complex one. Although bands are made up from members of many different clans they are built around a core membership of people who have close association with part or all of the range over which the band forages. The core tends to be drawn from people of the clan that owns the land or children of women of the clan. During their lifetime individuals are members of a number of different bands, but there tends to be a pattern in their membership (Peterson 1974). While they are young, children will tend to be wherever their mother is; after marriage, men will tend to spend a few years in the band of their wife's father and as they reach middle age they will tend to spend more time close to their own clan's estate. Throughout their lives people maintain a close relationship with their own clan's land, performing songs and paintings associated with it during rituals, and visiting it more frequently with advancing age. In this way people establish long-term relationships with areas of land and pass on knowledge of that land to their children, even if they spend much of their life away from it. Senior clan members provide the fulcrum around which groups coalesce, the fixed points in a mobile social landscape, in which the shape and composition of foraging groups varies according to seasonal and social factors.

Peterson argues that this system of clanship not only provides the basis for the orderly formation of foraging groups but also enables the long-term monitoring of the relationship between people and the environment. The people with the deepest environmental knowledge are in a position to regulate the size of groups that form at different times of the year. The authority vested in the elders through their long-term association with place may even facilitate population control by licensing infanticide in periods of severe hardship. In effect, this system of adaptation provides an orderly mechanism for adjusting the relationship between people and land. It operates, with some regional variation in detail, on an Australia-wide basis. The whole of Australia is divided into owned areas of land with which people establish long-term relationships. These relationships are religiously sanctioned and give people the authority to manage the land.

The unusual aspect of this system of land-management is that it creates an almost absolute separation between land-ownership and land-use. The land is owned not as an economic resource but as a spiritual endowment. While some land-owners may use the land they own, they use it as members of bands, not in their capacity as land-owners. In general, anyone who has permission can utilize the economic resources of the land. It is a system that requires cooperation on a wide basis. It is not possible for members of a clan to live exclusively off their own lands. Clan estates may consist of dispersed parcels of land often separated by a hundred kilometres or more. In many cases a clan's estate will not contain the resources necessary to feed the clan's members, even if it were logistically possible to range over it. The clan lands per se are not the ecological life spaces; it is not the clans who forage as a group over any area of land. Clan lands are arbitrary divisions of the landscape that take no account, in any simple way, of resource distribution. Band ranges cross-cut the territories of a number of different clans and the foraging bands are made up of members of a number of different clans. The system provides a mechanism for ordering the relationship between people and land and for the long-term monitoring of the environment, but it requires collaboration, negotiation, and the recognition of rights over a broad area.

The model I have just outlined is based on research undertaken after European colonization, but it really belongs to the space between the prehistoric past and the European era. It is the outcome of a process of hunter-gatherer adaptation to the changing environment of Australia and it was also the ideological basis of Aboriginal response to the colonists. In the rest of this chapter I will be taking the argument in two directions. The first involves a stepping-back in time to place the model in the context of Australian and, in particular, Arnhem Land prehistory. I will not come up with any answers as to precisely how and when the particular form of adaptation emerged; rather, I will sketch the terrain in which plausible explanations might be found. I will then move forward in time to show how Yolngu have responded to the changed environment resulting from the European invasion and European attitudes, and to consider what difference it might have made if their way of life had been accepted as valid and what lessons of mutual benefit might have been learnt as a result. My first excursion covers a period of more than fifty thousand years and my second little more than a hundred, since the effective colonization of Arnhem Land was comparatively late.

LOOKING BACK

According to current research it is most likely that Australia was first populated by the wave of fully modern humans who, some 100,000 years ago, moved out of Africa, replacing the earlier hominid populations as they went. Australia had to be populated from the sea. At no time in human history has the sea crossing been much less than 60 kilometres, that being the distance that separated the Australia-New Guinea land mass—the continent of Sahul—from Island Indonesia at the height of the great Ice Age. Landfall is likely to have been between 40,000 and 60,000 years ago, and was certainly not in Arnhem Land. For much of prehistory Arnhem Land, with its flood plains, its sinuous mangrove-lined rivers, its coastal dunes and oyster-encrusted rocks, has been an inland place (Jones 1985). The continental shelf joined Australia to New Guinea in a single land mass that was only finally separated at the Torres Strait some 7–8,000 years ago. While the coastline has fluctuated much since the first humans arrived it is likely that, whenever and wherever they did land for the first time, Arnhem Land was a long way from the sea.

The prehistory of Australia before 25,000 BP remains largely unknown. Time has compressed a thousand generations of human activity into the thin deposits of debris that on rare occasions can be found lining the floors of rock shelters. But since modern archaeology began with the work of John Mulvaney (1975), the myths of the uniform past have been dissolved and the bases of diversity have begun to emerge. The nature of archaeological evidence, its dependence on stone technology and bio-geographical data, means that, for the most part, fine-grained detail is lost.

Though in Australia rock art has added a rich complementary source of evidence (see Layton 1992), the further back in time the eye searches the fainter the image becomes.

The precise date of human arrival in Australia is unknown and we know very little of the way of life of the first Australians. It is possible that its first inhabitants had a major impact on the biogeography of Australia. Human action is one possible explanation for a whole range of environmental changes that have occurred over the past 100,000 years or more. Almost certainly the systematic use of fire by Australian foragers has had some impact on the environment (Pyne 1991). Pollen sequences from the Atherton tablelands, for example, suggest that around 45,000 years ago the *Eucalyptus* species began to make inroads into areas of tropical rainforest, a process that may have been encouraged by the regular use of fire in hunting (Singh *et al.* 1980). But most such hypotheses depend on indirect evidence, and alternative explanations can be found in the form either of climate change or the regular outbreaks of fire associated with lightening strikes. From the evidence of stone tools, the early population of Australia is not distinguishable from the population of the neighbouring region of Eastern Indonesia.

The general view of Australian hunters and gatherers which emerges from this early period right up to the Holocene is of people who were as 'advanced' as any in the world. In order to reach Australia, people must have developed, perhaps for the first time, means of long-distance water-transport. In the Kimberley region of Australia we have the world's earliest evidence of rock paintings, from 39,000 years ago (O'Connor and Fankhauser n.d.), and in Arnhem Land polished stone axes, considered to be a major advance in lithic technology, were produced more than 20,000 years ago, as early as anywhere else on earth (White 1967). At Lake Mungo in New South Wales the world's first cremation burial dates from 26,000 years ago. The high value accorded by contemporary prehistorians to innovation may reflect in part the desire of prehistorians and anthropologists to counter the nineteenth-century and popular view of Aborigines as living representatives of the Stone Age by showing that in the Stone Age Aborigines were at least as advanced as, if not more advanced than their European cousins.

As we move forward in time, evidence becomes richer and we can begin to identify some of the dynamic factors that may have resulted in the development of the form of Aboriginal adaptation that immediately preceded European colonization. Over the past 40,000 years Australia has been subject to considerable climatic change and to an ongoing process of coastal movement. There have been periods of higher rainfall in which considerable areas of inland Australia became more hospitable. With the advance of the Ice Age rainfall declined in many areas and the land mass extended outwards. As the ice-sheets melted and the sea level rose, land was lost and coastal regions were transformed.

This process has been best documented for the region of the Alligator Rivers in Western Arnhem Land. If we consider only the past 16,000 years or so, the changes have been quite dramatic and have been reflected in changes in the archaeological record (Taçon and Brockwell 1995, Hiscock forthcoming). At the beginning of this era the region was both colder and drier than it is today. The land mass was close to its maximum extent and the Arnhem Land escarpment was an inland massif 350 kilometres from the coast, occupied only sporadically by humans during favourable seasons. The magnificent rock art of the region extends back to this time and represents animals of the inland—kangaroos, emus, and extinct species such as the marsupial wolf or thylacine. Implements such as boomerangs that are no longer found in the region also occur in the rock art at this time. Around 15,000 years ago the climate began to warm up and the sea began to flood the continental shelf. By 10,000 years ago the Arnhem Land escarpment was less than 100 kilometres from the coast. The rise of the sea level continued until around 7000 BP and stabilized at its present level a thousand years later. The annual loss of coastal land during the period of the rise in sea level has been estimated at between 25 and 45 square metres per year, and at certain places and times was likely to have been quite catastrophic (Taçon and Brockwell 1995). However, in the Arnhem Land region itself the climate was becoming more and more favourable for human occupation. The steady increase in rainfall resulted in an increase in the biomass and a more stable environment for hunters and gatherers. Archaeological sites become more numerous as time goes by and the paintings on the rock surfaces over the last 10,000 years draw increasingly on coastal themes of fish and turtles.

The sometimes rapid movement of the sea would have made conditions difficult for the people who occupied the front line. It was not simply that the land was contracting: the coastal environment was continually changing, as it adjusted to new coastal topography and climatic change. Once the sea stopped moving, the problems for the hunter-gatherer population, far from being at an end, arrived at a new beginning. Around 7000–8000 BP the coastal portion of the Alligator Rivers region comprised a huge and perhaps unique mangrove forest, interspersed with fresh-water lakes. This forest remained for a period of perhaps 3,000 years, until increasing alluvial deposition from inland produced a vast salt-water plain, with the mangroves retreating to the river margins.

During this time the course of the rivers changed continuously and numerous ox-bow lakes were formed. These salt-flats were transformed as little as 1,500 years ago into fresh-water wetlands. Each of these environments required a different subsistence strategy, which in turn is reflected in the archaeological record. The mangrove swamp era saw distinctive economies on the coastal and the inland margins. Huge middens were formed along the coast, reflecting the intensive exploitation of shellfish, and a mixed economy developed in the inland river valleys on the edge of the escarpment, where people moved between exploiting the resources of the mangroves and the inland valleys (Hiscock forthcoming). With the development of the saline flats the focus of the economy seems to have moved to the edge of the mangroves and their immediate hinterland. There is some evidence that the saline environment was one of steady change and considerable unpredictability and that the period required considerable flexibility on the part of the local population. With the development of the extensive fresh-water wetlands the environment became highly productive for hunters and gatherers and the focus of the economy moved onto the floodplains, with evidence of a substantial increase in population. Perhaps 400–500 years ago a new factor entered the equation: with the annual visits of the Bugis traders from South Sulawesi, a period of intense contact with outsiders began.

As the lens of prehistory focuses in on a particular region of Australia, we begin to see the dynamic context in which Aboriginal social systems have developed. The myth of uniformity is replaced, certainly in the recent prehistoric past, by a picture of changing sea levels, transforming environments and climatic change. While the rise in sea level was concentrating the Aboriginal population into an increasingly smaller space, changes in climate and coastal environment required new strategies of resource exploitation and continual readjustment of population to resources. While many of these adjustments could be made slowly, the changing circumstances would have put a premium on flexibility.

The model of Aboriginal social organization that I have outlined could certainly be an adaptation to the changing environments that Aboriginal people have faced since colonizing the continent. Most importantly, it could respond both to short-term or seasonal changes and to long-term trends in environmental change. The Aboriginal mode of adaptation enables the establishment of long-term relationships between people and land, while at the same time encouraging the development of widespread linkages of kinship, ritual, and residence with people in surrounding areas.

The rise in sea level, the salinization of the coastal plains, and the development of the wetlands would all have required a careful monitoring of the environment by its human occupants and a sharing of knowledge on a regional basis if they were to be successfully accommodated. Aboriginal groups would have been able rapidly to share knowledge of changing environments and to respond proactively to encroachment of the salt flats or the wet season inundation of the floodplains. Their flexible social organization allowed them to modify group size on a seasonal basis and yet maintain a wider polity that could span both space and time.

Long-term changes are not, however, the most significant factors in human adaptation: rather, it is the short-term events that require an immediate and adequate response. The picture of long-term change I have outlined for the Alligator Rivers region contains within it hundreds, perhaps thousands, of short-term disasters that have been a continuing feature of Australia prehistory. The battle with drought, for example— the fact that populations in inland regions may have to abandon vast tracts of land for many years, perhaps even decades—has been a crucial factor in Aboriginal adaptation. As the sea moved in and salination occurred, there would have been periods of inundation when a band's main seasonal resources would have been washed away or dramatically changed.

In many parts of the world such catastrophes would have resulted in starvation or increasing conflict between social groups. In times of drought, the desert-dwelling bands would have been fighting each other for the same limited permanent water resources; the coastal group whose beds of shellfish were washed away would have moved to compete for the resources of inland groups. Aborigines, by combining long-term knowledge of the environment with an extensive network of relationships, were able to manage these catastrophes well. People in the desert expected severe drought to occur periodically and anticipated the formation of large groups in times of hardship. They also knew that such periods of drought did not last for ever and were able to keep alive the knowledge of the landscape in distant places so that when conditions changed they would be able to reoccupy the country. They had social and religious imperatives to move out and exploit outlying resources when they became available through a succession of good seasons. Populations are not limited by the number of people who can be supported in good times, but by the number of people who survive in harsh times, and the Australian mode of adaptation appears to have developed in such a way as to enable the population to cope well with times of hardship.

Thus far I have established a model of a mode of adaptation that existed at the time of European colonization, and outlined the prehistoric context in which it must have arisen. Given the existence of short-term and long-term environmental pressures, the kind of regulatory system I have modelled for maintaining long-term relationships between people and land would always have been advantageous. As Butlin (1993: 55) wrote: 'In strategic terms Aborigines evolved in Australia from hunters and gatherers to resource managers and improvers.' And at this stage this is almost as far as the evidence allows us to go. Until recently, it was thought most likely that the immediate pre-contact system developed around 6,000–8,000 years ago at the time the sea was reaching its present-day level. There is considerable evidence from around that time for changes in material culture, rock art, and a small population increase, which could be associated with the development of new forms of social organization. For example the increasing regional differentiation of art styles could be associated with the development of local systems of attachment to land. There is also some evidence for linguistic change occurring around that time, with the spread of Pama-Nyungan languages across much of Australia. However it is equally possible that the change occurred 1,500–2,000 years ago. There is evidence of increased population densities throughout Australia over the past 1,000–1,500 years, in particular, what amounts to a reoccupation of areas of Central Australia. This increase does not seem to be associated with climate change or with the development of new technology, though again it may be associated with the development of new art styles. The Wanjina paintings of the Kimberley region of Western Australia were first produced some 1,500–2,000 years ago.

STRANGERS ARRIVE

Whatever its origins, the present-day system of local organization was well in place throughout Australia at the time of European colonization. People had deep long-term attachments to land, and incorporated their neighbours in regional systems of exchange, which at their outer limits had the potential to link groups across the length and breadth of Australia. It was from this base that Aborigines encountered strangers who visited their land and tried to incorporate them into their world. Aborigines had established relationships with outsiders many years before Europeans arrived. On Cape York Peninsula contact with outsiders was continuous. Relations of trade and exchange have occurred across the Torres Strait for as long as people have lived in Australia. In Arnhem Land and along the Kimberley Coast there was a shorter history of contact with outsiders, but a much more intense and disruptive one.

Bugis traders from Eastern Indonesia arrived each wet season with the monsoon to collect and process trepang (*bêche-de-mer*) (MacKnight 1976). They established close relations with Aboriginal groups who lived along the coast, entering into trading relationships with them and recognizing their land rights. Macassans were incorporated into the myth and ritual cycles of the region, and some Aboriginal people went back with the boats to spend time in Macassar. It is possible to identify some changes to Arnhem Land society that resulted from the annual visits of the Macassans. There was an increasing focus on the coast, as people were attracted by trading opportunities. The Macassans probably introduced sea-going dugout canoes, which enabled the more effective hunting of dugong and turtles. There may have been an increase in warfare as a result of the increased competition for resources along the coast. But on the whole memories handed on from Macassan times are positive. The Macassans respected Aboriginal land rights and fitted in with the system that they found in place. Encounters with Europeans took a quite different form.

Fortunately for the people of Eastern Arnhem Land, Europeans arrived later there than elsewhere in the continent. Europeans took no account of the history of Australia before their arrival. Australia was *terra nullius*, an unpeopled land (see Williams 1986, in particular chapter 7, for a discussion of the relevant legal history). As David Lowenthal (1997: 134) writes:

At the outset, imperial settlers were hardly aware of indigenous impacts, blind to signs of non-European occupation. They assumed that they saw virtually untouched virgin lands, 'almost fresh from the Maker's hands'. That indigenes without permanent farms or advanced tools had over millennia, profoundly altered New World landscapes, and were still doing so, long went unrecognised.

Australia rapidly became what some historians refer to as a settler society, in which people established their own relationship to land without reference to what had existed before, treating the land as a *tabula rasa* in imposing their own way of life, modelled on the Europe that they had left behind (see Griffiths 1997). The speed and nature of change was staggering: the landscape was transformed rapidly by a process of deforestation into pasture for the monoculture of sheep or cattle. As Butlin puts it, vividly but not altogether accurately: 'The British takeover was more a confrontation between British livestock on the one hand and Aboriginal mammals and plants on the other rather than a clash between British and Aboriginal persons. The livestock won, hooves down' (1993: 228). By 1900 the process of 'mindless destruction', in Michael Williams' words (1997: 173), had reduced the forests of New South Wales alone from 10.1 million to 4.5 million hectares. The frontier moved rapidly across Australia: the herds ate up the new land, almost literally, until natural barriers of desert and flood halted the process in parts of the North and Centre. The Aborigines were simply pushed off their land, dispersed. The balanced relationship they had established with the land meant that coexistence with the pastoral economies was impossible; they were competing for the same resources, their own way of life already adjusted to the severe limitations of the environment. In the early years of settlement the pastoralists depended on Aborigines for their survival and in subsequent years relied on them as a cheap source of labour. Without Aboriginal labour the pastoral industry over most of Australia could never have survived. But although they depended on Aborigines, the colonists did not learn from them. In 1935 Francis Ratcliffe, an Oxford biologist and student of Huxley, was commissioned to write a report on the dust-bowl conditions that were beginning to be evident in some parts of southeastern Australia. He concluded that

[the] essential features of white pastoral settlement—a stable home, a circum-scribed area of land, and a flock or herd maintained on this land year-in year-out—are a heritage of life in the reliable kindly climate of Europe. In the drought-risky semi-desert Australian inland they tend to make settlement self destructive. (Ratcliffe 1938: 322)

Ratcliffe's recommended solution was a conscious strategy to 'decrease . . . the density of the pastoral population of the inland' (1938: 331). In the words of the American historian Thomas Dunlap (1997: 79), his approach was ecological, being concerned with 'relationships, processes, and limits imposed by the environment, and the solution was to fit the social order to the natural one'. It is interesting how precisely the strat-egy of the colonists contradicted that of the Aborigines. Aborigines had established long-term sentimental attachments to the land and they did so in a way that took account of variability of climate and resources. In many respects, their social order was fitted to the natural one. Noel Butlin has explored the dynamics of the relationships between Aborig-ines and pastoralists and one of his conclusions is that: 'Large scale pas-toralists had the incentive to go a considerable distance in destroying the ecology of the Aborigines but to preserve at least a substantial number alive, dependent and living on their properties' (1993: 210).

People in northeast Arnhem Land avoided this settler stage, mainly because of the difficulties their environment raised for pastoralism, but partly because they actively defended their country. The factors that make coastal Arnhem Land one of the most resource-rich areas for hunter-gatherers—extensive coastal mud-flats, mangrove-lined river estuaries, and seasonally flooded wet-lands—make it highly unsuitable for cattle. The combination of high Aboriginal population densities and difficult terrain halted the march of the frontier in southern Arnhem Land until around the time of the Second World War. In the 1930s, after a number of skirmishes between Yolngu and outsiders which resulted in the death of some Japanese fishermen and a few Europeans, including one of the policemen sent to investigate what had occurred, mission stations were established at Milingimbi, Elcho Island and Yirrkala. Even in this, the timing was fortunate. Originally, the Commonwealth government had planned to send a military expedition to pacify the region and 'disperse' the Aborigines, as had often happened in earlier times in other parts of the continent. But times had changed and the outcry in the southern press resulted in an alternative strategy. An anthropologist, Donald Thomson, was sent to investigate, and the Methodist and Anglican Churches were encouraged to establish mission stations. Simultaneously, according to Yolngu oral history, Wonggu, a great Yolngu clan leader, encouraged his people to establish cooperative and peaceful relations with Europeans.

The interpretation of events depends so much upon the position of the interpreter. While the view in the south was that the little local difficulty was over, that the Aborigines had at last been pacified and incorporated within the structure of state, the understanding *in situ* was very different. The missionaries presented themselves not as representatives of the state but as individuals who were committed to protecting the Yolngu from outside encroachment. The Yolngu had decided to make peace and to allow the missionaries to establish their settlement in one small area of land. Just as the Yolngu had incorporated the Macassans into their world, so too did they incorporate Europeans, who appeared a few at a time in manageable numbers, posing no threat to their resources or their ownership of the land. And this was the situation until the 1960s. While the mission settlements, like the Macassans, provided a focal point of attraction, Yolngu continued to support themselves by hunting and gathering and spent much of the year in their own lands. They maintained their autonomy but took account of the presence of another world on their doorstep, trying to engage it and to persuade the newcomers of the value of their way of life (Morphy 1983).

On countless occasions since the arrival of the missionaries Yolngu have taken the opportunity to persuade Europeans of the value of their culture and the need to respect their ownership of the land. Until the 1960s this must have seemed largely an unproblematic exercise. Yolngu developed a successful art and craft industry, provided accounts of their culture and society to visiting scientific expeditions, formed syncretic movements as a result of dialogues with missionaries, but were not conscious of any long-term threat to their way of life. Then one day a lease to mine bauxite was taken out, engineers arrived and began to survey the land, samples were taken, and temporary offices were built. No one had mentioned anything to the Yolngu, far less consulted them or asked for permission.

The Yolngu response was immediate. They sent a petition in the form of a bark-painting to the Commonwealth government in Canberra, and when that was of no avail took the government to court over land rights. The basis of their case was that they had a system of law that involved the management of land and that this law had been in place at the time of European colonization. Justice Blackburn's judgement recognized the validity of their arguments, though he failed to understand the relationship between land-ownership and land-use. He concluded, however, that they had no claim over the land, since native title was not recognized under Australian law. The fiction of Australia as a *terra nullius* remained unchallenged (Williams 1986). The mining company, Nabalco, was granted a lease and began, literally, to rip the surface off Yolngu land. But again this was the beginning rather than the end of the story. Justice Blackburn implied that the law might be out of step with the times and the incoming Labor government, by way of the Woodward Commission, introduced land rights legislation for the Northern Territory that would grant many Aboriginal people title to their land. Finally, in 1992, native title was recognized in common law by the Mabo judgement of the High Court (Attwood 1996).

As a result of their experience of the European colonial process Yolngu draw a contrast between European relationships to land and their own, which reverses commonly held European assumptions about the nature of their society. The nomadism which Chatwyn sought in Aboriginal society is thought by Yolngu to characterize Europeans. Europeans see land in terms of extractable resources. They do not establish long-term relationships with the land and do not take account of its history. As far as Aboriginal people are concerned, moreover, Europeans disregarded an existing body of religiously sanctioned land-law which had served the Yolngu well for time immemorial. Daymbalipu Mununggurr, grandson of Wonggu and clan leader, would describe Europeans as nomads on a global scale with no home of their own, who wandered the earth, taking from it valuable resources, then moving on to somewhere else. Interestingly enough, a similar perspective on the European colonial process is provided by the economic historian Noel Butlin (1993: 190), when he described the Spanish, the Dutch, the British, and the French as 'hunting and gathering under their control vast areas of the rest of the world'. For Yolngu, land is embedded in a network of social relationships. Its use requires permission based on activating these relationships. The system of land-use takes into account the historical relationships between people and resources and allows for stable processes of transition. By way of contrast, Europeans are seen to be concerned with restricting the number of right-holders in any enterprise, focusing on the rights of those who provide the capital, and, until recently, disregarding the history of place. In building the township of Nhulunbuy, little account was taken of the importance of particular sites to Aboriginal people. The mining operation cleared land irrespective of its pre-existing significance to Yolngu. The town sewers emptied into the lagoon where people had fished and collected water-chestnuts for generations. The red mud-settling ponds converted many hectares of hunting land to an eerie desert landscape. The days were punctuated with explosions, as the bauxite was blasted out of the ground. It was then transported some 15 kilometres from the crusher to the treatment plant by what was proudly advertised as the longest conveyor belt in the southern hemisphere, and finally loaded onto bulk ore carriers in Melville Bay for shipment to Japan, from a wharf built out from a beach which was a rich source of marine food.

Aboriginal people continually tried to influence the development of the mine and the township, and to reduce its impact on the Yolngu population, but with little success. Many of the facilities offered by the mining town, in particular the ready availability of alcohol, were things that Yolngu campaigned against for fear of the consequences they might have on their own society. Certainly, the company has put considerable efforts into restoring the environment once the ore has been extracted. As one of the officials said: 'the landscape will be exactly the same as before only 12 feet lower'. However, restoring a sacred landscape to which people have developed attachments over generations when it has been lowered by 12 feet and has been out of bounds for thirty years is clearly not going to be an easy task (Dunlop 1995). Without the continual involvement of Aboriginal people, even apparently straightforward tasks such as regenerating the vegetation can prove problematic. On one occasion an environmental officer proudly informed Daymbalipu of the amount of research that had gone into selecting replacement flora, including some exotic species like African mahogany. Daymbalipu somewhat sceptically responded that the area had previously been a main source of stringy bark used for bark-painting and shelters and he would like the landscape exactly as it was before, right down to the indigenous grasses.

CONCLUSION

In Australia today there are both encouraging signs of changing attitudes in the settler population and discouraging signs that nothing has really changed. In the past two decades there appears to have been a significant shift in the ideology and practice of some mining corporations. The passing of land rights legislation has enabled Aboriginal people to negotiate more effectively with mining companies, gaining improved environmental and social preconditions for mining developments and some compensation and return, through royalty agreements, for the exploitation of their land. Thus there has been some improvement in relationships between mining companies and indigenous peoples in Australia and some other parts of the world, and a greater sensitivity to the environmental and social impacts of mining. Significantly, large mining companies such as CRA, in contrast, for example, to pastoralists, have not seen the recognition of native title as being incompatible with their economic objectives.

On the other hand, the Australian government has in the 1990s moved to a position which waters down native title legislation to limit and restrict the process of consultation with indigenous right-holders. This is consistent with a more general lack of government sympathy to environmental issues and an increasing emphasis on short-term economic returns rather than long-term economic goals. Australia suffers as much if not more than any other country from the effects of the reduction of the ozone layer, the intensification of the El Niño effect, and global warming. Yet it has negotiated significant exemptions from agreements to control greenhouse gases and, indeed, will be proudly increasing its own emissions. Aboriginal systems of land management have something important to teach about long-term management of resources in the interests of the population as a whole, because they belong to people who value the long-term attachment of people to place. Local nomads may know much more about the sustainability of resources than nomads who operate on a global scale.

REFERENCES

Attwood, B. (ed.) (1996). *In the Age of Mabo: History, Aborigines and Australia.* St Leonards (NSW): Allen and Unwin.

Butlin, N. (1993). *Economics and the Dreamtime*. Cambridge: Cambridge University Press.

Chatwyn, B. (1987). *The Songlines*. London: Jonathan Cape.

Crosby, A. W. (1986). *Ecological Imperialism: The Biological Expansion of Europe, 900–1900*. Cambridge: Cambridge University Press.

Dunlap, T. R. (1997). 'Ecology and environmentalism in the Anglo settler colonies', in T. Griffiths and L. Robin (eds), *Ecology and Empire: Environmental History of Settler Societies*. Melbourne: Melbourne University Press.

Dunlop, I. (1995). *This is my Thinking*. Sydney: Film Australia.

Durkheim, E. (1971). *The Elementary Forms of the Religious Life* (trans. Joseph Ward Swain). London: George Allen and Unwin.

Griffiths, T. (1997). 'Ecology and empire: towards an Australian history of the world', in T. Griffiths and L. Robin (eds), *Ecology and Empire: Environmental History of Settler Societies*. Melbourne: Melbourne University Press.

Hiscock, P. forthcoming. 'Holocene coastal occupation of Western Arnhem Land', in J. Hallard and I. McNiven, *Australian Coastal Archaeology*.

Jones, R. (ed.) (1985). *Archaeological Research in Kakadu National Park*. Canberra: Australian National Parks and Wildlife Service.

Layton, R. (1992). *Australian Rock Art: A New Synthesis*. Cambridge: Cambridge University Press.

Lee, R. B. and Devore, I. (1968). *Man the Hunter*. Chicago: Aldine.

Lowenthal, D. (1997). 'Empire and ecologies: reflections on environmental history', in T. Griffiths and L. Robin (eds), *Ecology and Empire: Environmental History of Settler Societies*. Melbourne: Melbourne University Press.

MacKnight, C. (1976). *The Road to Marege: Macassan Trepangers in Northern Australia*. Melbourne: Melbourne University Press.

Morphy, H. (1983). 'And now you understand: an analysis of the way Yolngu have used sacred knowledge to retain their autonomy', in N. Peterson and M. Langton (eds), *Aborigines, Land and Land Rights*. Canberra: Australian Institute of Aboriginal Studies.

Morphy, H. (1991). *Ancestral Connections: Art and an Aboriginal System of Knowledge*. Chicago: University of Chicago Press.

Morphy, H. (1993). 'Cultural Adaptation', in G. Harrison (ed.), *Human Adaptation*. Oxford: Oxford University Press.

Mulvaney, J. (1975). *The Prehistory of Australia* (revised edition). Harmondsworth: Penguin.

O'Connor, S. and Fankhauser, B. (n. d.). 'Art at 40,000 BP? One step closer, an ochre covered rock from Carpenter's Gap shelter 1'. Kimberley region, WA.

Peterson, N. (1972). 'Totemism yesterday: sentiment and local organisation among the Australian Aborigines'. *Man* (n.s.) 7 (12): 12–32.

Peterson, N. (1974). 'The importance of women in determining the composition of residential groups in Aboriginal Australia', in F. Gale (ed.), *Women's Role in Aboriginal Society*. Canberra: Australian Institute of Aboriginal Studies.

Peterson, N. (1975). 'Hunter-gatherer territoriality: the perspective from Australia'. *American Anthropologist*, 77: 53–68.

Peterson, N. (1986). *Australian Aboriginal Territorial Organisation* (Oceania Monographs 30). Sydney: Oceania Monographic.

Pyne, S. (1991). *Burning Bush: A Fire History of Australia*. New York: Holt.

Ratcliffe, F. (1938). *Flying Fox and Shifting Sand: The Adventures of a Biologist in Australia*. London: Angus and Robertson.

Singh, G., Kershaw, A. P., and Clark, R. L. (1980). 'Quaternary vegetation and fire history in Australia', in A. M. Gill, R. A. Groves and I. R. Nobel (eds), *Fire and the Australian Biota*. Canberra: Australian Academy of Science.

Spencer, W. B. (1921). Presidential address at the 15th Australian and New Zealand Association for the Advancement of Science. Hobart/Melbourne.

Taçon, P. and Chippindale, C. (1994). 'Australia's ancient warriors: changing depictions of fighting in the rock art of Arnhem Land, N.T.' *Cambridge Archaeological Journal*, 4: 211–48.

Taçon, P. S. C., and Brockwell, S. (1995). 'Arnhem Land prehistory in landscape: stone and paint'. *Antiquity*, 69: 676–95.

White, C. (1967). 'Early stone axes in Arnhem Land'. *Antiquity*, 41: 149–52.

Williams, N. (1986). *The Yolngu and their Land: A System of Land Tenure and the Fight for its Recognition*. Canberra: Australian Institute of Aboriginal Studies.

Williams, M. (1997). 'Ecology, Imperialism and Deforestation', in *Ecology and Empire*: T. Griffiths and L. Robin (eds), *Environmental History of Settler Societies*. Melbourne: Melbourne University Press.

INDEX